Dean LeBaron's
Book of Investment Quotations

Dean LeBaron's
Book of
Investment
Quotations

Dean LeBaron
Romesh Vaitilingam
Marilyn Pitchford

John Wiley & Sons

Published by John Wiley & Sons, Inc., New York.
Published simultaneously in Canada.

This publication is designed to provide accurate and authoritative information in regard to the subject matter covered. It is sold with the understanding that the publisher is not engaged in rendering professional services. If professional advice or other expert assistance is required, the services of a competent professional person should be sought.

Library of Congress Cataloging-in-Publication Data:

Dean LeBaron's book of investment quotations/[compiled by] Dean LeBaron,
    Romesh Vaitilingam, Marilyn Pitchford.
     p. cm.
    Includes index.
    ISBN 0-471-15350-8 (cloth : alk, paper)
    1. Money—Quotations, maxims, etc. 2. Investments—Quotations,
maxims, etc. I. Title: Book of investment quotations. II. LeBaron,
Dean. III. Pitchford, Marilyn. IV. Vaitilingam, Romesh.

PN6084.M56 D43 2001
332.6—dc21
                                                 2001045362

Previously published in 1999 as *The Ultimate Book of Investment Quotations* by Capstone Publishing Limited, Oxford, United Kingdom.

Printed in the United States of America.
10 9 8 7 6 5 4 3 2 1

Contents

99 99 99

Preface

99 99 99

I love deadlines. I like the whooshing sound they
make as they fly by.

Douglas Adams, 1952–2001
writer and producer

Investing is serious business. But it has its moments—chaos and ter-
ror, reward and sublimity—sometimes all within the space of twenty-
four hours. Most things are not as good or as bad—and certainly not
as permanent—as they seem at the moment. James Thurber said:
"Humor is emotional chaos remembered in tranquility." Time and
tranquility have a way of reorienting the moment. Sometimes our
worst experience becomes our most cherished, because it is so hilari-
ous in the retelling.

In the age of sound bytes, quotes take on new importance. The
phrase, "I wish I had said that," captures significant meaning and often
humor in just a few words. And the words become memorable by being
passed on from one to another.

We hope these quotes about and as applied to investment and finance become memorable to you and are useful in provoking new
thoughts, providing content for conversation and speeches, as well as

just casual, fun skimming. They have been collected from many sources, some literary, some friends, and some personal. By bringing them together for you, we hope to enhance your reading as they have ours.

> Dean LeBaron
> Romesh Vaitilingam
> Marilyn Pitchford

Note: Individual authors are customarily listed with their affiliation at the time of the quotation attributed to them.

Dean LeBaron's
Book of
Investment
Quotations

Active Portfolio Management

99 99 99

Perfect Portfolios

To be in the game, you have to endure the pain.
George Soros, b. 1930, Budapest, financier,
philanthropist, author

Is it possible to outperform the market? If your answer is no, if you believe the market is efficient, then passive investing or indexing is probably the way to go. But if your answer is yes, it is possible to beat the market, then you should pursue active portfolio management. Among the arguments for this approach is the possibility that anomalies in securities markets can be exploited to outperform passive investments and the fact that many investors and managers have outperformed passive investing for long periods of time.

Investment Management: An exercise where you make major decisions, in public, on the basis of flimsy information in a system largely governed by chance, when you may be wrong slightly more than 50% of the time, and . . . you have to go back and do it again.

Richard Vancil, b. ~1930, Harvard Business School

The periods of boredom have grown shorter and shorter—and the terrors last a bit longer.

Arthur Cashin, floor broker, New York Stock Exchange, 1987

I think the fact that I don't look at the stock market every hour is very helpful, and the fact that I don't look at the relative performance [of different funds]. Because you can't manage a portfolio as if you're running a race every five minutes.

Gerald Tsai, Primerica Corp., 1987

The actual, private object of the most skilled investment today is to "beat the gun," as the Americans so well express it, to outwit the crowd, and to pass the bad, or depreciating, half-crown to the other fellow.

John Maynard Keynes, 1883–1946, British economist,
1st Baron Keynes of Tilton

With very little training, you can translate and transfer your knowledge as a trader in one commodity to another. There is an old saw that goes, "A real good trader walks on the floor and listens to where the noise is coming from, and that's where he goes to trade." Pit trading is a seat-of-the-pants game. It's go with the flow.

Leo Melamed, b. ~1932, former Chairman,
Chicago Mercantile Exchange

It's difficult to find a portfolio manager who will continue to provide superior performance after he is retained.

Eugene B. Burroughs

Nobody works as hard for his money as the man who marries it.

Kin Hubbard, 1868–1930, American humorist and journalist

The road to success in investing is paved with independence of spirit, decisiveness and the courage of one's conviction.

Peter L. Bernstein, b. ~1919, investment manager,
economic commentator

There's no luck to professional portfolio investing: you can no more pile up a superlative record by luck or accident than you can win a chess tournament by luck or accident.

John Train

Aim to be independent of any one vote, of any one fashion, of any one century.

Baltasar Gracian, 1601–1658, Spanish priest and writer

Men may change their climate, but they cannot change their nature. A man that goes out a fool cannot ride or sail himself into common sense.

Joseph Addison, 1672–1719, writer

Your only assets are your people. And only the top 10 percent of the people in this business add value. Average people are worthless.

Peter Vermilye, investment manager, Baring America
Asset Management Co., 1987

My grandfather once told me that there are two kinds of people: those who do the work and those who take the credit. He told me to try to be in the first group. There was much less competition there.

Indira Gandhi, 1917–1984, prime minister of India

One only gets to the top rung on the ladder by steadily climbing up one at a time, and suddenly all sorts of powers, all sort of abilities which you thought *never* belonged to you—suddenly become within your own possibility and you think, "Well, I'll have a go, too."

Margaret Thatcher, b. 1925, British prime minister

Some one must play the minor parts,
Some one must hold the spear,
And some one, when the music starts,
Must follow in the rear.
Not every one can be the star,
That shines with great white light,
But some must twinkle from afar
To harmonize the night.

Exchange, publication

Success in business does not depend upon genius. Any young man of ordinary intelligence who is normally sound and not afraid to work should succeed in spite of obstacles and handicaps if he plays the game fairly and keeps everlastingly at it.

J. C. Penney, 1875–1971, American retailer

The best place I know for a young man to succeed is where he is by better using what he has.

Charles M. Schwab, 1862–1939, 1st president of U.S. Steel Corp.

The old adage of investment cynics that "managers do not pick markets, markets pick managers" is not quite true. Rather, because investment styles radiate from the developed to the emerging markets, managers can freely roam the world looking for an investment style that suits them.

Dean LeBaron, b. 1933, investment manager and contrarian thinker

The real difference between men is energy. A strong will, a settled purpose, an invincible determination, can accomplish almost anything; and in this lies the distinction between great men and little men.

Buckminster Fuller, 1895–1983, American designer

Big corporations are the ultimate run-sheep-run guys: "If that's good enough for General Mills, that's sure good enough for us." We went from *nothin'*, like a rocket ship, to a billion-and-a-half dollars under management. You know, we really thought we were magic. We all felt like World War I fighter pilots—daring young men pushing out the frontiers. We spun in from nowhere and were eating the big banks' lunch.

Robert Kirby, investment manager, Capital Guardian Trust Co., 1987

To know the world, one must construct it.

Cesare Pavese, 1908–1950, Italian author

Trifles make perfection and perfection is no trifle.

Michaelangelo, 1475–1564, Italian artist

What one does easily, one does well.

Andrew Carnegie, 1835–1919, steel manufacturer and philanthropist

An amazing number [of investment managers] that come to see me don't know how to listen. It's like they've been wound up and they have rehearsed this proposal in front of a mirror and, come hell or high water, they're going to take me through their three-ring binder.

John English, b. ~1933, Ford Foundation

What we hope ever to do with ease, we must learn first to do with diligence.

Samuel Johnson, 1709–1784, British author

At one time, say in the early '60s, when half-a-dozen banks had half the pension fund business in the country, the total pension business was less than $50 billion.

> *Peter Vermilye, investment manager, Baring America*
> *Asset Management Co., 1987*

Whether you believe you can do a thing or not, you are right.

> *Henry Ford, 1863–1947, American automobile manufacturer,*
> *founder of Ford Motor Co.*

The specialists had a wonderful deal—and we came along and screwed it up. We made real markets. We embarrassed a lot of them. The concept of fair and orderly markets with some specialists was their credo, but with others they couldn't spell it. They didn't make a market at all.

> *Will Weinstein, former head trader, Oppenheimer & Co., 1987*

A stockbroker is someone who invests other people's money until it's all gone.

> *Woody Allen, b. 1935, American film maker*

Average investors who try to do a lot of trading will just make their brokers rich.

> *Michael Jensen, finance professor, Harvard*

I remember an occasion, early in my career, when I was practically wiped out in my personal account.

> *George Soros, b. 1930, Budapest, financier, philanthropist, author*

To the investment manager, soft dollars are someone else's money and hard dollars are your own.

> *Dean LeBaron, b. 1933, investment manager and contrarian thinker*

There are three classes of people who don't think markets work: the Cubans, the North Koreans and active managers.

Rex Sinquefield, Dimensional Fund Advisors

Action is the last resource of those who know not how to dream.

Oscar Wilde, 1854–1900, Irish-British author

Creative minds have always been known to survive any kind of bad training.

Anna Freud, 1895–1982, psychoanalyst

At that time [1956] it was rare to have a European who had spent so much time in the United States, and we brought something to Europe about which little was known here: U.S. methods of investment research.

Yves Oltramare, former general partner, Lombard, Odier & CIE, 1987

Do what you can, with what you have, where you are.

Theodore Roosevelt, 1858–1919, 26th U.S. president

His head was turned by too great success.

Seneca, ~45 B.C.–A.D. 65, Roman statesman and philosopher

If a pension manager is lucky, and few of us are, he spends 50 percent of his time on the portfolio and the rest talking to the clients. That's a problem in itself, but the nature of the conversation makes it worse. Because the client focuses on the 3-W list: What Went Wrong?

Robert Kirby, investment manager, Capital Guardian Trust Co., 1987

I sometimes try to be miserable that I may do more work.

William Blake, 1757–1827, British poet and artist

If anything is evident about people who manage money, it is that the task attracts a very low level of talent, one that is protected in its highly imperfect profession by the mystery that is thought to enfold the subject of economies in general and of money in particular.

John Kenneth Galbraith, b. 1908, economist

Size of assets under management is the ultimate barrier to successful investing. The investment business is the perfect example of the Peter Principle: do well with $500 million, and they'll give you $5 billion.

Jeremy Grantham, investment manager, Grantham, Mayo, Van Otterloo

If I had known then what I know now, I would have made the same mistakes sooner.

Robert Half, employment agent

It ain't braggin' if you can do it.

Dizzy Dean, 1911–1974, American baseball player

It is always with the best intentions that the worst work is done.

Oscar Wilde, 1854–1900, Irish-British author

It is good to have an end to journey toward, but it is the journey that matters, in the end.

Ursula Le Guin, b. 1929, American author

Somebody said that I predicted that Mayday would be a "nonevent." What I did say was I didn't think that there would be enormous discounting on day one, and the discounting did come much faster than I would have thought. The biggest thing at work in bringing down commissions was the growth of the industry; and when it was freed up from this artificial structure, it just encouraged more people to do more trading.

Donald Marron, b. ~1934, Paine Webber

Life is a long lesson in humility.

James M. Barrie, 1860–1937, dramatist and novelist

Play so you may be serious.

Anarchis

Rest and motion, unrelieved and unchecked, are equally destructive.

Benjamin Cardozo, 1870–1938, Associate Supreme Court justice

If you start out as a macro-oriented money manager, in some sense the macro is made up of a lot of little micros.

Michael Steinhardt, investment manager, Steinhardt Partners, 1987

Striving for excellence motivates you; striving for perfection is demoralizing.

Harriet Braiker

The girl who can't dance says the band can't play.

Yiddish proverb

There are two kinds of talent, man-made and God-given. With man-made talent you have to work very hard. With God-given, to just touch it up once in a while.

Pearl Bailey, 1918–1990, singer

Average people are worthless and mediocrity breeds failure. A mediocre analyst gets between a portfolio manager and a good idea and obfuscates the situation.

Peter Vermilye, investment manager, Baring America Asset Management Co., 1987

There is no excellency without difficulty.

Ovid, 43 B.C.–A.D. 17, Roman poet

There is nothing either good or bad but thinking makes it so.

William Shakespeare, 1564–1616, English poet, playwright

- There is too much liquidity and not enough investment.
- In the United States, investment technology counts for nothing, wisdom counts for everything.
- Time is an enemy to investors.

Dean LeBaron, quoted in Five Eminent Contrarians, *by Steven L. Mintz, 1994*

Thinking without constructive action becomes a disease.

Henry Ford, 1863–1947, American automobile manufacturer, founder of Ford Motor Co.

True enjoyment comes from activity of the mind and exercise of the body; the two are united.

Alexander von Humboldt, 1769–1859, German scientist

Try first thyself, and after call in God; for to the worker God himself lends aid.

Euripides, ~484–406 B.C., Greek dramatist, tragic poet

People like Bill Sharpe were not saying that nobody can beat the market. They were saying the average person could not beat the market. But that academic research collided with the marketing pretensions and illusions of institutional investors.

Barr Rosenberg, b. ~1942, Rosenberg Institutional Equity Management

When a man is wrong and won't admit it, he always gets angry.

Thomas Haliburton, 1796–1865, Canadian jurist and humorist

When once a decision is reached and execution is the order of the day, dismiss absolutely all responsibility and care about the outcome.

William James, 1842–1910, American philosopher and psychologist

There are old traders around and bold traders around but there are no old, bold traders around.

Bob Dinda

An ego in this business is a dangerous thing.

Will Weinstein, former head trader, Oppenheimer & Co., 1987

Determine never to be idle. No person will have occasion to complain of the want of time who never loses any. It is wonderful how much may be done if we are always doing.

Thomas Jefferson, 1743–1826, 3rd U.S. president

When it comes to trading decisions, you can't discuss it with a lot of people. You have to follow your own judgment, and judgment cannot be discussed.

Hans-Joerg Rudloff, b. ~1940, Credit Suisse First Boston

I am only one, but still I am one; I cannot do everything, but still I can do something; and because I cannot do everything I will not refuse to do the something that I can do.

Edward E. Hale, 1822–1909, American author

More errors arise from inhibited indecision than from impulsive behavior.

Morris Ernst

There is nothing so stupid as an educated man, if you get him off the thing he was educated in.

Will Rogers, 1879–1935, American humorist and showman

To manage money successfully, I think you need exactly the same skills and talent that you always have. Above all, you need investment judgment. You need enormous curiosity. You need a sense of causality. You need to be able to identify the driving forces that make economies and industries and companies rise and fall and to sense the quality of managements and sense who moves the marketplace.

Peter Vermilye, investment manager, Baring America
Asset Management Co., 1987

One of my chief regrets during my years in the theater is that I couldn't sit in the audience and watch me.

John Barrymore, 1882–1942, American actor

Knowledge is our most powerful engine of production.

Alfred Marshall, 1842–1924, British educator and economist

It does not matter whether the cat is black or white, only that it catches mice.

Deng Xiaoping, 1904–1998, Chinese political leader

Nothing worthwhile comes easily. Half effort does not produce half results. It produces no results. Work, continuous work and hard work, is the only way to accomplish results that last.

Hamilton Holt

There is a cropping-time in the races of men, as in the fruits of the field; and sometimes, if the shock be good, there springs up for a time a succession of splendid men; and then comes a period of barrenness.

Aristotle, 384–322 B.C., Greek philosopher, educator, scientist

No wonder that so many cars collide;
Their drivers are accident prone,
When one hand is holding a coffee cup,
And the other a cellular phone.

Art Buck

Sloth, like rust, consumes faster than labor wears, while the key often used is always bright.

Benjamin Franklin, 1706–1790, statesman, scientist, public leader

The social object of skilled investment should be to defeat the dark forces of time and ignorance, which envelop our future.

*John Maynard Keynes, 1883–1946, British economist,
1st Baron Keynes of Tilton*

Good firms worry about competition. Great firms worry about clients.

Hugo Paulson, 1998, quoted in Goldman Sachs: The Culture of Success, *by Lisa Endlich*

Contrarian Investing

99 99 99

Contrarians and Controversies

Eagles don't flock.

> *H. Ross Perot, b. 1930, American businessman,*
> *presidential candidate*

Contrary thinking is intellectual independence with a healthy dash of agnosticism about consensus views. If a consensus grows to be a "crowd," the contrarian will flee, but not necessarily to the exact opposite. Instead, identification of a herd motivates the contrarian to be more rigorous in independent thinking. And the contrarian is more likely to be attracted to a point of view that has not yet been thought of—the "empty file drawer" idea—than one that has been considered and rejected.

The fact that other people agree or disagree with you makes you neither right or wrong. You will be right if your facts and reasoning are correct.

Benjamin Graham, 1894–1976, value investor

Contrary thinking is a deliberate shaking of the mind back and forth, reversing and reaffirming plausible views to separate out the non-essential, much as the gold panner shakes out unwanted pebbles.

Bradbury Thurlow in Rediscovering the Wheel: Contrary Thinking and Investment Strategy

Achetez aux canons, vendez aux clairons.
[Buy on the cannons and sell on the trumpets.]

French proverb

No great genius ever existed without some touch of madness.

Seneca, ~4 B.C.–A.D. 65, Roman statesman and philosopher

Sudden events quickly crystallize opinion.

Humphrey Neill, d. 1978, contrarian and author

A radical is a man with both feet firmly planted—in the air.

Franklin D. Roosevelt, 1882–1945, 32nd U.S. president

A very popular error—having the courage of one's convictions: rather it is a matter of having the courage for an attack upon one's convictions.

Friedrich Nietzsche, 1844–1900, German philosopher

Real revolutionaries are people who look with a deep sense of humour upon their institutions.

Ivan Illich, b. 1926, Austrian-born U.S. theologian and author

To buy when others are despondently selling and to sell when others are greedily buying requires the greatest fortitude and pays the greatest reward.

Sir John Templeton, b. ~1913, Tennessee-born British financier

Dogs come when they're called; cats take a message and get back to you.

Mary Bly

The central principle of investment is to go contrary to the general opinion, on the grounds that if everyone agreed about its merits, the investment is inevitably too dear and therefore unattractive.

John Maynard Keynes, 1883–1946, British economist,
1st Baron Keynes of Tilton

Every revolutionary is an optimist.

Unknown

When everyone thinks alike, everyone is likely to be wrong.

Humphrey Neill in The Art of Contrary Thinking, *1997*

Granting our wish is one of Fate's saddest jokes.

James Russell Lowell, 1819–1891, writer and diplomat

No one can possibly achieve any real and lasting success or "get rich" in business by being a conformist.

J. Paul Getty, 1892–1976, oil tycoon

I am only an average man, but, by George, I work harder at it than the average man.

Theodore Roosevelt, 1858–1919, 26th U.S. president

I never found the companion that was so companionable as solitude.

Henry David Thoreau, 1817–1862, American naturalist and writer

Imagination rules the world.

Napoleon Bonaparte, 1769–1821, French general

Immense power is acquired by assuring yourself in your secret reveries that you were born to control affairs.

Andrew Carnegie, 1835–1919, steel manufacturer and philanthropist

When everyone is bearish, a market must go up because there are no sellers left; conversely, when everyone is bullish, a market must go down because there are no buyers left.

Unknown

In the history of mankind, fanaticism has caused more harm than vice.

Louis Kronenberger, b. 1904, writer

People just like things status quo. One governor of the exchange said to me [in 1967], "And how many more are there behind you?" Like I was gonna lead a doggone parade onto the floor. And twenty years later, where are they? I am still the only woman to have bought a seat on the New York Stock Exchange.

Muriel Siebert, stockbroker, Muriel Siebert & Co., 1987

It is dangerous to be right in matters on which the established authorities are wrong.

Voltaire, 1694–1778, French philosopher and writer

One machine can do the work of fifty ordinary men. No machine can do the work of one extraordinary man.

Elbert G. Hubbard, 1856–1915, American writer and businessman

One man with courage makes a majority.

Andrew Jackson, 1767–1845, 7th U.S. president

One of the strongest characteristics of genius is the power of lighting its own fire.

John Foster, 1836–1917, American diplomat

Only the bold get to the top.

Publilius Syrus, 1st century B.C., Roman writer

Other people are quite dreadful. The only possible society is one's self.

Oscar Wilde, 1854–1900, author

Physical bravery is an animal instinct; moral bravery is a much higher and truer courage.

Wendell Phillips, 1811–1884, American social reformer

Some power that I little suspected in my student days took me in charge and carried me on from the obscure neighborhood of Plymouth Notch to the occupancy of the White House.

Calvin Coolidge, 1872–1933, 30th U.S. president

- Mistakes of commission have the same character as triumphs.
- If you are complacent about your investment decisions, they are wrong.
- Neutral is uncommitted.

Dean LeBaron, quoted in Five Eminent Contrarians, *by Steven L. Mintz, 1994*

Take the course opposite to custom and you will almost always do well.

Jean-Jacques Rousseau, 1712–1778, French philosopher

The extreme limit of wisdom—that's what the public calls madness.

Jean Cocteau, 1889–1963, French author

The great man is the man who does a thing for the first time.

Alexander Smith, 1830–1867, Scottish poet and writer

Worldly wisdom teaches us that it is better for reputation to fail conventionally than to succeed unconventionally.

John Maynard Keynes, 1883–1946, British economist,
1st Baron Keynes of Tilton

The proper office of a friend is to side with you when you are in the wrong. Nearly everybody will side with you when you are in the right.

Mark Twain, 1835–1910, American author

The will to do, the soul to dare.

Sir Walter Scott, 1771–1832, Scottish author

Unless a capacity for thinking be accompanied by a capacity for action, a superior mind exists in torture.

Benedetto Croce, 1866–1952, Italian philosopher

What the superior man seeks is in himself but what the small man seeks is in others.

Confucius, 551–479 B.C., Chinese philosopher

You will do foolish things, but do them with enthusiasm.

Colette, 1873–1954, French author

In sum, the purpose is to contest the popular view, because popular opinions are so frequently found to be untimely, misled (by propaganda), or plainly wrong.

Humphrey Neill in The Art of Contrary Thinking, *1997*

The way I learned from Humphrey Neill is that you buy stuff when it's quiet. A contrarian should look at all sides of a question or problem and not just follow the crowd. And if the crowd gets thick and heavy, then usually you should avoid it. It's more independent thinking than anything else.

James L. Fraser, author, publisher, contrarian thinker

Better eccentric vagaries than commonplace dullness.

Unknown

All men's friend, no man's friend.

John Wodroephe

America has had gifted conservative statesmen and national leaders. But with few exceptions, only the liberals have gone down in history as national heroes.

Gunnar Myrdal, 1898–1987, Swedish economist and sociologist

Courage is what it takes to stand up and speak; courage is also what it takes to sit down and listen.

Winston Churchill, 1874–1965, British prime minister

Discoveries are often made by not following instructions; by going off the main road; by trying the untried.

Frank Tyger

Speaking of her son: Dean is not a contrarian . . . he was a good baby.

Irene LeBaron, b. 1914, mother of Dean LeBaron

Every great advance in natural knowledge has involved the absolute rejection of authority.

Thomas H. Huxley, 1825–1895, British zoologist

Every new opinion, at its starting, is precisely a minority of one.

Thomas Carlyle, 1795–1881, Scottish author

Every society honors its live conformists and its dead troublemakers.

Mignon McLaughlin, b. 1915, American author and editor

For an idea that does not at first seem insane, there is no hope.

Albert Einstein, 1879–1955, German-American scientist

He was a bold man who first ate an oyster.

Jonathan Swift, 1667–1745, English churchman and writer, b. Dublin

He was like a cock who thought the sun had risen to hear him crow.

George Eliot, 1819–1880, British author

I cannot afford to waste my time making money.

Louis Agassiz, 1807–1873, Swiss-born naturalist

If thou are a man, admire those who attempt great things, even though they fail.

Seneca, ~4 B.C.–A.D. 65, Roman statesman and philosopher

It is your enemies who keep you straight. For real use one active, sneering enemy is worth two ordinary friends.

Edgar (Ed) Watson Howe, 1853–1937, American journalist and author

Man is not what he thinks he is, but what he thinks, he is.

Elbert G. Hubbard, 1856–1915, American writer and businessman

Strength alone knows conflict; weakness is below even defeat, and is born vanquished.

Anne Swetchine, 1782–1857

Success is the child of audacity.

> *Benjamin Disraeli, 1804–1881, British prime minister, author,*
> *1st Earl of Beaconsfield*

The errors of great men are venerable because they are more fruitful than the truths of little men.

> *Friedrich Nietzsche, 1844–1900, German philosopher*

The man with a new idea is a crank until the idea succeeds.

> *Mark Twain, 1835–1910, American author*

The mass of men lead lives of quiet desperation.

> *Henry David Thoreau, 1817–1862, American naturalist and writer*

The rewards of genius go to society. The price of being a genius is paid by the genius alone.

> *James Thorpe, 1886–1953, American athlete*

The visionary lies to himself, the liar only to others.

> *Friedrich Nietzsche, 1844–1900, German philosopher*

The worst solitude is to be destitute of sincere friendship.

> *Sir Francis Bacon, 1561–1626, poet, dramatist, thinker*

To die for an idea sets a high price on conjecture.

> *Anatole France, 1844–1924, French novelist and critic*

Too chaste a youth leads to a dissolute old age.

> *André Gide, 1869–1951, French author*

Try not to become a man of success, but rather try to become a man of value.

> *Albert Einstein, 1879–1955, German-American scientist*

Visionary people are visionary partly because of the very great many things they don't see.

Berkeley Rice

We mount to heaven mostly on the ruins of our cherished schemes, finding our failures were successes.

Amos Bronson Alcott, 1799–1888, American social reformer and abolitionist

What a man is is the basis of what he dreams and thinks, accepts and rejects, feels and perceives.

John Mason Brown, 1900–1969, American drama critic

When a true genius appears in the world, you may know him by this sign, that the dunces are all in confederacy against him.

Jonathan Swift, 1667–1745, English churchman and writer, b. Dublin

What this country needs is radicals who will stay that way regardless of the creeping years.

John Fischer

Corporate Governance

🙶 🙶 🙶

Shareholder Power

I've got to follow them. I am their leader.
*Alexandre Ledru-Rollin, 1807–1874, French
lawyer and politician*

Shareholders demand high returns on their equity investments, while executives of public companies typically want a peaceful life with good remuneration and minimal outside intervention. These conflicting interests and how to achieve some kind of alignment between them—to give corporate managers the incentives to act in the best interests of the owners—are the central questions of corporate governance. Challenges have come from activist shareholders who demand long-term value creation from the companies whose shares they own, companies that are underperforming in the light of strong underlying values and are susceptible to increased value through shareholder involvement.

First-rate people hire first-rate people; second-rate people hire third-rate people.

> *Leo Rosten, b. 1908, American writer*

My opinion is that, philosophically, I'm doing the right thing in trying to shake up some of these managements. It's a problem in America today that we are not nearly as productive as we should be. That's why we have the balance-of-payments problems. It's like the fall of Rome, when half the population was on the dole.

> *Carl Icahn, b. 1936, corporate raider*

I have made good judgments in the past. I have made good judgments in the future.

> *J. Danforth Quayle, b. 1947, vice president of the United States*

In naval leadership training, officers are taught that any decision that comes to the captain will not be made on facts; otherwise, it would already have been made at lower levels. So the captain's job is to make the decision on the basis of principles and to be decisive.

> *Dean LeBaron, b. 1933, investment manager and contrarian thinker*

My idea of a group decision is to look in the mirror.

> *Warren Buffett, b. 1930, American investor*

A "tired businessman" is one whose business is usually not a successful one.

> *Joseph R. Grundy*

A bank-managed industry will not change obsolete machinery for up-to-date equipment because their eyes are fixed too firmly on dividends. Such an industry runs down, ceases to be efficient and finally dies. With engineer management a business is constantly replenished with the best methods regardless of cost and the public gets a better product.

Henry Ford, 1863–1947, American automobile manufacturer, founder of Ford Motor Co.

A leader of men must make decisions quickly . . . be a fighter . . . speak openly, plainly, frankly . . . cooperate, co-ordinate, work with active faith . . . be loyal, true, faithful . . . have a high, intelligent, worthy purpose and ideal.

Henry Dodge, 1782–1867, American army officer and politician

All free governments are managed by the combined wisdom and folly of the people.

James A. Garfield, 1831–1881, 20th U.S. president

The lesson I needed to learn for this job was patience, how to deal with people, not to do everything yesterday. Accept frustration from time to time, but keep your eye on your same goal.

Gerald Tsai, Primerica Corp., 1987

Big business and little business will never again be exactly the same as they were in the booming '20s. Reactions may come, but we shall never swing back to where we were in business methods and the philosophy of business, exemplified by the old idea of every man for himself and the devil take the hindmost. Thinking men by now must see that neither cut-throat competition between business men nor ruthless disregard of the economic welfare of 90 percent of our people can be conducive to the welfare of business itself.

Senator Capper

Good management consists in showing average people how to do the work of superior people.

John D. Rockefeller, 1839–1937, American industrialist and philanthropist

He is a hard man who is only just, and a sad one who is only wise.

Voltaire, 1694–1778, French philosopher and writer

I believe in the capitalist system, but I believe it will work only if it is fair, and I think no one is blind to the fact that the bad employer at this moment is not only risking his own life but he is risking everything else, if he only knew it.

Lady Nancy Astor, 1879–1964, politician

CITIC has grown to be a diversified conglomerate with investments in about 180 enterprises. "Conglomerate" is the concept or terminology borrowed from the Western world; we call CITIC a socialist conglomerate.

Rong Yiren, b. ~1916, China International Trust and Investment Corp.

The corporate raider helps to keep management honest. And I say "honest" in the sense that they give shareholders a fair shake. Many managements thought they owned the company, that the company was run for their benefit. Many companies—not even giant companies, but mid-sized companies—had shooting lodges and apartments all over. They were like kings.

Saul Steinberg, founder, Reliance Group Holdings, 1987

It is said that if Noah's ark had had to be built by a company, they would not have laid the keel yet; and it may be so. What is many men's business is nobody's business. The greatest things are accomplished by individual men.

Charles Spurgeon

It's easy to have principles when you're rich. The important thing is to have principles when you're poor.

Ray Kroc, 1902–1984, founder of McDonald's

Leaders of men are later remembered less for the usefulness of what they have achieved than for the sweep of their endeavors.

Charles de Gaulle, 1890–1970, French president

Positive decisions have to be made by an individual. Groups can't do it.

Edward Johnson, founder of Fidelity Funds

No gain is so certain as that which proceeds from the economical use of what you already have.

Latin proverb

Putting off a hard thing makes it impossible.

George Horace Lorimer, 1867–1937, American editor

It was the right thing to establish a strong and well-capitalized bank, because in banking you cannot expand if you don't maintain the proper financial ratios. The Arab banks did not take advantage of the boom; they could have built much stronger banks [in the late 1970s], but nowadays they are no longer able to.

Abdulla Saudi, founder, Arab Banking Corp. (ABC), 1987

So much of what we call management consists in making it difficult for people to work.

Peter Drucker, b. 1909, author and consultant

The great menace to the life of an industry is industrial self-complacency.

David Sarnoff, 1891–1971, executive

The surest foundation of a manufacturing concern is quality. After that, and a long way after, comes cost.

Andrew Carnegie, 1835–1919, steel manufacturer and philanthropist

Wall Street had a certain cachet: It was the only aristocratic business in the United States. By that I mean [until the 1970s] the only business where a father, if he were a senior partner, could count on passing the business on to his son.

Leon Levy, Odyssey Partners, cofounder Oppenheimer Fund, 1987

The worst cliques are those which consist of one man.

George Bernard Shaw, 1856–1950, playwright

There's always room at the top—after the investigation.

Oliver Herford, 1863–1935, American poet and illustrator

I heard I was having a palace revolt. Things had been brewing, and I heard there was a candidate who wanted my job . . . I thought I was with gentlemen. Obviously, I was wrong. Breaks at that level are never clean. Parties on both sides are always bruised.

James Needham, b. ~1932, former chairman, New York Stock Exchange

What we seek is a return to a clearer understanding of the ancient truth that those who manage banks, corporations and other agencies handling or using other peoples' money are trustees acting for others.

Theodore Roosevelt, 1858–1919, 26th U.S. president

When prosperity comes, do not use all of it.

Confucius, 551–479 B.C., Chinese philosopher

These conflicts about management practices and basic corporate mission were quite fundamental, and they created a situation in which it was much easier to stop innovation than to carry it out.

David Rockefeller, b. 1915, Chase Manhattan Bank,
American financier, son of John D. Rockefeller, Jr.

You have not converted a man because you have silenced him.

John Morley, 1838–1923, British politician and biographer

A liar will not be believed, even when he speaks the truth.

Aesop, d. 565 B.C., Greek storyteller

An administration, like a machine, does not create. It carries on.

Antoine de Saint-Exupéry, 1900–1944, French aviator and author

An intellectual is someone whose mind watches itself.

Albert Camus, 1913–1960, French journalist and philosopher

Factions within the industry were continually at war. By 1974 we were in one of the real granddaddies of bear markets. Trading volumes were very bad. There was really a feeling that the exchange [NYSE] probably only had a couple of years to go.

John Phelan, Jr., New York Stock Exchange, 1987

Big shots are only little shots who keep shooting.

Christopher Morley, American author

Corporation: An ingenious device for obtaining individual profit without individual responsibility.

Ambrose Bierce, 1842– ~1914, American writer and journalist

Today in America too many large corporations are the property no longer of shareholders but of management and investment bankers. Together they're having a ball [having] forgotten who their owners are. We don't think there needs to be a great revolution, but we think that maybe shareholders shouldn't take a totally passive role. We have to be more activist.

> *Edward (Ned) Johnson III, b. 1930, chairman, Fidelity Investments*

Do not wait for extraordinary circumstances to do good actions; try to use ordinary circumstances.

> *Jean Paul Richter, 1763–1825, German writer and humorist*

Everything which is properly *business* we must keep carefully separate from *life*. Business requires earnestness and method; life must have a freer handling.

> *Johann Goethe, 1749–1832, German writer*

Oil did help bring some of the few Arab bankers into the arena. But I think the problem lies in the Arab system, the way that the Arab countries operate. The fortunes or money generated through oil were either in the hands of governments or of private individuals [who] lacked the experience.

> *Abdulla Saudi, founder, Arab Banking Corp. (ABC), 1987*

Happiness is not the end of life, character is.

> *Henry Ward Beecher, 1813–1887, American religious leader, reformer*

I have long been profoundly convinced that in the very nature of things, employers and employees are partners, not enemies; that their interests are common, not opposed; that in the long run the success of each is dependent upon the success of the other.

> *John D. Rockefeller, Jr., 1874–1960, businessman,*
> *built Rockefeller Center*

I don't want any yes-men around me. I want everyone to tell the truth—even though it costs him his job.

Samuel Goldwyn, 1882–1974, American movie producer

I have yet to hear a man ask for advice on how to combine marriage and a career.

Gloria Steinem, b. 1934, American social reformer

If you would grow great and stately, you must try to walk sedately.

Robert Louis Stevenson, 1850–1894, Scottish author

Indolence is the dry rot of even a good mind and a good character, the practical uselessness of both. It is the waste of what might be a happy and useful life.

Tryon Edwards, 1809–1894

In this [takeover] game, if you have the stock, you should win. The guy who has the most stock and the fortitude to hold on to it can go ahead and can win this thing. But it's a tough game.

Carl Icahn, b. 1936, corporate raider

It is difficult to get a man to understand something when his salary depends upon his not understanding it.

Upton Sinclair, 1878–1968, American author

It is frequently a misfortune to have very brilliant men in charge of affairs; they expect too much of ordinary men.

Thucydides, 460– ~400 B.C., Greek historian

Kind hearts are more than coronets, and simple faith than Norman blood.

Alfred, Lord Tennyson, 1809–1892, English poet

Leadership is the ability to get men to do what they don't want to do and like it.

Harry S. Truman, 1884–1972, 33rd U.S. president

If you own 10 percent or 20 percent of a company, the chief executive should at least meet with you. Those managements pay greenmail because they don't want any large shareholder: not because the large shareholder's going to take over the company but because a large shareholder spends more time on the investment, on the company, asks more questions.

Saul Steinberg, founder, Reliance Group Holdings, 1987

Never is work without reward or reward without work.

Livy, 59 B.C.–A.D. 17, Roman historian

I think there are some people who think that if you pay someone a large salary, you can alter their integrity and their value system.

James Needham, b. ~1932, former chairman, New York Stock Exchange

Nothing gives one person so much advantage over another as to remain always cool and unruffled under all circumstances.

Thomas Jefferson, 1743–1826, 3rd U.S. president

Of all the incentives for work, money is the most popular—and the most unreliable.

Cullen Hightower

One can always be kind to people about who one cares nothing.

Oscar Wilde, 1854–1900, Irish-British author

Our minds need relaxation, and give way,
Unless we mix with work a little play.

Molière, 1622–1673, French dramatist

Perpetual devotion to what a man calls his business is only to be sustained by perpetual neglect of many other things. And it is not by any means certain that a man's business is the most important thing he has to do.

Robert Louis Stevenson, 1850–1894, Scottish author

Quality is never an accident; it is always the result of intelligent effort.

John Ruskin, 1819–1900, writer and critic

As more and more money became institutionalized, it led to stocks moving up and down more, and corporate managements became very aware of this and managed their affairs [maximizing short-term earnings instead of looking to the future] with this in mind.

Peter Vermilye, investment manager, Baring America Asset Management Co., 1987

Some people with great virtues are disagreeable, while others with great vices are delightful.

La Rochefoucauld, 1613–1680, French author

The father in praising the son extols himself.

Chinese proverb

The thing that impresses me most about America is the way parents obey their children.

Duke of Windsor, 1894–1972

The worst misfortune that can happen to an ordinary man is to have an extraordinary father.

Austin O'Malley

Every business should have its biographer—not after its head is dead but to show that he's very much alive.

Frank Romer

Companies have always bought back their own shares from large stockholders, usually at a premium for a large block. That's been going on with us for years. It became a dirty word when the term "greenmail" was coined. I've always believed that all shareholders should get the same offer. But you almost always have to accept greenmail. The offer is usually coupled—I'm basically giving you my experience—with a threat.

Saul Steinberg, founder, Reliance Group Holdings, 1987

There is nothing so fatal to character than half-finished tasks.

David Lloyd George, 1863–1945, British prime minister

Those who bring sunshine to the lives of others cannot keep it from themselves.

James M. Barrie, 1860–1937, dramatist and novelist

Those who do not find time for exercise will have to find time for illness.

Earl of Derby, British prime minister

Those who do the least always seem to have the least time.

Arnold Glasow, American humorist

We are most of us very lonely in this world; you who have any who love you, cling to them and thank God.

William Makepeace Thackeray, 1811–1866, British author

When a manager with a reputation for brilliance tackles a business with a reputation for bad economics, the reputation of the business remains intact.

Warren Buffett, b. 1930, American investor

When I do good, I feel good. When I do bad, I feel bad. And that's my religion.

Abraham Lincoln, 1809–1865, 16th American president

While the right to talk may be the beginning of freedom, the necessity of listening is what makes the right important.

Walter Lippmann, 1889–1974, American journalist

You can have peace. Or you can have freedom. Don't ever count on having both at once.

Robert A. Heinlein, 1907–1988, American author

You will find, as you look back upon your life, that the moments that stand out, the moments when you have really lived, are the moments when you have done things in the spirit of love.

Henry Drummond, 1851–1897, British clergyman and writer

I expect to pass through life but once. If, therefore, there be any kindness I can show, or any good thing I can do to any fellow being, let me do it now and not defer or neglect it, as I shall not pass this way again.

William Penn, 1644–1718, American colonial leader

Until the government enforces the fiduciary laws respecting conflicting interests, there has been an attitude of benign neglect in the Anglo-American world. Thus, we have the irony that among institutional investors, only those least qualified by education, training and outlook are free to be activist.

Robert A. G. Monks, b. ~1936, investor, shareholder activist, author

Corporate Restructuring

Remaking Corporations

It's often wrong to do the thing you have a right
to do.

Frank Tyger

One of the most high profile features of the business and investment worlds is corporate restructuring—mergers and acquisitions
(M&A), leveraged buyouts, divestitures, spin-offs and the like. The
number and value of mega-mergers in 1998 set new records. This has
reawakened the populist cry that such mergers do not create new wealth,
that they merely represent the trading of existing assets—rearranging
the deck chairs on the Titanic. The primary argument in favor of M&A
is that they are good for industrial efficiency. Takeovers are a radical solution for remedying poor performance and safeguarding against economic mediocrity.

This [takeover] game gets in your blood, though, because when you're in it, it's like being in the middle of a tiger hunt, and the tigers are coming at you and you've just got a spear.

Carl Icahn, b. 1936, corporate raider

[In 1968, while I was at the SEC, World Bank head Robert McNamara] asked me what I thought about investment bankers, and I told him the truth—which was that I was trying to indict most of them under the Sherman Act. He asked me what I thought of commercial bankers, and I said I thought they sailed around in little ships on Long Island Sound in the summertime and wore white buck shoes.

Eugene Rotberg, b. ~1929, World Bank

Before you organize you ought to analyze and see what the elements of the business are.

Gerard Swope, 1872–1957, American electrical engineer,
president of General Electric

Disease makes men more physical; it leaves them with nothing but body.

Thomas Mann, 1875–1955, German author

Effective action is always unjust.

Jean Anouilh, 1910–1987, French dramatist

How the past perishes is how the future becomes.

Alfred North Whitehead, 1861–1947, English mathematician
and philosopher

The merger environment then [1967], compared to what it is today, was like comparing a Mozart quartet to Mick Jagger.

Felix Rohatyn, Lazard Frères & Co.

Make the most of yourself, for that is all there is to you.

> *Ralph Waldo Emerson, 1803–1882, American essayist and poet*

Risk arbitrage in those days [1949] basically depended upon the bankruptcy proceedings of the railroads [and] some public utility holding companies. And the consensus was that after these things came out, there'd be no more arbitrage business.

> *Alan Greenberg, b. 1928, Bear, Stearns & Co.*

As quoted in 1929: Neither patents, processes nor secrets are any longer an assurance of success. The men responsible for the financing of industry have come to recognize that scientific methods have largely leveled down the advantages between one product and another. There are no longer any secrets in business—at least not in the most successful business.

> *Bruce Barton, 1886–1957, American advertising*
> *executive and politician*

Syndicate business was not just a matter of firms. It was a matter of personalities.

> *Frederick Whittemore, Morgan Stanley & Co.*

I called my guys together and I said, "Fellas, the single or double won't work now. We need a home run." And that was Gulf Oil. We believed that we could take that big position in Gulf, show them how to restructure the company and enhance the value of our stock along with everybody else's. That was it. We were not trying to acquire them.

> *T. Boone Pickens, Jr., Mesa (Petroleum) LP, 1987*

Spring makes everything young again, save man.

> *Jean Paul Richter, 1763–1825, German writer and humorist*

The chains of habit are too weak to be felt until they are too strong to be broken.

Samuel Johnson, 1709–1784, British author

There will not be a Red revolution or a social catastrophe in the United States in five or fifty years. Big business has got us into a jam, and it will be most natural for leaders of business to show the way out. Since this will involve a financial loss by capitalists, who are powerful and hard of upsetting, drastic changes will not be immediately forthcoming.

Albert Bushnell Hart, 1854–1943, American historian

People have always said I overpay for companies. They're wrong. The reason I was willing to overpay was because I was analyzing them like stocks. I'm interested in three things: in managing, in growing the company internally and, of course, in making acquisitions. Because through internal growth, let's face it, unless you're a scientific company, to grow much more than 15 percent is not easy.

Gerald Tsai, Primerica Corp., 1987

Now, when I arrived at the exchange [1972], needless to say, the floor members were very concerned that they were going to go out of existence. There were lawsuits threatening Rule 390 that required that all trading by member firms of listed stocks be done on the exchange. So the floor members were very, very upset about that. Upstairs firms were burning, and the floor was angry with the upstairs firms over other matters. And there were, of course, a lot of failures to dispose of. In the end, I walked into a situation of hysteria.

James Needham, b. ~1932, former chairman, New York Stock Exchange

Whatever a man's age, he can reduce it several years by putting a bright-colored flower in his buttonhole.

Mark Twain, 1835–1910, American author

Banking may well be a career from which no man really recovers.

John Kenneth Galbraith, b. 1908, economist

Beauty, though injurious, hath strange power,
After offence returning to regain
Love once possessed.

John Milton, 1608–1674, English poet

You'd have the lawyer acting as a public relations man, and the investment banker acting as a lawyer, and the PR guy second-guessing everybody.

Joseph Flom, lawyer, Skadden, Arps, Slate, Meagher & Flom

First Boston achieved victory for DuPont [in its takeover of Conoco], mainly because of the deal's complex structure, the so-called Big Rube, after [cartoonist] Rube Goldberg. We nicknamed it the double-barreled two-step.

Joseph Perella, b. ~1941, Wasserstein Perella,
formerly at First Boston Corp.

Failure is only the opportunity to begin again, more intelligently.

Henry Ford, 1863–1947, American automobile manufacturer,
founder of Ford Motor Co.

Having outlived so many of my contemporaries, I ought not to forget that I may be thought to have outlived myself.

James Madison, 1751–1836, 4th U.S. president

I have always thought it would be easier to redeem a man steeped in vice and crime than a greedy, narrow-minded, pitiless merchant.

Albert Camus, 1913–1960, French journalist and philosopher

After Rule 415 [on shelf registration] came in [in the 1970s], you heard a lot of firms talking about the need for capital. They acquired capital and they have all grown, but I would raise the question of whether it was all necessary. I think the desire to cash in was what caused the public offerings of investment banking firms, not the "need for capital."

John Whitehead, Goldman, Sachs & Co., 1987

There were conglomerateurs, as they were called, buying companies by issuing preferred stock, warrants. The more complex the merger, the greater the arbitrage opportunity.

Leon Levy, Odyssey Partners, cofounder Oppenheimer Fund, 1987

I want to thank everybody who made this day necessary.

Yogi Berra, b. 1925, baseball player, coach, and manager

Never have so many people made so much money for contributing so little to the world.

Paul Miller, investment manager, Miller, Anderson & Sherrerd

Investment Banker: He thinks morals are paintings on walls, and scruples are money in Russia.

Sabrina, *the movie, 1995*

I have always believed that it's important to show a new look periodically. Predictability can lead to failure.

T. Boone Pickens, Jr., Mesa (Petroleum) LP, 1987

Nothing impresses the mind with a deeper feeling of loneliness than to tread the silent and deserted scene of former flow and pageant.

Washington Irving, 1783–1859, American author

Of course people are getting smarter; they are letting lawyers instead of their conscience be their guides.

Will Rogers, 1879–1935, American humorist and showman

It started just absolutely exploding, till by the late '60s, [the arbitrage business] was very, very active. By then there were many takeovers, and the conglomerateurs were getting tremendous heat because they were issuing paper that people were very suspicious of, just like they are now—only it was called Chinese paper instead of junk bonds.

Alan Greenberg, b. 1928, Bear, Stearns & Co.

Our whole life is but a greater and longer childhood.

Benjamin Franklin, 1706–1790, statesman, scientist, public leader

Restructuring is good insofar as it enhances the productivity of capital and labor. Restructuring is bad insofar as it lays a lot of debt on a company that it then has to pay interest on and pay off as opposed to developing products and plants and a more efficient operation over time.

Peter Vermilye, investment manager, Baring America Asset Management Co., 1987

The best description of "utter waste" would be a busload of lawyers going over a cliff with three empty seats.

Lamar Hunt, member, Professional Football Hall of Fame

We are reformers in the spring and summer; in autumn and winter we stand by the old; reformers in the morning, conservers at night.

Ralph Waldo Emerson, 1803–1882, American essayist and poet

We'd had a long historical relationship with Credit Suisse and felt that, of the three big Swiss banks, they were the most investment-banking minded; they knew all facets of the business. Then Rainer Gut came on the scene. He was a real international investment banker and a top strategist. He immediately realized he had a problem and an opportunity. The small participation was both too much and too little. That is when he and I negotiated the full association and Credit Suisse added its name to the venture, taking a large interest and making it its chosen instrument for supranational investment banking.

Robert Genillard, former chairman, Credit Suisse White Weld, 1987

The hair, it seems, is less involved in the Resurrection than the other parts of the body.

St. Thomas Aquinas, 1225–1274, Christian theologian and philosopher

You may not realize it when it happens, but a kick in the teeth may be the best thing in the world for you.

Walt Disney, 1901–1966, animator and film producer

Body and mind, like man and wife, do not always agree to die together.

Charles Caleb Colton, 1780–1832, writer

I'll tell you what led to the presence of so many corporate raiders. There were tremendous values in a lot of companies that shareholders weren't getting. So smart guys went out and said, "Hey, if they won't realize these values, if these guys won't do the job, I'll do it and make the money for myself."

Saul Steinberg, founder, Reliance Group Holdings, 1987

Bankruptcy is perhaps the greatest and most humiliating calamity which can befall an innocent man. The greater part of men, therefore, are sufficiently careful to avoid it. Some, indeed, do not avoid it; as some do not avoid the gallows.

Adam Smith, 1723–1790, political economist

One should . . . be able to see things as hopeless and yet be determined to make them otherwise.

F. Scott Fitzgerald, 1896–1940, novelist

At least 75 percent of farming is unscientific. If the same conditions of lack of modern business methods were applied to American industries and manufacturers, we would be a bankrupt nation today. This condition will not be corrected by Federal Farm Relief laws or any one panacea. Relief must come through education along right lines and through cooperation between individuals and communities.

Franklin D. Roosevelt, 1882–1945, while governor, State of New York

The gigantic corporate form of business, suspected and harrassed during the years of its evolution, is now accepted as not only useful, but necessary.

John D. Rockefeller, 1839–1937, American industrialist and philanthropist

Whatever needs to be maintained through force is doomed.

Henry Miller, 1891–1980, American writer

At the time [1977], people worked out mergers on the back of envelopes rather than through the management-consulting-type, by-the-pound analysis that's fairly standard now.

Bruce Wasserstein, Wasserstein Perella, formerly at First Boston Corp., 1987

A just cause needs no interpreting: It carries its own case. But the unjust argument, since it is sick, needs clever medicine.

Euripides, ~484–406 B.C., Greek dramatist, tragic poet

I still thought that I could convince Gulf to go along with my royalty trust spin-off. See, I probably can identify a dry hole quicker than most other people can, but I'm optimistic and a bit of a dreamer at times, and I want things to work.

T. Boone Pickens, Jr., Mesa (Petroleum) LP, 1987

I regret that I have but one law firm to give for my country.

Adlai E. Stevenson, 1900–1965, U.S. ambassador to the United Nations

On the legal nature of a corporation: It has neither a soul to damn nor a body to kick.

American jurist

I worried about whether I was really with it anymore. After all, I was a relationship banker, and I thought that that system was better for the clients than this wild bidding system in which the relationships counted for nothing.

John Whitehead, Goldman, Sachs & Co., 1987

Before 1980 the investment banker was the intermediary between borrower and investor; he did not have to judge the market, because he took no risk whatsoever.

Hans-Joerg Rudloff, b. ~1940, Credit Suisse First Boston

When you are through changing, you're through.

Alfred P. Sloan, Jr., 1875–1966, chairman of General Motors Corporation

Takeovers are, to my mind, almost as risk-free as [classical] arbitrage, in that you're buying assets, you're buying value in the marketplace, and what stands between you and the value is management. So if you can take control of a company, it's the greatest thing in the world. There's a certain enjoyment in the chess game—the fighting to get control.

Carl Icahn, b. 1936, corporate raider

Nothing so needs reforming as other people's habits.

Mark Twain, 1835–1910, American author

When one door closes another door opens; but we often look so long and so regretfully upon the closed door that we do not see the ones which are open for us.

Alexander Graham Bell, 1847–1922, American inventor and educator

In America, the young are always ready to give to those older than themselves the full benefit of their inexperience.

Oscar Wilde, 1854–1900, author

The worst bankrupt in the world is the man who has lost his enthusiasm. Let a man lose everything else in the world but his enthusiasm and he will come through again to success.

H. W. Arnold

Business is a combination of war and sport.

André Maurois, 1885–1967, French novelist and biographer

Common sense is genius dressed in its working clothes.

Ralph Waldo Emerson, 1803–1882, American essayist and poet

Most business problems require common sense rather than legal reference. They require good judgment and honesty of purpose rather than reference to the courts.

Edward N. Hurley

When we are too young our judgment is weak; when we are too old, ditto.

Blaise Pascal, 1623–1662, French philosopher

The late '60s really saw the origin of junk bonds. Drexel Burnham did not invent them. The companies issuing the bonds were the companies trying to do the takeovers, and Bear Stearns was active in trading and arbitraging them.

Alan Greenberg, b. 1928, Bear, Stearns & Co.

One of the things I learned the hard way was it does not pay to get discouraged. Keeping busy and making optimism a way of life can restore your faith in yourself.

Lucille Ball, 1911–1989, comedienne

Of Bruce Wasserstein, Perella's cohead of investment banking at First Boston: Ours is a unique relationship on Wall Street. It's almost like a marriage.

Joseph Perella, b. ~1941, Wasserstein Perella,
formerly at First Boston Corp.

I hadn't given up on exploration, but at the same time I saw that acquisitions would bring cheaper reserves than exploration. I was trying to upgrade the value of the assets. People used to say to me, "You should go out and drill because you're in the oil business." That's ridiculous. I mean, if it isn't economically sound, you're a fool to do it. I'd be a sap to go out and try to find oil at $15 a barrel when I could buy three barrels for the same price. It didn't take a financial genius to figure all that out.

T. Boone Pickens, Jr., Mesa (Petroleum) LP, 1987

Most controversies would soon be ended if those engaged in them would first accurately define their terms and then adhere to their definitions.

Tryon Edwards, 1809–1894

I've also felt that a shortage of capital is not necessarily a bad thing. It forces you to make choices as to what businesses you engage in and don't engage in. Any business that has all the capital it could possibly need is in trouble, because nobody is there making choices as to how it uses its capital.

John Whitehead, Goldman, Sachs & Co., 1987

Takeovers have increased the leverage in corporations. In the '60s when mergers were made, they were made with stock, mostly. There were not so many cash deals, so that didn't add debt. The leverage came in the '70s, when the stocks were undervalued and managements didn't want to use undervalued stock, so they started to borrow money.

Saul Steinberg, founder, Reliance Group Holdings, 1987

Reporters never ask, "What are these guys really up to?" The real rea-son for a bid in some cases is because you were being forced into it. With Cities Service we had an average price on our stock of $44, and the stock was selling for something like $36. I was afraid we'd get out and have an eight-point loss. That was $30 million. I didn't want to take the loss so I had to force something to happen.

T. Boone Pickens, Jr., Mesa (Petroleum) LP, 1987

Way back in 1973, Felix Rohatyn [Lazard Frères] was on the cover of *Business Week*, and I remember reading about all the fees he had col-lected working on [M&A] deals. I was so impressed. You don't use any of the firm's capital—at least you didn't in those days—and you make all these nice fees. You know, this is a *great* business. It wasn't like underwriting, where you actually had to take a capital risk.

Joseph Perella, b. ~1941, Wasserstein Perella,
formerly at First Boston Corp.

Things refuse to be mismanaged long.

Ralph Waldo Emerson, 1803–1882, American essayist and poet

In the takeover business, if you want a friend, you buy a dog.

Carl Icahn, b. 1936, corporate raider

Economic Forecasting

"" "" ""

Fantasies, Fudges, and Forecasts

Forecasts can be injurious to your wealth.
Dean LeBaron, b. 1933, investment manager
and contrarian thinker

Economic forecasts are derived from models—usually of the aggregate national or global economy—that simply extrapolate the past or that attempt to understand the sources of past changes and build them into the forecasts. Interpretations of economic data may give some clues as to how the financial markets will react, though more often than not, they are explaining why the markets have already reacted as they did. This discipline is teased for forecasting three recessions for every one that actually happens. No wonder it is called the dismal science.

An economist is an expert who will know tomorrow why the things he predicted yesterday didn't happen today.

Unknown

I'm a creature of the stock market. So my big successes are in getting secular swings in the stock market right.

Barton Biggs, Morgan Stanley & Co., 1987

I believe we are on an irreversible trend toward more freedom and democracy—but that could change.

J. Danforth Quayle, b. 1947, vice president of the United States

The clairvoyant society of London will not meet Tuesday because of unforeseen circumstances.

Advertisement in the London Financial Times

If economists could get themselves thought of as humble, competent people, on a level of dentists, that would be splendid.

John Maynard Keynes, 1883–1946, British economist,
1st Baron Keynes of Tilton

Why did it take Alan Greenspan ten years to get around to marrying his girlfriend? Because it took her ten years to figure out what he was talking about.

Richard Russell, author of Dow Theory Letters, *newsletter*

The golden rule for economic forecasters is: forecast what has already happened and stay at the cautious end. Forecasts tell us more about the present and the recent past than about the future.

Sir Samuel Brittan, Financial Times *columnist*

Wall Street economists set their CPI projections to the nearest one tenth of one percent to prove they have a sense of humor.

Edgar R. Fiedler

We were not happy with the way the media and other circles talked about petrodollars. We were not trying to use our investments to gain influence here or there. It was never political. I was never taken in by the idea that we would be rich forever. From the beginning we never felt it was good for the oil-producing countries—and especially us— to push oil prices up and up and up. We wanted an oil price to be reasonable and to be sustainable.

Mohammed Ali Abalkhail, Minister of Finance and National Economy, Saudi Arabia, 1987

When it comes to forecasting, there are only two kinds of economists, those who don't know and those who don't know that they don't know.

Ray Marshall, U.S. Secretary of Labor, 1977–1981

Economists don't know very much. And other people know even less.

Herbert Stein, former chairman, U.S. Council of Economic Advisers

One thing has not changed. Bear markets still correlate with tightening money more than anything else. If I ever see the Fed tightening money significantly, I'm going to sell stocks hard.

Peter Vermilye, investment manager, Baring America Asset Management Co., 1987

During that short time when high midsummer descends upon us and we are for once in a while drenched in nothing but sunshine, I lose my hold on reality.

J. B. Priestley, 1894–1984, dramatist

First there is a time when we believe everything, then for a little while we believe with discrimination, then we believe nothing whatever, and then we believe everything again—and, moreover, give reasons why we believe.

Georg C. Lichtenberg, 1742–1799, German physicist and philosopher

For four dreary years [1929–1933] the world has writhed under the cruel thumb of economic disaster. Many have thought that happiness had forever fled the earth. All this heaviness of night is surely but the prelude to a better dawn. The voice of God and the voice of Nature proclaim that the best is yet to be—always, the best is yet to be.

Robert Cromie

I have had a long, long life full of troubles, but there is one curious fact about them—nine-tenths of them never happened.

Andrew Carnegie, 1835–1919, steel manufacturer and philanthropist

The ideas of economists and political philosophers, both when they are right and when they are wrong, are more powerful than is commonly understood. Indeed, the world is ruled by little else.

John Maynard Keynes, 1883–1946, British economist,
1st Baron Keynes of Tilton

Then there is America's debt. It's like an astronomer's black hole, it is of such a magnitude and so complex. I think we will all go into the black hole—and I am sure that on the other side another light will come—but in the hole you will discover that the laws of physics are different.

Yves Oltramare, former general partner, Lombard, Odier & CIE, 1987

If a man looks sharply and attentively, he shall see fortune; for though she be blind, yet she is not invisible.

Sir Francis Bacon, 1561–1626, poet, dramatist, thinker

If theorists will cease to scare lenders with indiscriminate talk of currency inflation, and if the public encourages lending institutions which borrow freely from reserve sources—instead of running from them as if they had the plague—we will soon see the end of the depression.

Franklin W. Fort, Federal Home Loan Bank Board

Ireland is a country in which the probable never happens and the impossible always does.

J. P. Mahaffy, 1839–1919

Economists are smarter and smarter about fewer and fewer subjects. They tend to focus only on their narrow field of interest. That makes many of them very uninteresting, and irrelevant.

Ed Yardeni, chief economist and global investment strategist, Deutsche Bank Securities in New York

It is a mistake to look too far ahead. Only one link of the chain of destiny can be handled at a time.

Winston Churchill, 1874–1965, British prime minister

It isn't so much that hard times are coming; the change observed is mostly soft times going.

Groucho Marx, 1890–1977, comedian

Mass production is making a joke of old-time economies.

Coleman Livingston Blease, 1868–1942, American politician

Much wisdom often goes with fewer words.

Sophocles, 496–406 B.C., Athenian tragedian

Forecasts usually tell us more of the forecaster than of the future.

Warren Buffett, b. 1930, American investor

Oft expectation fails, and most oft there where most it promises.

William Shakespeare, 1564–1616, English poet, playwright

On the whole, I think we shall survive . . . The outlook is as bad as it has ever been, but thinking people realize that, and therein lies hope of its getting better.

Jawaharlal Nehru, 1889–1964, prime minister of India

The circumstances of the world are so variable, that an irrevocable purpose or opinion is almost synonymous with a foolish one.

W. H. Seward, 1801–1872, American political leader

The present contains nothing more than the past, and what is found in the effect was already in the cause.

Henri Bergson, 1859–1941, French philosopher

Things that I felt absolutely sure of but a few years ago, I do not believe now; and this thought makes me see more clearly how foolish it would be to expect all men to agree with me.

F. D. Van Amburgh

This time, like all other times, is a very good one, if we but know what to do with it.

Ralph Waldo Emerson, 1803–1882, American essayist and poet

I never felt good about being called Dr. Gloom, but I never worried about it either, because I think you should try to say it as it is. You're not in a popularity contest here.

Henry Kaufman, b. 1927, chief economist, Salomon Brothers

Unemployment may be due to good management which causes technological unemployment or to bad management which creates seasonable unemployment. It may be due to a temporary and superficial situation like the conditions created by the change in the Ford model last Fall, to deep lying recurrent fevers like cyclical disturbances, or to an acute situation due to fundamental change in national economy such as has taken place in England or Austria. It may be the price of progress or the sign of decay. And we can never be sure which is cause and which is effect.

Sam A. Lewisohn, American Management Association

What is all our knowledge worth? We do not even know what the weather will be tomorrow.

Berthold Auerbach, 1812–1882, German writer

When you come right down to it, almost any problem eventually becomes a financial problem.

Frederic G. Donner, former chief executive, General Motors

What's the matter, you dissentious rogues, that, rubbing the poor itch of your opinion, make yourself scabs.

William Shakespeare, 1564–1616, English poet, playwright

If you want to forecast the outcome of a beauty contest, look at the judges, not the beauties.

John Maynard Keynes, 1883–1946, British economist,
1st Baron Keynes of Tilton

Personally, I think everybody who predicts the future with a straight face should be required (by federal law) to change out of the business suit, wrap him/herself in a gypsy shawl, wear one of those pointed wizard's hats with a picture of a crescent moon on it, and make conjuring sounds over a crystal ball. That way, everybody would know exactly what's going on and how much credibility to give the answer.

Robert N. Veres, "The Vision Thing," Investment Advisor RR

Remember the First Law of Economics: For every economist, there is an equal and opposite economist—so for every bullish economist, there is a bearish one. The Second Law of Economics: They are both likely to be wrong.

> *William A. Sherden in* The Fortune Sellers: The Big Business of Selling and Buying Predictions

Murphy's Law of Economic Policy: Economists have the least influence on policy where they know the most and are most agreed; they have the most influence where they know the least and disagree the most vehemently.

> *Alan Blinder, economics professor and former Federal Reserve governor*

On October 14, 1929, ten days before the start of the Great Crash: Stock prices have reached what looks like a permanently high plateau.

> *Irving Fisher, 1867–1947, American economist*

The human mind craves clairvoyance, but anyone's ability to see the future is extremely limited.

> *Frederick L. Muller, chartered financial analyst (CFA)*

The trouble with our times is that the future isn't what it used to be.

> *Paul Valéry, 1871–1945, French writer*

False conclusions which have been reasoned out are infinitely worse than blind impulse.

> *Horace Mann, 1796–1859, American educator*

Fate laughs at probabilities.

> *Edward Bulwer-Lytton, 1803–1873, British author*

Give your decisions, never your reasons; your decisions may be right, your reasons are sure to be wrong.

William Murray, 1705–1793, British jurist, 1st Earl of Mansfield

The farther back you can look, the farther forward you are likely to see.

Winston Churchill, 1874–1965, British prime minister

In all recorded history there has not been one economist who has had to worry about where his next meal would come from.

Peter Drucker, b. 1909, author and consultant

Is today's crisis really earthshaking? Will you still think so next week? Next month? Next year?

A. I. Velander

Man's real life is happy, chiefly because he is ever expecting that it soon will be so.

Edgar Allan Poe, 1809–1849, writer

There is no harm in being sometimes wrong—especially if one is promptly found out.

John Maynard Keynes, 1883–1946, British economist,
1st Baron Keynes of Tilton

Minor surgery is surgery someone else is having.

J. Carl Cook

On December 6, 1996, when the Dow was at 6381.94: But how do we know when irrational exuberance has unduly escalated asset values, which then become subject to unexpected and prolonged contractions as they have in Japan over the past decade?

On January 20, 1999, when the Dow was at 9335.91: The level of equity prices would appear to envision substantially greater growth of profits than has been experienced of late.

> *Alan Greenspan, b. 1926, chairman of the U.S. Federal Reserve*

Silence is an answer to a wise man.

> *Euripides, ~484–406 B.C., Greek dramatist, tragic poet*

The best thing about the future is that it comes only one day at a time.

> *Abraham Lincoln, 1809–1865, 16th U.S. president*

The chief value of money lies in the fact that one lives in a world in which it is overestimated.

> *H. L. Mencken, 1880–1956, American journalist and writer*

The reason why so few people are agreeable in conversation is that each is thinking more about what he intends to say than about what others are saying, and we never listen when we are eager to speak.

> *La Rochefoucauld, 1613–1680, French author*

Two great talkers will not travel far together.

> *George Borrow, 1803–1881, British philologist, traveler, and writer*

What a people talk about means something. What they don't talk about means something.

> *William Saroyan, 1908–1981, American author*

You can observe a lot by just watching.

> *Yogi Berra, b. 1925, baseball player, coach, and manager*

It was the best of times, it was the worst of times, it was the age of wisdom, it was the age of foolishness, it was the epoch of belief, it was the epoch of incredulity, it was the season of Light, it was the season of Darkness, it was the spring of hope, it was the winter of despair.

Charles Dickens, 1812–1870, novelist

We moved through a number of squeezes and crises. We had the '66 crunch; '70 was Penn Central; '74 was Franklin National and City of New York; then we had that period of '79, '80 and '81, where we had Penn Square and Continental Illinois. The level of interest rates seemed to suggest that these stringencies were very severe. But in terms of market perception and requirements, it took higher and higher levels of interest rates to have markets recoil.

Henry Kaufman, b. 1927, chief economist, Salomon Brothers

In the long run we are all dead.

John Maynard Keynes, 1883–1946, British economist,
1st Baron Keynes of Tilton

[Forecasting] is like being in the entertainment business. You're only as good as your last call.

Barton Biggs, Morgan Stanley & Co., 1987

The future will be better tomorrow.

J. Danforth Quayle, b. 1947, vice president of the United States

Never prophesy, especially about the future.

Samuel Goldwyn, 1882–1974, American movie producer

When my forecast doesn't happen, I examine what led the market astray when it failed to act the way I thought it would.

Peter L. Bernstein, b. ~1919, investment manager,
economic commentator

Emerging Markets

99 99 99

Emerging Fortunes

> Brazil is the country of the future and always will be.
>
> *Brazilian joke*

This relatively new focus of investor enthusiasm is always exciting with something happening all the time, somewhere in the world, promising the opportunity for huge profits. However, emerging market investing may be a long-term cyclical phenomenon and not a steady, one-way path to riches. Certainly, the emerging market investment phase of more than the last decade is over. Not only has capital been destroyed and confidence shattered but the idea of capital flows for superior return from developed countries to needy, developing ones is gone.

We like it when markets are bearish. It's an interesting psychological phenomenon that when markets are bullish, I feel very uncomfortable and not too happy, because it's more difficult for us to find bargains. When markets are down, I'm a much happier person. When we hear about recessions, disasters, revolutions, we know there will be an opportunity.

Mark Mobius, investment manager, Templeton Emerging Markets Group

Gold always flows to where the most new wealth is being created: booming China could alone absorb the entire South African output in one or two years.

David Fuller

I was recently on a tour of Latin America, and the only regret I have was that I didn't study Latin harder in school so I could converse with those people.

J. Danforth Quayle, b. 1947, vice president of the United States

God didn't create emerging markets to enrich foreigners. Investment in them is getting to look a lot like colonization. The first few colonies made money; then the rest followed on a mistaken premise.

Marc Faber, b. ~1945, investment manager based in Hong Kong

Some cause happiness wherever they go; others whenever they go.

Oscar Wilde, 1854–1900, Irish-British author

The most sublime courage I have ever witnessed has been among that class too poor to know they possessed it, and too humble for the world to discover it.

George Bernard Shaw, 1856–1950, playwright

When written in Chinese the word crisis is composed of two characters. One represents danger and the other represents opportunity.

John F. Kennedy, 1917–1963, 35th U.S. President

Asia provides us with a unique opportunity to make strategic moves that will increase our presence and our participation in what we know will be one of the world's great markets of the 21st century.

Jack Welch, b. 1935, American executive

A great step towards independence is a good-humored stomach.

Seneca, ~4 B.C.–A.D. 65, Roman statesman and philosopher

All of us who grew up before World War II are immigrants in time, immigrants from an earlier world, living in an age essentially different from anything we knew before.

Margaret Mead, 1901–1978, American anthropologist

Both foreign business people and Chinese had their worries; after so many years of a closed-door policy, Chinese were afraid of having contacts with foreign partners.

Rong Yiren, b. ~1916, China International Trust and Investment Corp.

And he shall judge among the nations, and shall rebuke many people: and they shall beat their swords into plowshares, and their spears into pruning hooks: nation shall not lift up sword against nation, neither shall they learn war any more.

Isaiah 2:4, from The Bible

Democracy is the recurrent suspicion that more than half the people are right more than half of the time.

Elwyn Brooks White, 1899–1985, American author

It was always macroeconomic; we couldn't tell a country, "You shouldn't spend so much money for buying airplanes; spend more for something else." That was not considered to be the fund's field.

Johannes Witteveen, former managing director,
International Monetary Fund, 1987

Every human mind is a great slumbering power until awakened by keen desire and by definite resolution to do.

Edgar F. Roberts

Everything that is done in the world is done by hope. No merchant or tradesman would set himself to work if he did not hope to reap benefit thereby.

Martin Luther, 1483–1546, German religious leader

I have convinced myself that progress today is made not by the single genius, but the common people. The genius raids but the common people occupy and possess.

T. E. Lawrence, 1888–1935, British soldier and writer

Idealism increases in direct proportion to one's distance from the problem.

John Galsworthy, 1867–1933, British author

In emerging markets investments, it is necessary to be optimistic since the world belongs to optimists; the pessimists are only spectators. The fact remains that there have always been problems and there will continue to be so in the coming years throughout the world. But we are entering an era which is perhaps unparalleled in the history of mankind. With better communications, improved travel, more international commerce and generally better relations between nations, the opportunities for emerging markets investors are better than they have ever been before.

Mark Mobius, investment manager, Templeton Emerging Markets Group

A man doubtful of his dinner, or trembling at a creditor, is not much disposed to abstracted meditation, or remote inquiries.

Samuel Johnson, 1709–1784, British author

If you would trust men, you must train them.

Thomas Jefferson, 1743–1826, 3rd U.S. president

In no other country but the United States could a boy from a country village, without inheritance or influential friends, look forward with unbounded hope.

Herbert Hoover, 1874–1964, 31st U.S. president

Markets are people, not places.

Dr. Julius Klein

Nothing in life is to be feared. It is only to be understood.

Marie Curie, 1867–1934, chemist

One does not leave a convivial party before closing time.

Winston Churchill, 1874–1965, British prime minister

Some will always be above others. Destroy the inequality today, and it will appear again tomorrow.

Ralph Waldo Emerson, 1803–1882, American essayist and poet

The basis of individual and national progress is the willingness to sacrifice the present for the future. That is the way nations get ahead, and that is the way individuals get ahead.

William Feather, 1889–1981, American author, publisher

In 1967 Japan was still a very small country; the GNP was then $173 million. Today [1987] it's $2 trillion. Beginning in 1967 we entered a period of growth with stability.

Yusuke Kashiwagi, Bank of Tokyo, 1987

The greatest realities are physical and economic, all the subtleties of life come afterward.

Joyce Carol Oates, b. 1938, American author

The influence of each human being on others in this life is a kind of immortality.

John Quincy Adams, 1767–1848, 6th U.S. president

The lower unemployed man in America today is better fed, better clothed, and better housed than the highest paid manual laborer in Russia.

Dr. Will Durant, 1885–1981, American historian

The moral progression of a people can scarcely begin till they are independent.

Harriet Martineau, 1802–1876, British social reformer

Among a democratic people, where there is no hereditary wealth, every man works to earn a living, or is born of parents who have worked. The notion of labor is therefore presented to the mind, on every side, as the necessary, natural, and honest condition.

Alexis de Tocqueville, 1805–1859, French historian
and political philosopher

The real price of everything, what everything really costs to the man who wants to acquire it, is the toil and trouble of acquiring it.

Adam Smith, 1723–1790, political economist

There is a serious tendency towards capitalism among the well-to-do peasants.

Mao Zedong, 1893–1976, Chinese soldier and Communist leader

What a vast difference there is between the barbarism that precedes culture and the barbarism that follows it.

Friedrich Hebbel, 1813–1863, German dramatist

You won't learn to hold your own in the world by standing on guard, but by attacking and getting well hammered yourself.

George Bernard Shaw, 1856–1950, playwright

In 1994: What is happening in the emerging markets is not a mania, like the Mississippi Bubble in the early 18th century. It's a fundamental development, like the rise of the United States in the 19th century or the rise of Japan in the second half of the 20th century.

Barton Biggs, Morgan Stanley & Co., 1994

When the capital development of a country becomes the by-product of the activities of a casino, the job is likely to be ill-done.

John Maynard Keynes, 1883–1946, British economist,
1st Baron Keynes of Tilton

Unless you're tolerant, you can't have an open mind. If you don't have an open mind, you can't be a good investor. You've got to let everything in and be willing to digest it.

Mark Mobius, investment manager, Templeton Emerging Markets Group

The fund required a reduction of the deficit, and a government did it not by reducing military spending but by reducing consumer subsidies. Then there were riots in the streets, and the IMF was blamed for this policy.

Johannes Witteveen, former managing director,
International Monetary Fund, 1987

An idea does not pass from one language to another without change.

Miguel de Unamuno, 1864–1937, Spanish author

Anyone who says you can't see a thought simply doesn't know art.

Wynetka Ann Reynolds

Change does not necessarily assure progress, but progress implacably requires change. Education is essential to change for education creates both wants and the ability to satisfy them.

Henry Steele Commager, b. 1902, American historian

Fortune favors the brave.

Terence, ~186–159 B.C., Roman playwright

He who cannot change the very fabric of his thought will never be able to change reality.

Anwar Sadat, 1918–1981, Egyptian president

History is rapidly becoming a race between education and catastrophe.

H. G. Wells, 1866–1946, English novelist, sociologist, and historian

In life as in the dance, grace glides on blistered feet.

Alice Abrams

It is the studying that you do after your school days that really counts. Otherwise, you know only that which everyone else knows.

Henry L. Doherty, 1870–1939, American engineer and utility magnate

Success seems to be largely a matter of hanging on after others have let go.

William Feather, 1889–1981, American author, publisher

Men of genius do not excel in a profession because they labor in it; they labor in it because they excel.

William Hazlitt, 1778–1830, British author

Nothing will ever be attempted, if all possible objections must first be overcome.

Samuel Johnson, 1709–1784, British author

Speculation is the romance of trade, and casts contempt upon its sober realities. It renders the stock-jobber a magician, and the exchange a region of enchantment.

Washington Irving, 1783–1859, American author

Success is not searching for you. You must do the seeking.

Frank Tyger

The attempt and not the deed confounds us.

William Shakespeare, 1564–1616, English poet, playwright

The interval between the decay of the old and the formation and establishment of the new constitutes a period of transition which must always necessarily be one of uncertainty, confusion, error, and wild and fierce fanaticism.

John C. Calhoun, 1782–1850, American political leader

The fund [the IMF] is not meant to be an institution specially designed to help developing countries. It is meant to help all its member countries when their balance-of-payments situation requires some assistance.

Johannes Witteveen, former managing director,
International Monetary Fund, 1987

There are a terrible lot of lies going around the world, and the worst of it is half of them are true.

Winston Churchill, 1874–1965, British prime minister

If this nation is going to survive meaningfully, and then perhaps grow decently, it has got to begin to know and accept enormous deprivation.

William Saroyan, 1908–1981, American author

Reform must come from within, not from without. You cannot legislate for virtue.

James Cardinal Gibbons, 1834–1921, American religious leader

The highest and best form of efficiency is the spontaneous cooperation of a free people.

Woodrow Wilson, 1856–1924, 28th U.S. president

To preserve their [our] independence, we must not let our rulers load us with perpetual debt. We must make our election between economy and liberty, or profusion and servitude.

Thomas Jefferson, 1743–1826, 3rd U.S. president

The progress of democracy seems irresistible, because it is the most uniform, the most ancient and the most permanent tendency which is to be found in history.

Alexis de Tocqueville, 1805–1859, French historian
and political philosopher

Money is the most important thing in the world. It represents health, strength, honor, generosity, and beauty as conspicuously as the want of it represents illness, weakness, disgrace, meanness, and ugliness. Not the least of its virtues is that it destroys base people as certainly as it fortifies and dignifies noble people.

George Bernard Shaw, 1856–1950, playwright

Culture is the sum of all the forms of art, of love and of thought, which, in the course of centuries, have enabled man to be less enslaved.

André Malraux, 1901–1976, French author and political activist

Labor rids us of three great evils—irksomeness, vice and poverty.

Voltaire, 1694–1778, French philosopher and writer

Necessity is the constant scourge of the lower classes, ennui of the higher ones.

Arthur Schopenhauer, 1788–1860, German philosopher

The forces of a capitalist society, if left unchecked, tend to make the rich richer and the poor poorer.

Jawaharlal Nehru, 1889–1964, prime minister of India

"Emerging markets" may be a euphemism but it is also a declaration of hope and faith. Although some of the stock markets of developing nations may sometimes seem "submerged," they are generally emerging into bigger and better things.

Mark Mobius, investment manager, Templeton Emerging Markets Group

Experience and enthusiasm are two fine business attributes seldom found in one individual.

William Feather, 1889–1981, American author, publisher

In great attempts it is glorious even to fail.

Longinus, 1st century A.D., *Greek critic*

I said at the annual meeting in '76 that now the policy should shift toward adjustment [due to the oil deficits]. I think at that time countries, especially the developing countries that were borrowing so heavily, should have adjusted more and the banks should have become more reserved. But they were still in their big lending spree. They felt there was no sovereign risk and it was a marvelous thing to do—the expanded lending with nice margins and so on.

Johannes Witteveen, former managing director,
International Monetary Fund, 1987

It is very much easier for a rich man to invest and grow richer than for a poor man to begin investing at all. And this is also true of nations.

Barbara Ward, 1914–1981, British economist and journalist

Financial Engineering

99 **99** **99**

Instruments of Torture
or Engineering Profit

The revenge of the nerds.

Andrew Lo, professor, Massachusetts Institute of
Technology and director and founder of its
Laboratory for Financial Engineering

Financial engineering is, in essence, the phenomenon of innovation in the financial industries: securities innovation; innovative financial processes; and creative solutions to corporate finance problems. The biggest challenges over the next few decades for financial engineering will focus on aspects of human judgment that are now considered impossible to mimic computationally: fear, greed, and other emotional aspects of decision making. Recent advances in the cognitive sciences, neurobiology, and computer science may provide some clues to solving these tantalizing problems in financial contexts.

The advent of affordable desktop microcomputers and machine-readable real-time and historical data have irrevocably changed the way financial markets function. The outcome is nothing short of an industrial revolution in which the old-boys network has been replaced by the computer network; where what matters more is *what* you know, not *who* you know; and where graduates of Harvard and Yale suddenly find themselves less employable than graduates of MIT and Caltech. It is, in short, the revenge of the nerds!

Andrew Lo, MIT finance professor

I am sorry to say that there is too much point to the wisecrack that life is extinct on other planets because their scientists were more advanced than ours.

John F. Kennedy, 1917–1963, 35th U.S. president

Traditional banking is dying. But the grieving throng around the deathbed face a long and expensive vigil.

Peter Martin, Financial Times *columnist*

Banking is essential; bankers are not.

Bill Gates, b. 1955, Microsoft founder

A man is really at his best, when he's on his way to becoming what he's going to become. After he's become it, he loses an infinitesimal bit of sharpness, like a star after his best role.

Edward Johnson, founder of Fidelity Funds

Anything that has been done in the same way for the past five years needs an investigation or change.

Percy S. Straus, R. H. Macy & Co.

Change is scientific, progress is ethical.

Bertrand Russell, 1872–1970, British philosopher, mathematician

[It's] time for the human race to enter the solar system.

J. Danforth Quayle, b. 1947, vice president of the United States

For everything you have missed you have gained something else.

Ralph Waldo Emerson, 1803–1882, American essayist and poet

How do I work? I grope.

Albert Einstein, 1879–1955, German-American scientist

- A time series is a fallacy.
- Make volatility of events and markets your ally.
- Be an investment guerrilla; strike back fast, unpredictably . . . and withdraw.
- Unless you become right within twenty-four months, you are wrong.

Dean LeBaron, quoted in Five Eminent Contrarians, *by Steven L. Mintz, 1994*

If I have been able to see farther than others, it was because I stood on the shoulders of giants.

Isaac Newton, 1642–1727, English scientist

It is the mind that makes the body rich.

William Shakespeare, 1564–1616, English poet, playwright

In science, read by preference the newest works; in literature, the oldest. The classics are always modern.

Lord Lytton, 1803–1873, English novelist and politician

Change is the handmaiden Nature requires to do her miracles with.

Mark Twain, 1835–1910, American author

It is essential to the triumph of reform that it never succeed.

William Hazlitt, 1778–1830, British author

Just because everything is different doesn't mean anything has changed.

Irene Peter

Technology changes, economic laws do not.

Hal Varian and Carl Shapiro in Information Rules, *1998*

Man is a dog's idea of what God should be.

Holbrook Jackson, 1874–1948

No age or time of life, no position or circumstance, has a monopoly on success. Any age is the right age to start doing!

Gerard, d. 1108, Archbishop of York

My own view, that the invisible hand could work its magic through mere humans, is an essential part of Adam Smith's insight. Not many thousands of years ago, men like this would have clubbed each other over hunting rights. A few hundred years ago they would have hacked each other with axes and swords. Now they yelled at trainees while they brought together the supply and demand of home mortgages on a world-wide scale.

Harry Markowitz, Nobel laureate for economics

No army can withstand the strength of an idea whose time has come.

Victor Hugo, 1802–1885, French writer

No great advance has ever been made in science, politics, or religion, without great controversy.

Lyman Beecher, 1775–1863, American religious leader

Obsolescence is a factor which says that the new thing I bring you is worth more than the unused value of the old thing.

Charles F. Kettering, 1876–1958, engineer and inventor

On "pushing the envelope:" If a thing is worth doing, it's worth doing to excess.

Dean LeBaron, b. 1933, investment manager and contrarian thinker

One change always leaves the way open for the establishment of others.

Niccolò Machiavelli, 1469–1527, Florentine diplomat and writer

Out of every fruition of success, no matter what, comes forth something to make a new effort necessary.

Walt Whitman, 1819–1892, American poet

Change is inevitable in a progressive country. Change is constant.

Benjamin Disraeli, 1804–1881, British prime minister, author, 1st Earl of Beaconsfield

Innovation happened at the Merc [in 1967] because we were hungrier . . . than the Chicago Board of Trade. The Merc was on the make.

Leo Melamed, b. ~1932, former chairman, Chicago Mercantile Exchange

Progress is not how long you can keep a thing, but how quickly you can economically scrap it.

Owen D. Young, 1874–1962, American lawyer and financier

Progress might have been all right once, but it's gone on too long.

Ogden Nash, 1902–1971, American poet

Man is still the most extraordinary computer of all.

John F. Kennedy, 1917–1963, 35th U.S. president

Restlessness and discontent are the first necessities of progress.

Thomas A. Edison, 1847–1931, inventor and industrialist

Some have an idea that the reason we in this country discard things so readily is because we have so much. The facts are exactly opposite—the reason we have so much is simply because we discard things so readily. We replace the old in return for something that will serve us better.

Alfred P. Sloan, Jr., 1875–1966, chairman of General Motors Corporation

The greatest events—these are not our loudest but our stillest hours.

Friedrich Nietzsche, 1844–1900, German philosopher

The most successful businessman is the man who holds onto the old just as long as it is good and grabs the new just as soon as it is better.

Robert P. Vanderpoel

The war has demanded the most resolute daring and imaginative qualities in the history of American industry. This is not without its benefits to every one of us. In the past three years it explored new fields, applied newly discovered principles and developed a new variety of industrial products almost beyond belief. These benefits for mankind are withheld now only by the prior needs of war. Once the war is won this new American production, this vigorous team of industry and research, will be one of the major results of that victory. Let us then put it to work for a world at peace.

Admiral Chester W. Nimitz, 1885–1966, fleet admiral

There is no genius in life like the genius of energy and activity.

D. C. Mitchell

Among the things I regret most is that this liberalization in the financial field was not as fast as I expected.

Haruo Mayekawa, former governor, Bank of Japan, 1987

There is nothing wrong with change, if it is in the right direction.

Winston Churchill, 1874–1965, British prime minister

This is a world of action, and not for moping and droning in.

Charles Dickens, 1812–1870, novelist

Name the greatest of all inventors. Accident.

Mark Twain, 1835–1910, American author

Unless the reformer can invent something which substitutes attractive virtues for attractive vices, he will fail.

Walter Lippmann, 1889–1974, American journalist

War will disappear, like the dinosaur, when changes in world conditions have destroyed its survival value.

Robert A. Millikan, 1868–1953, American physicist

The early days were the greatest period. It was really fun, because you felt you were creating something, building up an entirely new structure, an entirely new market. It wasn't just dealing in abstract financial paper—it wasn't just a financier's job. It was really an architect's job. It was building a house, building a structure.

Robert Genillard, former chairman, Credit Suisse White Weld, 1987

We can change our whole life and the attitude of people around us simply by changing ourselves.

Rudolf Dreikurs, 1897–1972, American psychiatrist

We have more power than will, and it is only to exculpate ourselves that we often say that things are impracticable.

La Rochefoucauld, 1613–1680, French author

Work is a necessity for man. Man invented the alarm clock.

Pablo Picasso, 1881–1973, artist

You can judge your age by the amount of pain you feel when you come in contact with a new idea.

John Nuveen

You have a dollar. I have a dollar. We swap. Now you have my dollar—I have your dollar. We are no better off . . . You have an idea, I have an idea. We swap. Now you have two ideas and I have two ideas—both are richer . . . What you gave you have; what I got you did not lose. This is Cooperation.

The Outlook

Imagination is more important than knowledge.

Albert Einstein, 1879–1955, German-American scientist

You'll find as you grow older that you weren't born such a very great while ago after all. The time shortens up.

William Dean Howells, 1837–1920, American author

Everything that can be invented has been invented.

Charles H. Duell, director of U.S. Patent Office, 1899

The market is not an invention of capitalism. It has existed for centuries. It is an invention of civilisation.

Mikhail Gorbachev, b. 1931, Soviet leader and Nobel laureate

Recently we worked on a project that involved users rating their experience with a computer. When we had the computer the users had worked with ask for an evaluation of its performance, the responses tended to be positive. But when we had a second computer ask the same people to evaluate their encounters with the first machine, the people were significantly more critical. Their reluctance to criticize the first computer "face to face" suggested they didn't want to hurt its feelings, even though they knew it was only a machine.

Bill Gates, b. 1955, Microsoft founder, in The Road Ahead

We started working closely with the [NYSE] member firms to expand our system to handle 100 million shares a day. Some of the members were very much opposed to building a system that would handle 100 million shares. I wasn't willing to risk the continued existence of the New York Stock Exchange. If the volume came and the industry and the exchange were not prepared, we could count on very serious intervention by the government. Then one day we traded 82 million shares. Well, that eliminated most of the skeptics.

William Batten, former chairman,
New York Stock Exchange, 1976–1984

A determined soul will do more with a rusty monkey wrench than a loafer will accomplish with all the tools in a machine shop.

Rupert Hughes

American businessmen are always ready to scrap worn-out machines but slow to scrap worn-out ideas.

Eugene G. Grace, d. 1960, American businessman

Education, however indispensable in a cultivated age, produces nothing on the side of genius. When education ends, genius often begins.

Isaac Disraeli, 1766–1848, English author

From men, man learns to speak, from the gods to keep silent.

Plutarch, d. A.D. 431 or 432, Greek philosopher

Have you not learned that not stocks or bonds or stately homes, or products of mill or field are our country? It is the splendid thought that is in our minds.

Benjamin Harrison, 1726–1791, American patriot

During the crunch of 1968 we once ran the computer 43 straight days without shutting it off. And it never bombed out.

William Tuite, former senior vice president for data processing, Drexel Burnham Lambert

I like talking to engineers best. They build bridges, they're very precise, very disciplined, yet I find they have roving minds.

Ralph Richardson, 1902–1983, English writer

If there were no bad people, there would be no good lawyers.

Charles Dickens, 1812–1870, novelist

There's a way to do it better . . . find it.

Thomas A. Edison, 1847–1931, inventor and industrialist

If youth knew, if age could.

Henri Estienne, 1531–1598, French printer and publisher

We're going to have the best-educated American people in the world.

J. Danforth Quayle, b. 1947, vice president of the United States

Necessity is the mother of taking chances.

Mark Twain, 1835–1910, American author

Intelligent discontent is the mainspring of civilization.

Eugene V. Debs, 1855–1926, American labor leader

It has recently been discovered that research causes cancer in rats.

Unknown

It is quite wrong to think of old age as a downward slope. On the contrary, one climbs higher and higher with the advancing years, and that, too, with surprising strides. Brain-work comes as easily to the old as physical exertion to the young.

George Sand, 1804–1876, French author

As quoted in 1987: It's amazing the fantastic speed at which it goes. The Big Bang in London will lead to a world financial market and to deregulation, and the competition is going to be fierce and free.

Yves Oltramare, former general partner, Lombard, Odier & CIE, 1987

Make it idiot-proof and someone will make a better idiot.

Bumper sticker

Men of lofty genius when they are doing the least work are the most active.

Leonardo da Vinci, 1452–1519, Italian artist,
architect, engineer, and scientist

Most of us are about as eager to be changed as we were to be born, and go through our changes in a similar state of shock.

James Baldwin, 1924–1987, novelist

When the music stops, forget the old music!

Edward Johnson, founder of Fidelity Funds

Talent is a gift which God has given us secretly, and which we reveal without perceiving it.

Charles de Montesquieu, 1689–1755, French philosopher, author

That there is an evolution of one sort or another is now common ground among scientists. Whether or not that evolution is directed is another question.

Pierre Chardin, 1881–1955, French philosopher

No one can examine the panorama of business and finance in America during the past half-dozen years without realizing that we are living in a new era.

John Moody, founder of the credit agency, 1927

The most important thought I ever had was that of my individual responsibility to God.

Daniel Webster, 1782–1852, American statesman

I've seen people who stayed too long in a leading position. If they are creative people, they invent a new religion, and then sooner or later they believe their religion is infallible. They start believing in their own myths, and they are not able to rejuvenate themselves.

Robert Genillard, former chairman, Credit Suisse White Weld, 1987

There is a woman at the beginning of all great things.

Alphonse de Lamartine, 1790–1869, French writer and statesman

Thought breeds thought. It grows under your hands.

Henry David Thoreau, 1817–1862, American naturalist and writer

When a distinguished but elderly scientist states that something is possible, he is almost certainly right. When he states that something is impossible, he is probably wrong.

> *Arthur C. Clarke, b. 1917, author of science fiction*

Engineering, by the very nature of its development and application, builds on whatever is accepted theory at any given stage of the cycle. Investment theories tend to lurch forward in leaps, usually after the disappointment of a prolonged bear market. New theories emerge, correcting the ills exposed by a calamitous decline, and engineering applies the new wisdoms.

> *Dean LeBaron, b. 1933, investment manager and contrarian thinker*

Within us all there are wells of thought and dynamos of energy which are not suspected until emergencies arise.

> *Thomas J. Watson, 1874–1956, American businessman, IBM chairman*

Worry compounds the futility of being trapped on a deadend street. Thinking opens new avenues.

> *Cullen Hightower*

The second step was diversification, and that was in 1971. The rulebook was now in place; we [the Merc] were successfully doing the meat business . . . but where could you go with that? You can't invent another meat.

> *Leo Melamed, b. ~1932, former chairman, Chicago Mercantile Exchange*

Progress is the mother of problems.

> *G. K. Chesterton, 1874–1936, English journalist and writer*

Without these breakthroughs [in computer technology, data collection, and organization], much of the financial technology developed over the past thirty years would be irrelevant academic musings, condemned to the moldy oblivion of unread finance journals in university library basements.

Andrew Lo, MIT finance professor

Nothing is, but thinking makes it so.

William Shakespeare, 1564–1616, English poet, playwright

The nation that has the schools has the future.

Prince Otto Eduard Leopold von Bismarck, 1815–1898,
1st chancellor of the German Empire

Fixed Income

Bonds and Bonding

The first hundred years are the hardest.

Sidney Homer

Fixed income securities are generally thought of as safe rather boring investments, lacking the risks associated with equities. In practice, though, it is possible to lose vast amounts of money by getting the bond markets wrong. Inflation is bad for bonds, eroding their value as prices and yields, unless index-linked, fail to keep pace with rising prices. Inflation drives interest rates higher and bond prices down. In terms of inflation-adjusted returns, bonds have actually been more risky than equities for most of the nineteenth and twentieth centuries. However, many believe that bonds may outperform stocks over the next few years as stocks' recent strong performance makes them less attractive and as deflation becomes a more potent force than inflation.

$1,000 left to earn interest at 8% a year will grow to $43 quadrillion in 400 years, but the first hundred years are the hardest.

Sidney Homer

We do not believe that the way to cope with high interest rates is to borrow at floating rates. The way to resolve high interest rates is not to borrow. A floating rate is society's proxy for discontent; it means, "I don't want my future to be fixed." So short-term borrowings at floating rates are not bad per se; they simply reflect the unease of a culture.

Eugene Rotberg, b. ~1929, World Bank

Loss of capital is a far more regrettable alternative than loss of opportunity.

Kenneth Safian

Most of today's 30-something investors would rather burn their money than watch it molder in a money market fund.

Jim Grant

I used to think that if there was reincarnation, I wanted to come back as the president or the pope. But now I want to be the bond market— you can intimidate everybody.

James Carville, b. 1946, U.S. political advisor and author

Some people claim that the Eurobond market actually got started with the Autostrade issue of Warburgs in 1963. But that issue was only one of several occurring around that time. The Autostrade issue, though, was a key factor because it was a more structured effort and syndicated in more of a Eurobond fashion.

Robert Genillard, former chairman, Credit Suisse White Weld, 1987

"Easy come easy go" is a saying as applicable to knowledge as to wealth.

Herbert Spencer, 1820–1903, British philosopher

Creditors have better memories than debtors.

Benjamin Franklin, 1706–1790, statesman, scientist, public leader

Mountains of junk bonds were sold by those who didn't care to those that didn't think—and there was no shortage of either.

Warren Buffett, b. 1930, American investor

Sickness is felt, but health not at all.

Thomas Fuller, 1654–1734, doctor and writer

Now, there was an event in 1962 that people didn't pay that much attention to. It was the year in which Citicorp issued the first negotiable CD. It was the beginning of the liberalization of the Regulation Q ceilings on time and savings deposits. It was, I think, the birth of the restructuring of the financial markets, because it was then that the banks started gradually to bid for funds; previously, people just went into the bank to deposit.

Henry Kaufman, b. 1927, chief economist, Salomon Brothers

Sign in a bank window: "Little by little you can safely stack up a strong reserve here, *but not until after you start.*"

Unknown

Sleep, riches and health to be truly enjoyed must be interrupted.

Jean Paul Richter, 1763–1825, German writer and humorist

Investing in bonds requires attention to more than one event at a time. Driving a car requires a foot on the gas, hands on the wheel, and eyes on the road. Navigating the bond market requires a foot on interest rates, a handle on the prospects of being repaid, and an eye on inflation.

Steven Mintz, financial journalist, in Beyond Wall Street: The Art of Investing, *1998*

Perfection is obtained by slow degrees, it requires the hand of time.

Voltaire, 1694–1778, French philosopher and writer

A precedent embalms a principle.

Benjamin Disraeli, 1804–1881, British prime minister, author,
1st Earl of Beaconsfield

There is something infinitely healing in the repeated refrains of nature—the assurance that dawn comes after night, and spring after the winter.

Rachel Carson, 1907–1964, American biologist

You know you are an experienced investor when wide ties have been "in" three times in your investment career.

Steve Leuthold, investment manager, The Leuthold Group

I think the British have the distinction above all other nations of being able to put new wine into old bottles without bursting them.

Clement Atlee, 1883–1967, British prime minister

Love at first sight is easy to understand. It's when two people have been looking at each other for years that it becomes a miracle.

Sam Levinson

Permanence is a man-made fantasy smiled on by time.

Paul von Ringelheim

Then we had the New York City fiscal crisis. The city was selling this paper, and people weren't paying all that much attention. It's like somebody challenging the figures of the U.S. Treasury Department. How do you know what the national debt is?

Walter Wriston, formerly Citibank, 1987

Whatever limits us we call Fate.

> *Ralph Waldo Emerson, 1803–1882, American essayist and poet*

There is only one thing about which I am certain, and that is that there is very little about which one can be certain.

> *W. Somerset Maugham, 1874–1965, author*

An investment in knowledge always pays the best interest.

> *Benjamin Franklin, 1706–1790, statesman, scientist, public leader*

The financial institution had become part of the mechanism that was pushing credit and would allow the system to operate at a higher level of interest rates. Heretofore [before the 1970s] the financial institutions really were part of the braking mechanism. They got squeezed and suffered losses when interest rates went up.

> *Henry Kaufman, b. 1927, chief economist, Salomon Brothers*

Blessed are the young, for they shall inherit the national debt.

> *Herbert Hoover, 1874–1964, 31st U.S. president*

Obstinacy in opinions holds the dogmatist in the chains of error, without hope of emancipation.

> *John C. Granville*

Enjoyment is *not* a goal, it is a feeling that accompanies important ongoing activity.

> *Paul Goodman, 1911–1972, writer, educator, analyst*

Down cycles are not fun. Because when you're in a down cycle, you never know whether this is a down cycle or the beginning of the end.

> *Robert Rubin, b. ~1940, Goldman, Sachs, former U.S. treasury secretary*

The sage has one advantage: He is immortal. If this is not his century, many others will be.

Baltasar Gracian, 1601–1658, Spanish priest and writer

If the idea is good it will survive defeat. It may even survive victory.

Stephen Vincent Benet, 1898–1943, American author

The older I get, the better I used to be.

William D. Keogh

There are people whose watch stops at a certain hour and who remain permanently at that age.

Charles Sainte-Beuve, 1804–1869, French critic

If we open a quarrel between the past and the present, we shall find that we have lost the future.

Winston Churchill, 1874–1965, British prime minister

Success consists of a series of little daily victories.

Laddie F. Hutar

After the ship has sunk, everyone knows how she might have been saved.

Italian proverb

I sensed as we moved into that '68–'69 period that there was something changing in the financial system where we were removing all kinds of impediments to interest rates. And we were also gradually removing constraints for markets, for financial institutions to be in different types of businesses.

Henry Kaufman, b. 1927, chief economist, Salomon Brothers

He that fails today may be up again tomorrow.

Cervantes, 1547–1616, Spanish writer

Man is a history-making creature who can neither repeat his past nor leave it behind.

W. H. Auden, 1907–1973, British poet

If you would like to know the value of money, go and try to borrow some.

Benjamin Franklin, 1706–1790, statesman, scientist, public leader

Nothing comes easy that is done well.

Harry F. Banks

Inflation: Historical phenomenon that used to adversely affect stocks.

Steve Leuthold, investment manager, The Leuthold Group

All great changes are irksome to the human mind, especially those which are attended with great dangers and uncertain effects.

John Adams, 1735–1826, 2nd U.S. president

One can always trust to time. Insert a wedge of time, and nearly everything straightens itself out.

Norman Douglas, b. 1914, American agronomist

At this stage, in the 1960s really, there were two phases to the growth of the [Eurobond] market. At first, it was very difficult to convince anybody to float an issue: The market wasn't respectable, it was unproven, the concept was esoteric, it was legally complicated. Then in the second stage, the interest equalization tax passed by the United States gave a new dimension to the market by bringing in top-grade U.S. corporate borrowers for both straight and convertible bonds.

Robert Genillard, former chairman, Credit Suisse White Weld, 1987

The past not merely is not fugitive, it remains present.

Marcel Proust, 1871–1922, French novelist

The remedy of time is patience.

Arabian proverb

We boil at different degrees.

Ralph Waldo Emerson, 1803–1882, American essayist and poet

Experience is the hardest kind of teacher. It gives you the test first and the lesson afterward.

Unknown

And then, of course [in the 1970s], we had the advent of floating-rate financing, which helped you structure the maturity of an asset and the rate of return on an asset and have it spread against the liability side. So you were able to take the interest rate risk out of many a financing arrangement for a financial intermediary, although the financial intermediary kept the credit risk.

Henry Kaufman, b. 1927, chief economist, Salomon Brothers

What happens when the future has come and gone?

Robert Half, employment agent

The easy way to teach children the value of money is to borrow from them.

Unknown

Money talks and it is the only conversation worth hearing when times are bad.

Fred Allen, 1894–1956, American humorist

In investing money, the amount of interest you want should depend on whether you want to eat well or sleep well.

J. Kenfield Morley

Foreign Exchange

99 99 99

Dollars and Deutschmarks

Give me only lucky generals.

Napoleon Bonaparte, 1769–1821, French general

Foreign exchange (forex or FX) markets form the core of the global financial market, a seamless twenty-four hour structure dominated by sophisticated professional players, and often extremely volatile. As the 1997 Asian crisis and its aftermath vividly reveal, foreign exchange these days tends to lead economic activity. And the foreign exchange markets are huge, growing, and increasingly powerful. The size of forex trade has played its part in the series of currency crises in emerging nations during the 1990s. Currency attacks are becoming a depressingly common feature of the global economy.

The main discussion [in 1974] was about how far governments should intervene in exchange markets. And the feeling in the United States was that it should not be done at all. Instead, there should be "clean floating;" all intervention in exchange markets was called "dirty floating," and the United States was opposed to that.

Johannes Witteveen, former managing director,
International Monetary Fund, 1987

We invented money and we use it, yet we cannot either understand its laws or control its actions.

Lionel Trilling, 1905–1975, critic and writer

About how to get more stable exchange rates: Intervention will not help very much. You must have better coordination of macroeconomic policy between the United States and Germany and Japan that will be conducive to stabilizing the exchange rate. The United States has a particular responsibility.

Yusuke Kashiwagi, Bank of Tokyo, 1987

How can we be so willfully blind as to look for causes in nature, when nature herself is an effect?

Joseph de Maistre, 1753–1821, French diplomat and philosopher

I said to the traders of the Merc, "Look, you've got to leave your cattle pit, your hog pit, your belly pit; you've got to come help us launch currencies [currency futures market]."

Leo Melamed, b. ~1932, former chairman, Chicago Mercantile Exchange

If there is one fact in finance more firmly fixed than another, it is the certainty that the unrestricted issue of paper currency culminates in disaster.

Sir Charles Gordon, president, Bank of Montreal, 1933

In skating over thin ice our safety is in our speed.

Ralph Waldo Emerson, 1803–1882, American essayist and poet

It is the mark of a good action that it appears inevitable in retrospect.

Robert Louis Stevenson, 1850–1894, Scottish author

The strength or weakness of the dollar is crucial to the profitability of a number of our industries, so you have to think in those terms. The world is awash with liquidity, and how that is going to slosh into this country is vital in appraising the U.S. stock market.

Peter Vermilye, investment manager, Baring America Asset Management Co., 1987

The theory that a country strengthens its competitive position by depreciating its money is deceptive and utterly unsound. One country adopting this course may gain a temporary advantage in export trade by offering goods at the same nominal price in cheaper money, but once the competition is entered upon there is no stopping place short of the zero point for all. It is the most uncontrollable, demoralizing and fruitless competition that can be imagined.

National City Bank Bulletin

The ECU, curiously, started to be a currency without anyone telling it to do so. We started by using the ECU as an intervention instrument for central banks; now it is used as a currency for operations, accounting, settlements.

Valéry Giscard d'Estaing, b. 1926, former French president

I want the whole of Europe to have one currency; it will make trading much easier.

Napoleon Bonaparte, 1769–1821, French general

Worry affects the circulation, the heart, the glands, the whole nervous system. I have never known a man who died from overwork, but many who died from doubt.

Charles H. Mayo, 1865–1939, American surgeon

Worry is interest paid on trouble before it becomes due.

William Ralph Inge, 1860–1954, English prelate, dean of
St. Paul's, London

If you don't risk anything, you risk even more.

Erica Jong, b. 1942, writer

I recognized that while Bretton Woods was in existence, currency fluctuations, at least in the open, weren't likely—except on nights when finance ministers got together and devalued 2 percent or 5 percent or 10 percent and suddenly you have this giant move overnight and the rest of the time it's fixed.

Leo Melamed, b. ~1932, former chairman, Chicago Mercantile Exchange

Kites rise against, not with, the wind. No man ever worked his passage anywhere in a dead calm.

Robert Herrick, 1591–1674, English poet

Repartee is what you wish you'd said.

Heywood Broun, 1888–1938, American journalist

I think we were among the first European firms to make trips to the United States to tell American institutions that someday they would not rely entirely on the dollar, but would have to be multicurrency and multinational in their investments.

Yves Oltramare, former general partner, Lombard, Odier & CIE, 1987

Success is simple. Do what's right, the right way, at the right time.

Arnold Glasow, American humorist

Take time to deliberate, but when the time for action arrives, stop thinking and go in.

Andrew Jackson, 1767–1845, 7th U.S. president

It is not possible to diversify away all risk in a world economy where speculative frenzies and the rapid movement of capital make history a poor guide to the future.

James Surowiecki, Slate

I told [the head of international at the Japanese Finance Ministry in early 1973] if you once float the yen, it is very difficult to return to a fixed exchange rate. You might have to float it, but never do it unilaterally. You should always do it together with the Europeans. Don't let Japan float alone. That was my recommendation.

Yusuke Kashiwagi, Bank of Tokyo, 1987

The difference between genius and stupidity is that genius has its limits.

Unknown

The most savage controversies are those about matters as to which there is no good evidence either way.

Bertrand Russell, 1872–1970, British philosopher and mathematician

Portfolio capital inflows from overseas lead to interactions between two inherently unstable markets: the stock and currency markets.

Dean LeBaron, b. 1933, investment manager and contrarian thinker

There is a limit at which forbearance ceases to be a virtue.

Edmund Burke, 1729–1797, English political leader

There is a time for departure even when there's no certain place to go.

Tennessee Williams, 1911–1983, American dramatist

Water taken in moderation cannot hurt anybody.

Mark Twain, 1835–1910, American author

He who thinks everything must be in bloom when the strawberries are in bloom doesn't know anything about apples.

Greek proverb

Muddy water let stand will clear.

Chinese proverb

There can be no final truth in ethics any more than in physics, until the last man has had his experience and said his say.

William James, 1842–1910, American philosopher and psychologist

If Milton Friedman's view that Bretton Woods would indeed come apart in the near future was anywhere near correct, then my ideas for a currency futures market could work. In December of 1971, when the gold window was closed, I knew we were on the right track.

Leo Melamed, b. ~1932, former chairman, Chicago Mercantile Exchange

Anybody who is any good is different from anybody else.

Felix Frankfurter, 1882–1965, associate justice,
U.S. Supreme Court

Ask your neighbor only about things you know better yourself. Then his advice could prove invaluable.

Karl Kraus, 1874–1936, Austrian satirist

If ever there was a man who would fit the stereotype of the Judaeo-plutocratic Bolshevik Zionist world conspirator, it is me. And that is, in fact, how I am increasingly depicted in Eastern Europe and also to some extent in Western Europe, but not so much in America. This is a prime example of how good deeds don't go unpunished.

George Soros, b. 1930, in Soros on Soros

Fortune favors the audacious.

Desiderius Erasmus, ~1466–1536, Dutch philosopher

Man can believe the impossible, but man can never believe the improbable.

Oscar Wilde, 1854–1900, Irish-British author

Our doubts are traitors and make us lose the good we oft might win by fearing to attempt.

William Shakespeare, 1564–1616, English poet, playwright

The consistent policy of the Japanese [before the 1970s] was to defend the $1-to-¥360 rate that was set in 1950 and to never devalue the currency. That was to be the key economic policy. Fixed exchange rates exercise a kind of international discipline on the economy. You can have growth with stability with a fixed exchange rate.

Yusuke Kashiwagi, Bank of Tokyo, 1987

The soul that sees beauty may sometimes walk alone.

Johann Goethe, 1749–1832, German writer

Faith is believing what you know ain't so.

Mark Twain, 1835–1910, American author

Behind many acts that are thought ridiculous there lie wise and weighty motives.

La Rochefoucauld, 1613–1680, French author

No man ever made a great discovery without the exercise of the imagination.

George Henry Lewes, 1817–1878, British author

Vision is the art of seeing things invisible.

Jonathan Swift, 1667–1745, English churchman and writer

You don't launch currencies from your back pocket. If it is meaningful, then we ought to advise the movers and shakers of the world. I wanted people to salute it.

Leo Melamed, b. ~1932, former chairman, Chicago Mercantile Exchange

Life is like playing a violin solo in public and learning the instrument as one goes on.

Samuel Butler, 1612–1680, English author

Skill and confidence are an unconquered army.

George Herbert, 1593–1633, British poet

The essence of the liberal outlook lies not in *what* opinions are held but in *how* they are held: Instead of being held dogmatically they are held tentatively, and with a consciousness that new evidence may at any moment lead to their abandonment.

Bertrand Russell, 1872–1970, British philosopher and mathematician

Improvement makes straight roads; but the crooked roads without improvement are the roads of genius.

William Blake, 1757–1827, British poet and artist

Miracles sometimes occur, but one has to work terribly hard for them.

Chaim Weizmann, 1874–1952, Israeli statesman

Trying to determine what is going on in the world by reading newspapers is like trying to tell the time by watching the second hand of a clock.

Ben Hecht, 1894–1964, American author, playwright

If one could divine the nature of the economic forces in the world, one could foretell the future.

Robert Heilbroner, b. 1919, professor, author, American economist

Nine-tenths of wisdom consists in being wise in time.

Theodore Roosevelt, 1858–1919, 26th U.S. president

So in February of '73 we entered the age of floating . . . all the currencies floated and the academics didn't realize that what would happen with exchange rates would produce greater volatility and larger imbalances in terms of surpluses and deficits.

Yusuke Kashiwagi, Bank of Tokyo, 1987

Money is created by trade, not trade by money.

A. B. Barker

America has the world's best money. Every U.S. dollar is secured by the universal demand for it.

Cullen Hightower

You couldn't squeeze and corner the currencies. Nobody was worried about some people getting together and saying, "Hey, let's corner the deutsche mark tomorrow." You knew it was economics that was going to dictate that market. Supply and demand was going to determine the value, nothing else.

Leo Melamed, b. ~1932, former chairman, Chicago Mercantile Exchange

The great source of pleasure is variety.

Samuel Johnson, 1709–1784, British author

The prevailing wisdom is that markets are always right. I take the opposite position. I assume that markets are always wrong. Even if my assumption is occasionally wrong, I use it as a working hypothesis.

George Soros, b. 1930, in Soros on Soros

A billion dollars here, a billion dollars there, and pretty soon you're talking about real money.

Everett Dirksen, 1896–1969, American political leader

Global Investing

99 99 99

Investing in the World

Business is beginning to run the world.
James Davis, U.S. Secretary of Labor

Global investing is, in the first instance, about asset allocation between equities, bonds, cash, and other instruments; and second, about investing in global markets. International investors benefit by diversifying their portfolios across assets in a range of different countries. With many national markets often highly uncorrelated, this form of diversification would seem to offer the strongest potential for reducing risk, while at the same time promising enhanced returns. But the more markets move together, the fewer will be the benefits of international diversification.

About international researchers: The gunslingers had smooth, placid faces and faraway looks in their eyes. They were a little spaced out from looking at the tape for too long.

Barton Biggs, Morgan Stanley & Co., 1987

My ventures are not in one bottom trusted,
Nor to one place; nor is my whole estate
Upon the fortune of this present year:
Therefore, my merchandise makes me not sad.

Antonio in The Merchant of Venice, *by William Shakespeare, 1564–1616, English poet, playwright*

The selfish spirit of commerce knows no country, and feels no passion or principle but that of gain.

Thomas Jefferson, 1743–1826, 3rd U.S. president

European-Arab consortium banks were good for the '70s because the Arabs were emerging in the international market and they needed someone to sponsor them. Banking is not something where you just step into the market and say you want to do banking. We had a *presence* but never a real *participation*.

Abdulla Saudi, founder, Arab Banking Corp. (ABC), 1987

The stock market is people.

Bernard Baruch, 1870–1965, American financier and statesman, adviser to presidents, and popular sage

People are always blaming their circumstances for what they are. I don't believe in circumstances. The people who get on in this world are the people who get up and look for the circumstances they want and, if they can't find them, make them.

George Bernard Shaw, 1856–1950, playwright

It was our mission to be an explorer of new possibilities, to push the borders of this market.

> *André George, former financial director and treasurer, European Investment Bank, 1987*

Little progress can be made by merely attempting to repress what is evil; our great hope lies in developing what is good.

> *Calvin Coolidge, 1872–1933, 30th U.S. president*

The ever-present phenomenon ceases to exist for our senses. It was a city dweller, or a prisoner, or a blind man suddenly given his sight, who first noted natural beauty.

> *Remy de Gourmont, 1858–1915, French writer*

A laugh is worth a hundred groans in any market.

> *Charles Lamb, 1775–1834, essayist*

I had been told that in negotiating transactions in Japan there's a lot of ritual, that everything's very formal. I knew the cost of borrowing was going to end up at about 7 percent, and I didn't want to spend two months drinking tea until we got down to that point. Two weeks later, after a lot of tea, we ended up at 7 percent.

> *Eugene Rotberg, b. ~1929, World Bank*

For NASA, space is still a high priority.

> *J. Danforth Quayle, b. 1947, vice president of the United States*

Commerce is the great civilizer. We exchange ideas when we exchange fabrics.

> *Robert Ingersoll, 1833–1899, American lawyer*

I am convinced that when confidence has been established amongst all nations of the world, the present capacity of industrial countries will not be sufficient to satisfy the demand.

Oskar Sempell

Investment decisions should focus first and foremost on markets or asset classes. Over time, that's going to explain roughly ninety percent of investment returns.

Gary Brinson, Brinson Partners

I have traveled more than anyone else, and I have noticed that even the angels speak English with an accent.

Mark Twain, 1835–1910, American author

The world has been for many years on the verge of a nervous breakdown and the best thing the depression can do is to restore normal living.

Prof. C. U. Ariens Kappers, director, Central Institute for Brain Research of Amsterdam, 1933

We are now one business world, one financial world. You can no longer make a decision about the attractiveness of U.S. chemical stocks without knowing what's going on in Europe.

Peter Vermilye, investment manager, Baring America Asset Management Co., 1987

'Tis sweet to know that stocks will stand
When we with daisies lie,
That commerce will continue,
And trades as briskly fly.

Emily Dickinson, 1830–1886, American poet

The ambitious man climbs up high and perilous stairs, and never cares how to come down; the desire of rising hath swallowed up his fear of a fall.

Thomas Adams

Having been a country of refuge, we were also a country of international fund management. Switzerland has always had to manage internationally, because our domestic markets were far too small to absorb the amount of money we were given.

Yves Oltramare, former general partner, Lombard, Odier & CIE, 1987

There is but one bond of peace that is both permanent and enriching: The increasing knowledge of the world in which experiment occurs.

Walter Lippmann, 1889–1974, American journalist

Trade is a companion of peace, and flourishes only in her presence. Yet trade, seen through eyes prejudiced by a too selfish nationalism, becomes an excuse for war. Peoples are too easily led by leaders into thinking that the stimulating rivalries of the marketplace are summons to war.

The Library, *1929*

Twenty thousand years ago the family was the social unit. Now the social unit has become the world, in which it may truthfully be said that each person's welfare affects that of every other.

Arthur H. Compton, 1892–1962, American physicist

A great many people treated the Eurobond market as a flash in the pan.

Stanislas Yassukovich, Merrill Lynch Europe

We have assumed heavy world responsibilities that must be discharged. Our true strength is in the power of our purposes and of our way of life. This was the secret weapon which really destroyed Hitler and Japan. From our basic virtues as a freedom-loving nation came the strength which beat back the aggressors. And that strength is the natural possession of all right-minded people throughout the world. From a unity of all the people for the purposes of peace and from the dignity of man will come a continuing power to maintain peace in the world and heal the wounds this war has inflicted.

William D. Leahy, 1875–1959, admiral, U.S. Navy, World War II

We have been and still are conscious of the allegation of having too much power.

Wilfried Guth, Deutsche Bank

Fetter not commerce! Let her be as free as air. She will range the whole creation, and return on the four winds of heaven to bless the land of plenty with plenty.

Patrick Henry, 1736–1799, American political leader

For big money, stock picking is irrelevant. Asset allocation is the whole game.

Barton Biggs, Morgan Stanley & Co., 1987

I do not want my house to be walled in on all sides and my windows to be stuffed. I want the cultures of all lands to be blown about my house as freely as possible. But I refuse to be blown off my feet by any.

Mahatma Gandhi, 1869–1948, Indian nationalist and spiritual leader

In great affairs we ought to apply ourselves less to creating chances than to profiting from those that offer.

La Rochefoucauld, 1613–1680, French author

About the Asian economic crisis: Rather than a failure of the free-market system, I would argue that the move to more open markets simply exposed the fault lines created in economies where market forces were being suppressed or distorted by government intervention, crony capitalism and a lack of financial transparency.

> *Martin Barnes, editor,* Bank Credit Analyst

In the dark days and darker nights when England stood alone—and most men save Englishmen despaired of England's life—he [Churchill] mobilized the English language and sent it into battle.

> *John F. Kennedy, 1917–1963, 35th U.S. president*

Speech is civilization itself. The word—even the most contradictory word—preserves contact. It is silence which isolates.

> *Thomas Mann, 1875–1955, German author*

We cannot remain consistent with the world save by growing inconsistent with our past selves.

> *Havelock Ellis, 1859–1939, British psychologist*

If the structure of law and order in the global financial community breaks apart, all bets are off. We have a very, very dangerous situation developing globally.

> *Mark Mobius, investment manager, Templeton Emerging Markets Group*

Our sun is one of 100 billion stars in our galaxy. Our galaxy is one of the billions of galaxies populating the universe. It would be the height of presumption to think that we are the only living things within that enormous immensity.

> *Wernher von Braun, 1912–1977, German-American engineer*

The word impossible is not in my dictionary.

> *Napoleon Bonaparte, 1769–1821, French general*

The United States dominates the world's financial markets. Our interest rate changes explain more of the German or Japanese stock market shifts than their rate changes do.

Jeremy Grantham, investment manager, Grantham, Mayo, Van Otterloo

You work that you may keep pace with the earth and the soul of the earth. For to be idle is to become a stranger unto the seasons, and to step out of life's procession.

Kahlil Gibran, 1883–1931, Syrian-born poet and artist

Amongst democratic nations, each generation is a new people.

Alexis de Tocqueville, 1805–1859, French historian and political philosopher

I am always of the view that Japan lives with the world. As Japan gets bigger and bigger, we must share the prosperity. We benefit because the world is prosperous.

Yusuke Kashiwagi, Bank of Tokyo, 1987

It is wonderful how preposterously the affairs of the world are managed. We assemble parliaments and councils to have the benefit of collected wisdom, but we necessarily have, at the same time, the inconvenience of their collected passions, prejudices and private interests: for regulating commerce an assembly of great men is the greatest fool on earth.

Benjamin Franklin, 1706–1790, statesman, scientist, public leader

Only those cities and countries that are free can achieve greatness . . . In free countries we also see wealth increase more rapidly, both that which results from the culture of the soil and that which is produced by industry and art; for everybody gladly multiplies those things, and seeks to acquire those goods the possession of which he can tranquilly enjoy.

Niccoló Machiavelli, 1469–1527, Florentine diplomat and writer

We looked at companies as investments in the context of their international competition. We believed that the best company *worldwide* would win and that you could not just choose the best one in your own country. These ideas that today are *élémentaires* were not known at all at that time [1960].

Yves Oltramare, former general partner, Lombard, Odier & CIE, 1987

Self-interest is not only a legitimate but a fundamental cause for national policy, one which needs no cloak of hypocrisy.

Alfred Thayer Mahan, 1840–1914, American admiral and author

The experience of the last decade [1923–1933] including years of so-called prosperity and very real adversity, does not teach any important new lessons. It merely teaches the same lessons that experience had taught in this and every other civilized country ever since the industrial era began. Increased wealth and incomes are produced by the exertions of the people themselves, not by paternalism in government.

The Railway Age

I did not think that Chase could or should remain the way it was when I joined it [in 1946]. Things had begun to evolve quickly from a 1940s atmosphere in which the manager of our Paris office could pride himself on the fact that he could not and would not speak a word of French and saw no reason why this was important.

David Rockefeller, b. 1915, formerly Chase Manhattan Bank,
American financier, son of John D. Rockefeller, Jr.

For people to say just because I'm a resident of the United States that I'm going to restrict my investments to the United States is terribly myopic, and numerous studies have shown that it really curtails investment opportunities. The more one thinks about global investment opportunities, the greater the chances of success.

Gary Brinson, Brinson Partners

What has been the effect of coercion? To make one-half of the world fools and other half hypocrites.

Thomas Jefferson, 1743–1826, 3rd U.S. president

Only those who respect the personality of others can be of real use to them.

Albert Schweitzer, 1875–1965, philosopher, medical missionary

In a talk I gave [in 1970] to some treasurers in New York, I said that in a decade our clients would be investing rather seriously in international markets. They sort of laughed.

George Russell, Jr., Frank Russell Co., 1987

They can conquer who believe they can.

William Dryden

This world is warfare; I love to carry it on, it puts life into me.

Voltaire, 1694–1778, French philosopher and writer

I believed that if we were to take a share of the market, we had to be from day one what we call "born big." It's a good calling card; when we open doors they say, "Look at this billion-dollar bank."

Abdulla Saudi, founder, Arab Banking Corp. (ABC), 1987

What helps luck is a habit of watching for opportunities, of having a patient, but restless mind, of sacrificing one's ease or vanity, of uniting a love of detail to foresight; and of passing through hard times bravely and cheerfully.

Victor Cherbuliez, 1829–1899, Swiss novelist and critic

What I admire in Columbus is not his having discovered a world, but his having gone to search for it on the faith of an opinion.

A. Robert Turgot, French government official during the 1700s

The guideline the corporation [CITIC] follows is to become a window opening to the outside world.

Rong Yiren, b. ~1916, China International Trust and Investment Corp.

A life spent in making mistakes is not only more honorable but more useful than a life spent doing nothing.

George Bernard Shaw, 1856–1950, playwright

Gullibility is the key to all adventures. The greenhorn is the ultimate victor in everything; it is he that gets the most out of life.

G. K. Chesterton, 1874–1936, English journalist and writer

Foreign investing usually involves boom/bust sequences. I have been in the foreign investment business from the beginning of my career. I have seen many cycles. And I concluded early on that foreign investors acting as a herd always prove to be wrong.

George Soros, b. 1930, Budapest, financier, philanthropist, author

I must go down to the seas again,
To the lonely sea and the sky;
And all I ask is a tall ship
And a star to steer her by.

John Masefield, 1878–1967, English writer

Restlessness is the hallmark of existence.

Arthur Schopenhauer, 1788–1860, German philosopher

The world turns aside to let any man pass who knows whither he is going.

David S. Jordan, 1851–1931, American biologist

I am in hearty favor of an amendment, a change or some modification of the Sherman Law that would permit American manufacturers to honestly, legally and legitimately conduct the distribution of their business in a better manner.

Charles M. Schwab, 1862–1939, first president of U.S. Steel Corp.

We all had a dream of the Eurobond market becoming *the* supranational capital market. This has happened to such an extent that the market is no longer a Eurobond market, but the world capital market.

Robert Genillard, former chairman, Credit Suisse White Weld, 1987

Trust everybody, but yourself most of all.

Danish proverb

The best augury of a man's success in his profession is that he thinks it is the finest in the world.

George Eliot, 1819–1880, British author

Though we travel the world over to find the beautiful, we must carry it with us or we will find it not.

Ralph Waldo Emerson, 1803–1882, American essayist and poet

Getting [international research] started in 1973 was very fortuitous because we just scooped it at the bottom of a bear market and then we had the wind at our back.

Barton Biggs, Morgan Stanley & Co., 1987

Welcome to President Bush, Mrs. Bush, and my fellow astronauts.

J. Danforth Quayle, b. 1947, vice president of the United States

No person who is enthusiastic about his work has anything to fear from life.

Samuel Goldwyn, 1882–1974, American movie producer

They are able because they think they are able.

Virgil, 70–19 B.C., Roman poet

Never before has man had such capacity to control his own environment, to end thirst and hunger, to conquer poverty and disease, to
banish illiteracy and massive human misery. We have the power to
make this the best generation of mankind in the history of the world
or to make it the last.

John F. Kennedy, 1917–1963, 35th U.S. president

The journey of a thousand miles starts with a single step.

Chinese proverb

The first, pre-1962 wave of international investing turned out to be a
wave of vast speculation, just a short-term fad. American managers
thought they were in for the long term, but when they lost a lot of
money, they lost their jobs.

Yves Oltramare, former general partner, Lombard, Odier & CIE, 1987

Bronze is the mirror of the form; wine, of the heart.

Aeschylus, 525–456 B.C., writer of Greek tragedy

Americanism is a question of principle, of purpose, of idealism, of
character; it is not a matter of birthplace or creed or line of descent.

Theodore Roosevelt, 1858–1919, 26th U.S. president

You must not lose faith in humanity. Humanity is an ocean; if a few
drops of the ocean are dirty, the ocean does not become dirty.

Mahatma Gandhi, 1869–1948, Indian nationalist and spiritual leader

To be a true Marxist-Leninist is more than just reading some books; it is more important to have a clear understanding, an analysis of the international situation and of things developing in an economic world and to combine the objective situation with the real situation.

Rong Yiren, b. ~1916, China International Trust and Investment Corp.

I have been told that one of the reasons the astronomers of the world cooperate is the fact that there is no one nation from which the entire sphere of the sky can be seen. Perhaps there is in that fact a parable for national statesmen, whose political horizons are all too often limited by national horizons.

Adlai E. Stevenson, 1900–1965, U.S. ambassador to the United Nations

Mendacity is a system that we live in.

Brick, in Tennessee Williams's Cat on a Hot Tin Roof

Growth Investing

99 99 99

Growing Up

Bears don't live on Park Avenue.
*Bernard Baruch, 1870–1965, American financier
and statesman, adviser to presidents,
and popular sage*

Growth investing tends to be based on qualitative judgments about the kind of companies that will offer remarkable growth rates and exceptional returns performance. The growth investor needs prescience about earnings or rate of growth or the market's willingness to pay for future events. And the argument runs backwards in that those equities that have appreciated are assumed to have growth characteristics. Growth stocks may see the future through the rear view mirror. Once a growth stock starts to fall, it loses its momentum attractions, followers of the trend start to desert, forcing the price down further and creating a downward spiral. Then, as fallen angels they become potential seeds for future value stocks.

On the Dow's new historic high:
Hip is Wow Dow
10 k . . . 16.3.99 . . . Internet Time @ 659 [0950 EST]

> *Dean LeBaron, b. 1933, investment manager and contrarian thinker*

Bull markets are born on pessimism, grow on skepticism, mature on optimism, and die on euphoria.

> *Michael B. Steele*

Opportunity knocks, it jiggles the doorknob, it will try the window if we don't have the alarm system on.

> *P. J. O'Rourke, American satirist*

If you don't advertise you fossilize.

> *Lord Dewar, 1864–1930, British distiller*

The harder the conflict, the more glorious the triumph. What we obtain too cheap, we esteem too lightly; 'tis dearness only that gives everything its value.

> *Thomas Paine, 1737–1809, political thinker*

At that time [1959] Graham-Dodd analysis, balance sheet strength and other "fundamentals" were the dominant measures of stocks' worth. But Rodney [White] understood the multiples that companies deserved if their earnings were very likely to improve dramatically.

> *Leon Levy, Odyssey Partners, cofounder Oppenheimer Fund, 1987*

We work not only to produce but to give value to time.

> *Eugene Delacroix, 1798–1863, French painter*

You can't economize your way to profits; you've got to sell your way.

> *Unknown*

Always take a job that is too big for you.

> *Harry Emerson Fosdick, 1878–1969, American religious leader*

Investor: One who bought stocks that went up.
Speculator: One who bought stocks that went down.

> *Malcolm Forbes, 1919–1990, publisher and author*

To stop advertising would be to stop growing.

> *Roger W. Babson, 1875–1967, American financial statistician*

Is it a stale remark to say that I have constantly found the interest excited at a playhouse to bear an exact inverse proportion to the price paid for admission?

> *Charles Lamb, 1775–1834, essayist*

Our philosophy here is identifying change, anticipating change. Change is what drives earnings growth, and if you identify the underlying change, you recognize the growth before the market and the deceleration of that growth.

> *Peter Vermilye, investment manager, Baring America Asset Management Co., 1987*

One of the funny things about the stock market is that every time one man buys, another sells, and both think they are astute.

> *William Feather, 1889–1981, American author, publisher*

We do not see things as they are, we see things as we are.

> *The Talmud, body of Jewish civil and religious law*

History repeats itself, but not exactly.

> *Robert Farrell*

The search for truth is really a lot of good fun.

Vernon Howard

There is nothing like a ticker tape except a woman—nothing that promises, hour after hour, day after day, such sudden developments; nothing that disappoints so often or occasionally fulfils with such unbelievable, passionate magnificence.

Walter K. Gutman

The portfolio took off like a rocket ship for about 90 days. And then the wings fell off. I now think that if you take good research people and ask for a stock that will do it *right now*, you end up with a missile whose power is gone, and all it's got left is momentum and soon it will crash. That was when [Bob Greenebaum, Inland Steel] called up and said: "Only an idiot would try to catch a falling anvil, Kirby. Send the money back."

Robert Kirby, investment manager, Capital Guardian Trust Co., 1987

Two elements are needed to form a truth—a fact and an abstraction.

Samuel Butler, 1612–1680, English author

So much of left-wing thought is a kind of playing with fire by people who don't even know that fire is hot.

George Orwell, 1903–1950, novelist

Often a convert is zealous not through piety, but because of the novelty of his experience.

Austin O'Malley

If an idea is fashionable, that is by itself a pretty good reason to regard it with extreme scepticism.

Paul Krugman, b. 1953, MIT economics professor, author

I am right and therefore shall not give up the contest.

Rutherford B. Hayes, 1822–1893, 19th U.S. president

'Tis with our judgements as our watches; none go just alike, yet each believes his own.

Alexander Pope, 1688–1744, English poet

Bodies in motion tend to stay in motion (Newton's First Law). Earnings and stock prices with great yearly momentum tend to keep moving in the same direction for awhile, perhaps because economic cycles are, on average, longer than a year.

Jeremy Grantham, investment manager, Grantham, Mayo, Van Otterloo

I will utter what I believe today, if it should contradict all I said yesterday.

Wendell Phillips, 1811–1884, American social reformer

When a man has spent the major portion of his life learning to sing bass, he had better think twice before accepting an offer to sing tenor.

K. V. P. Philosopher

Fortune is ever seen accompanying industry.

Oliver Goldsmith, 1730–1774, British playwright and poet

If at first you do succeed it can give you a false sense of importance.

Frank Tyger

Take a nice little company that's been making shoelaces for 40 years and sells at a respectable six-times-earnings ratio. Change the name from Shoelaces, Inc. to Electronics and Silicon Furth-Burners. In today's market, the words electronic and silicon are worth 15 times earnings. However, the real play comes from the word furth-burners, which no one understands. This entitles you to double your entire score. Thus, we have six times earnings for the shoelace business and 15 times earnings for electronics and silicon, or a total of 21 times earnings. Multiply this by two for furth-burners, and we now have a score of 42 times earnings for the new company.

> *Jack Dreyfus, mutual fund pioneer, in* Time *magazine*

It is not enough to be industrious; so are the ants. What are you industrious about?

> *Henry David Thoreau, 1817–1862, American naturalist and writer*

The best place to succeed is where you are with what you have.

> *Charles M. Schwab, 1862–1939, first president of U.S. Steel Corp.*

There is certainly no exact standard of beauty. That precisely is what makes its pursuit so interesting.

> *John Kenneth Galbraith, b. 1908, economist*

All the statistics boil down to this: Too many investors are trying to find the next Home Depot. Too few are trying to find the next Chrysler . . . There are at least three dozen academic studies showing the long-term superiority of value strategies.

> *David Dreman, contrarian investor and author*

Education is an ornament in prosperity and a refuge in adversity.

> *Aristotle, 384–322 B.C., Greek philosopher, educator, scientist*

Growth stocks are a happy and haphazard category of investments, which, curiously enough, have little or nothing to do with growth companies. Indeed, the term "growth stock" is meaningless; a growth stock can only be identified with hindsight—it is simply a stock which went way up. But the concept of "growth company" can be used to identify the most creative, most imaginative management groups; and if, in addition, their stocks are valued at a reasonable ratio to their increase in earnings power over time, the odds are favorable for appreciation in the future.

Peter L. Bernstein, b. ~1919, investment manager, Harvard Business Review, *~1959*

Friendship being incompatible with truth, only the mute dialogue with our enemies is fruitful.

E. M. Cioran, b. 1911, French philosopher

There is only one thing in business that is certain and that's change. I don't know what tomorrow is going to be like, but I do know this— it's bound to be different from yesterday and today.

Henry Ford, 1863–1947, American automobile manufacturer, founder of Ford Motor Co.

Make three correct guesses consecutively and you will establish a reputation as an expert.

Laurence J. Peter, 1919–1990, Canadian author and educator

"Profitless Prosperity." Now, isn't such a situation ridiculous? It is bad enough to be profitless when there isn't any business, but it is even worse when there is lots of business not to have any profit.

George Puchta

Bull markets last longer than bear markets.

Mark Mobius, investment manager, Templeton Emerging Markets Group

I like the dreams of the future better than the history of the past.

Thomas Jefferson, 1743–1826, 3rd U.S. president

Trend is not destiny.

Unknown

When the rate of change outside exceeds the rate of change inside, the end is in sight.

Jack Welch, b. 1935, American executive

If we are to make the most of the opportunity which will be offered to us in the post-war period, there must be no inner demobilization. For this time, the duration will last longer than the war! We must mobilize all of the psychological, physical and spiritual resources at our command.

Walton E. Cole, D.D.

If equity markets continue to be so strong—particularly domestic equity markets—I worry that caution will no longer be a virtue, but a vice.

Jean-Marie Eveillard

Happiness is a rounding bottom.

Steve Leuthold, investment manager, The Leuthold Group

Where there is sunshine the doctor starves.

Flemish proverb

To turn $100 into $110 is work. To turn $100 million into $110 million is inevitable.

Edgar Bronfman, Canadian businessman

Start with a growing market. Swim in a stream that becomes a river and ultimately an ocean. Be a leader in that market, not a follower, and constantly build the best products possible.

Robert Noyce, one of the founders of Intel

Pessimism leads to weakness; optimism to power.

William James, 1842–1910, American philosopher and psychologist

The pessimist may be right in the long run, but the optimist has a better time during the trip.

Unknown

One must be thrust out of a finished cycle in life, and that leap is the most difficult to make—to part with one's faith, one's love, when one would prefer to renew the faith and recreate the passion.

Anaïs Nin, 1903–1977, American writer

The public is right during the trends, but wrong at both ends.

Humphrey Neill, d. 1978, contrarian and author

For best performance in a bull market, rent a kid.

John T. Bennett, Jr., investment manager, Bennett Management Co.

Hedge Funds

Hedging Your Bets

It wasn't raining when Noah built the Ark.

The Broadcaster

The name originally comes from the fact that hedge funds were able to deal in derivatives and short selling—in theory to protect or "hedge" their positions. Now, they borrow aggressively, sell short, leverage up to twenty times their paid-in capital, and generally make big but highly risky bets, usually with minimal disclosure to investors and regulators. It is often not clear if, when hedge funds perform spectacularly well, their high returns owe more to investment judgment, to leverage or to the chance outcomes of purely speculative bets. Indeed, their trading strategies can destabilize whole countries and markets that are not equipped to cope with mass selling of their currencies and equity markets.

About hedge funds: You can't tell who's swimming naked until the tide goes out.

> *Warren Buffett, b. 1930, American investor*

Conservative: Anyone without a margin account.

> *Steve Leuthold, investment manager, The Leuthold Group*

You can almost chart the rise of the bull market with the number of hedge funds that were started in the late '60s. That was really an ebullient period—the rise of the young, go-go performance money managers. But what people forget was that those guys really got wiped out in the 1970 bear market.

> *Barton Biggs, Morgan Stanley & Co., 1987*

There is no hard line between arbitrage and speculation; it is a continuum.

> *Stephen Ross, MIT finance professor*

The only perfect hedge is in a Japanese garden.

> *Eugene Rotberg, b. ~1929, World Bank*

A man with a surplus can control circumstances, but a man without a surplus is controlled by them, and often he has no opportunity to exercise judgment.

> *Harvey S. Firestone, 1868–1938, American businessman*

Better shun the bait than struggle in the snare.

> *John Dryden, 1631–1700, English author*

I'd like to live like a poor man with lots of money.

> *Pablo Picasso, 1881–1973, artist*

By the time the smoke has lifted, the train has left the station.

Unknown

If it isn't the sheriff, it's the finance company. I've got more attachments on me than a vacuum cleaner.

John Barrymore, 1882–1942, American actor

Do not bite at the bait of pleasure till you know there is no hook beneath it.

Thomas Jefferson, 1743–1826, 3rd U.S. president

No folly is more costly than the folly of intolerant idealism.

Winston Churchill, 1874–1965, British prime minister

Our thanks should be as fervent for mercies received as our petitions for mercies sought.

Charles Simmons

Skepticism is a hedge against vulnerability.

Charles Thomas Smith

Insofar as there is a dominant belief in our society today, it is a belief in the magic of the marketplace. The doctrine of laissez-faire capitalism holds that the common good is best served by the uninhibited pursuit of self-interest. Unless it is tempered by the recognition of a common interest that ought to take precedence over particular interests, our present system—which, however imperfect, qualifies as an open society—is liable to break down.

George Soros, b. 1930, Budapest, financier, philanthropist, author

Trust the friends of today as if they will be the enemies of tomorrow.

Baltasar Gracian, 1601–1658, Spanish priest and writer

When a man says money can do everything, that settles it; he hasn't any.

Edgar (Ed) Watson Howe, 1853–1937, American journalist and author

Before desiring something passionately, one should inquire into the happiness of the man who possesses it.

La Rochefoucauld, 1613–1680, French author

Good nature is the cheapest commodity in the world, and love is the only thing that will pay ten percent to both borrower and lender.

Robert Ingersoll, 1833–1899, American lawyer

Referring to hedge fund managers: Highwaymen of the global economy.

Mahathir Mohamad, Malaysian prime minister

I've learned that it's easier to stay out of trouble than to get out of trouble.

14-year-old's discovery

It is not the burden but the overburden that kills the beast.

Spanish proverb

Just because the river is quiet does not mean the crocodiles have left.

Malay proverb

Money is the seed of money, and the first guinea is sometimes more difficult to acquire than the second million.

Jean-Jacques Rousseau, 1712–1778, French philosopher

There are so many false rumours about our activities that they often obscure what we are really doing.

George Soros, b. 1930, Budapest, financier, philanthropist, author

Life would be infinitely happier if we could only be born at the age of 80 and gradually approach 18.

Mark Twain, 1835–1910, American author

Results are gained by exploiting opportunities, not by solving problems.

Peter Drucker, b. 1909, author and consultant

Slander cannot destroy the man . . . when the flood recedes, the rock is there.

Chinese proverb

Sometimes your best investments are the ones you don't make.

Donald Trump, b. 1946, American real estate developer

When you bet on a sure thing—hedge!

Robert Half, employment agent

By the former financial journalist credited with having founded the industry when he founded the first fund in 1949: The hedge fund doesn't have a terrific future.

Alfred Winslow Jones, 1977

A flood tide leads to fortune, but there is no tide table.

Unknown

Trust not the horse, O Trojans. Be it what it may, I fear the Greeks when they offer gifts.

Virgil, 70–19 B.C., Roman poet

The great enemy of clear language is insincerity. When there is a gap between one's real and one's declared aims, one turns, as it were, instinctively to long words and exhausted idioms, like a cuttlefish squirting out ink.

George Orwell, 1903–1950, novelist

It's true that the best minds are drawn to the hedge fund business. But there are not as many great minds out there as there are hedge funds being started.

Antoine Berheim, publisher, U.S. Offshore Funds Directory

A thick skin is a gift from God.

Konrad Adenauer, 1876–1967, German statesman

Associate yourself with men of good quality if you esteem your own reputation; for 'tis better to be alone than in bad company.

George Washington, 1732–1799, 1st U.S. president

Fate bestows its rewards on those who put themselves in the proper attitude to receive them.

Calvin Coolidge, 1872–1933, 30th U.S. president

If it wasn't for faith, there would be no living in this world; we couldn't even eat hash with any safety.

Josh Billings, 1818–1885, American author

One of the greatest pains to human nature is the pain of a new idea.

Walter Bagehot, 1826–1877, writer

Opposition inflames the enthusiast, never converts him.

Friedrich von Schiller, 1759–1805, German poet, playwright, and critic

To be engaged in opposing wrong affords but a slender guarantee for being right.

> *W. E. Gladstone, 1809–1898, British prime minister*

That which we call sin in others is experiment for us.

> *Ralph Waldo Emerson, 1803–1882, American essayist and poet*

The difference between intelligence and an education is this—that intelligence will make you a good living.

> *Charles F. Kettering, 1876–1958, engineer and inventor*

I have always harbored an exaggerated view of my self-importance. To put it bluntly, I fancied myself as some kind of god or even an economic reformer like Keynes or, even better, Einstein. My sense of reality was strong enough to make me realize these expectations were excessive, and I kept them hidden as a guilty secret. This was a source of considerable unhappiness through much of my adult life. As I made my way in the world, reality came close enough to my fantasy to allow me to admit my secret, at least to myself. Needless to say, I feel much happier as a result.

> *George Soros, b. 1930, Budapest, financier, philanthropist, author*

Trust everybody, but cut the cards.

> *Finley Peter Dunne, 1867–1936, American humorist and journalist*

If at first you don't succeed, skydiving's not for you.

> *Unknown*

We're pretty modern these days in Mississippi. We even know about sushi . . . but most folks call it bait.

> *Thad Cochran, senior senator from Mississippi*

It is by attempting to reach the top at a single leap that so much misery is caused in the world.

> *William Cobbett, 1762–1835, British journalist and social reformer*

You can't pull yourself up by the roots to see if you are growing.

> *Frank Lloyd Wright, 1869–1959, architect*

Whoever said "It's not whether you win or lose that counts," probably lost.

> *Martina Navratilova, b. 1956, tennis player*

About the economics of broader-based investment management: There's no way you're going to make more money than through the hedge fund.

> *Barton Biggs, Morgan Stanley & Co., 1987*

Every difficulty slurred over will be a ghost to disturb your repose later on.

> *Frederic-François Chopin, 1810–1849, Polish composer and pianist*

The past is a bucket of ashes, so live not in your yesterdays, nor just for tomorrow, but in the here and now. Keep moving and forget the post-mortems. And remember, no one can get the jump on the future.

> *Carl Sandburg, 1878–1967, poet*

A failure is a man who blundered, but is not able to cash in on the experience.

> *Elbert G. Hubbard, 1856–1915, American writer and businessman*

Humor is emotional chaos remembered in tranquility.

> *James Thurber, 1894–1961, American humorist*

Discern the chaos, and you could become rich.

> *George Soros, b. 1930, Budapest, financier, philanthropist, author*

Such is the state of life that none are happy but by the anticipation of change.

Samuel Johnson, 1709–1784, British author

Great men suffer hours of depression through introspection and self-doubt. That is why they are great. That is why you will find modesty and humility the characteristics of such men.

Bruce Barton, 1886–1957, American advertising executive and politician

My grandfather . . . used to say, "Don't get involved with frivolities."

Katharine Hepburn, b. 1909, American actress

We can't cross a bridge until we come to it; but I always like to lay down a pontoon ahead of time.

Bernard Baruch, 1870–1965, American financier and statesman, adviser to presidents, and popular sage

It is a socialist idea that making profits is a vice. I consider that the real vice is making losses.

Winston Churchill, 1874–1965, British prime minister

If all else fails, immortality can always be assured by spectacular error.

John Kenneth Galbraith, b. 1908, economist

Translating George Soros' calls for more international regulation of markets: "Stop me before I speculate again."

Paul Krugman, b. 1953, MIT economics professor

Indexing

99 99 99

Indexes and Benchmarks

An honest expression of incompetence.
Barr Rosenberg, b. ~1942, Rosenberg Institutional
Equity Management

Indexing is an investment practice that aims to match the returns of a specified market benchmark. An indexing manager or tracker attempts to replicate the target index by holding the securities in the index. The indexing approach, often described as passive, emphasizing broad diversification, low trading activity, and lower costs, derives originally from the concept of market efficiency. But markets are only efficient if investors study all available information and move prices to reflect the published data. This implies that as the market share of indexers rises, the market will become less efficient.

Index funds are an honest expression of incompetence. It's a vote for the inability to choose a good manager, so you put the money in an index fund. It's not saying I don't believe there is such a thing as a good manager. It's not saying I believe in efficient markets.

Barr Rosenberg, b. ~1942, Rosenberg Institutional Equity Management

Investment success is defined by the allocation of financial market returns between financial intermediaries and investors.

John C. Bogle, b. 1929, founder of the Vanguard Funds

Charisma means looking like everyone else.

Marshall McLuhan, 1911–1980, Canadian sociologist and critic

In speculation, as in most other things, one individual derives confidence from another. Such a one purchases or sells, not because he had any really accurate information as to the state of demand and supply, but because someone else has done so before him.

J. R. McCulloch in The Principles of Political Economy, *1830*

A foolish consistency is the hobgoblin of little minds. With consistency a great soul has simply nothing to do. He may as well concern himself with his shadow on the wall.

Ralph Waldo Emerson, 1803–1882, American essayist and poet

A friend who is near and dear may in time become as useless as a relative.

George Ade, 1866–1944, American author

If you want to outperform other people, you have got to hold something different from other people. If you want to outperform the market, the thing you mustn't hold is the market itself.

Anthony Bolton, Fidelity Investments

All mankind is divided into three classes: Those that are immovable, those that are movable, and those that move.

Arabian proverb

An educated man is one who knows a lot and says nothing about it.

Gracie Fields, 1898–1979, English comedienne

By the street of By-and-By, one arrives at the house of Never.

Cervantes, 1547–1616, Spanish writer

We always tried to have the dominant analyst in these industry groups. Our argument was that an average analyst was worthless because in order to achieve the averages all you had to do was to buy an index or buy a sector fund.

Barton Biggs, Morgan Stanley & Co., 1987

He who lives without folly is not so wise as he thinks.

La Rochefoucauld, 1613–1680, French author

Human affairs are not so happily arranged that the best things please the most men. It is the proof of a bad cause when it is applauded by the mob.

Seneca, ~4 B.C.–A.D. 65, Roman statesman and philosopher

I am already so popular that someone who vilifies me becomes more popular than I am.

Karl Kraus, 1874–1936, Austrian satirist

I have found that most people are about as happy as they make up their minds to be.

Abraham Lincoln, 1809–1865, 16th U.S. president

Maybe if there was no Mayday, volume wouldn't have gone up because of the high, fixed rates holding people back from trading. We certainly wouldn't have had program trading or index funds and all those things.

Donald Marron, b. ~1934, Paine Webber

If some period be not fixed, either by the Constitution or by practice, to the services of the First Magistrate, his office, though nominally elective, will, in fact, be for life, and that will soon degenerate into an inheritance.

Thomas Jefferson, 1743–1826, 3rd U.S. president

It is when we all play safe that we create a world of utmost insecurity.

Dag Hammarskjöld, 1905–1961, secretary-general of the United Nations

Man is a gregarious animal, and much more so in his mind than in his body. He may like to go alone for a walk, but he hates to stand alone in his opinions.

George Santayana, 1863–1952, Spanish-American poet and philosopher

Nothing is so dangerous as an ignorant friend; a wise enemy is worth more.

Henri-Marie Lafontaine, 1854–1943, Belgian politician and pacifist

Originality is undetected plagiarism.

William Inge, 1913–1973, American playwright

Read every day something no one else is reading. Think every day something no one else is thinking. It is bad for the mind to be always a part of a unanimity.

Christopher Morley, 1870–1957, American author

Given [the costs of active management and the semiefficiency of the U.S. stock market], indexing is hard to beat, and relative passivity is not a vice.

Jeremy Grantham, investment manager, Grantham, Mayo, Van Otterloo

Repetition is the death of art.

Alfred North Whitehead, 1861–1947, English mathematician and philosopher

The coward calls himself cautious.

Publilius Syrus, 1st century B.C., Roman writer

The surest way to corrupt a young man is to teach him to esteem more highly those who think alike than those who think differently.

Friedrich Nietzsche, 1844–1900, German philosopher

We are surer that we see a star when we know that others also see it.

Henry George, 1839–1897, American social reformer

Instead of its being the Nifty Fifty, it's [in 1987] the Nifty 500, whatever is in the S&P. All of the geniuses have figured out that the best way to have a glorious party is to all join the index . . . and the only problem is that all of the money is flowing into a limited number of securities and the index is no longer an index. It's making its own market.

Edward (Ned) Johnson III, b. 1930, chairman, Fidelity Investments

With the exception of the instinct of self-preservation, the propensity for emulation is probably the strongest and most alert and persistent of the economic motives proper.

Thorstein Veblen, 1857–1929, economist and philosopher

Children have never been very good at listening to their elders, but they have never failed to imitate them.

James Baldwin, 1924–1987, novelist

He who walks in another's tracks leaves no footprints.

Joan L. Brannon

No one goes there nowadays, it's too crowded.

Yogi Berra, b. 1925, baseball player, coach, and manager

We did the first indexed portfolios by hand, with rolls of calculator tape on a clothesline through the office.

Dean LeBaron, b. 1933, investment manager and contrarian thinker

Satan to a newcomer: The trouble with you Chicago people is that you think you are the best people down here, whereas you are merely the most numerous.

Mark Twain, 1835–1910, American author

The imagination imitates. It is the critical spirit that creates.

Oscar Wilde, 1854–1900, Irish-British author

For parlor use, the vague generality is a lifesaver.

George Ade, 1866–1944, American author

It is easy in the world to live after the world's opinion; it is easy in solitude to live after our own; but the great man is he who in the midst of the crowd keeps with perfect sweetness the independence of solitude.

Ralph Waldo Emerson, 1803–1882, American essayist and poet

Monotony is the awful reward of the careful.

A. G. Buckham

The stock market is always wrong, so that if you copy everybody else in the Wall Street, you're doomed to do poorly.

George Soros, b. 1930, Budapest, financier, philanthropist, author

A man should sleep sometime between lunch and dinner in order to be at his best in the evening when he joins his wife and friends at dinner.

Winston Churchill, 1874–1965, British prime minister

Knowledge dwells in heads replete with thoughts of other men; wisdom in minds attentive to their own.

William Cowper, 1731–1800, British poet

My advice to you, if you should ever be in a hold-up, is to line up with the cowards and save your bravery for an occasion when it may be of some benefit to you.

O. Henry (William Sydney Porter), 1862–1910,
American short-story writer

In matters of style, swim with the current. In matters of principle, stand like a rock.

Thomas Jefferson, 1743–1826, 3rd U.S. president

Anyway [while at AT&T], we discovered that with 111 managers, our performance in the aggregate was no better than the S&P 500's, minus fees and commissions. So we eventually created in-house index funds to manage some of the assets. I've learned a few things in the business, and one is that large pools of funds are market-driven. If the markets do well, the fund is going to do well. If the markets do poorly, the fund is going to do poorly.

John English, b. ~1933, Ford Foundation

You sometimes find something good in the lunatic fringe. In fact, we have got as part of our social and economic government a whole lot of things which in my boyhood were considered lunatic fringe, and yet they are now part of everyday life.

Franklin D. Roosevelt, 1882–1945, 32nd U.S. president

Lots of us get credit for enjoying our work when we are really only smiling over what we did last night.

Tom Sims, in Life

This business of measuring yourself by others means, of course, that you are never away from others, that you move with the crowd.

Marya Mannes

Professor [William] Sharpe noticed, as anyone else could have noticed, that if you add up everyone in the marketplace, by definition their average return is the market return. That just overwhelmed institutional investors.

Barr Rosenberg, b. ~1942, Rosenberg Institutional Equity Management

I looked for great men, but all I found were the apes of their ideals.

Friedrich Nietzsche, 1844–1900, German philosopher

More persons, on the whole, are humbugged by believing nothing, than by believing too much.

P. T. Barnum, 1810–1891, showman and businessman

The fellow that can only see a week ahead is always the popular fellow, for he is looking with the crowd. But the one that can see years ahead, he has a telescope but he can't make anybody believe he has it.

Will Rogers, 1879–1935, American humorist and showman

Nobody can think straight who does not work. Idleness warps the mind. Thinking without constructive action becomes a disease.

Henry Ford, 1863–1947, American automobile manufacturer, founder of Ford Motor Co.

When human beings are confronted with uncertainty, meaning they do not understand the rules or the terms of particular types of engagement they're having in the real world, they disengage. And in markets, disengagement, of necessity, means that prices fall. In other words, fear itself is something to be frightened of. It harms markets in its own right.

Alan Greenspan, b. 1926, chairman of the U.S. Federal Reserve

By annihilating desires you annihilate the mind. Every man without passions has within him no principle of action, nor motive to act.

Claude Adrien Helvétius, 1715–1771, French philosopher

If you do not ask, the answer is always no.

Owen Laughlin

There is no better measure of a person than what he does when he is absolutely free to choose.

Wilma Askinas, b. ~1924, writer

To drift is to be in hell, to be in heaven is to steer.

George Bernard Shaw, 1856–1950, playwright

Single-mindedness is all very well in cows or baboons; in an animal claiming to belong to the same species as Shakespeare, it is simply disgraceful.

Aldous Huxley, 1894–1963, English writer

Punctuality is the virtue of the bored.

Evelyn Waugh, 1903–1966, British author

There are only two ways to be quite unprejudiced and impartial. One is to be completely ignorant. The other is to be completely indifferent.

Charles P. Curtis, 1860–1936, American political leader

Faith is much better than belief. Belief is when someone else does the thinking.

Buckminster Fuller, 1895–1983, American designer

Initial Public Offerings

99 99 99

Straight to Market

It's a bad bargain where nobody gains.

English proverb

One of the most seemingly attractive areas of investment is that of initial public offerings (IPOs). Buying shares the first time they are offered to the public has considerable natural appeal, especially in a bull market, tempting investors with potentially phenomenal short-term returns as well as exposure to exciting new companies and industries. But a significant body of evidence indicates that, on aggregate, IPOs have underperformed the market, typically 30% to 50% below comparable companies over three- to five-year periods. Buying new issues should be no different from investing in existing quoted companies, with decisions made on the basis of as much knowledge as can be accumulated.

In olden times the pillory and the whipping-post were among the gentler forms of encouragement awaiting the inventor. Today we hail with enthusiasm a scientific discovery, and stand ready to make a stock company of it.

Thomas Bailey Aldrich, 1836–1907, American writer and editor

My career [while] at the SEC started in the early '60s, and at that time [we] were somewhat puzzled that stocks would double in price within minutes of coming to market. So we stuck a name on that—called them "hot issues"—and tried to figure out, quite unsuccessfully, why a stock price would double.

Eugene Rotberg, b. ~1929, World Bank

Nothing is so good as it seems beforehand.

George Eliot, 1819–1880, British author

Small opportunities are often the beginning of great enterprises.

Demosthenes, 384–322 B.C., Athenian orator and statesman

Strangers are what friends are made of.

Cullen Hightower

Wars almost never end the way starters had in mind.

Malcolm Forbes, 1919–1990, publisher, author

Investment banking is perhaps the most respectable department of the Wall Street community because it is here that finance plays its constructive role of supplying new capital for the expansion of industry.

Benjamin Graham, 1894–1976, in The Intelligent Investor, *1949*

Daring ideas are like chessmen moved forward. They may be beaten, but they may start a winning game.

Johann Goethe, 1749–1832, German writer

From fortune to misfortune is but a step; from misfortune to fortune is a long way.

Yiddish proverb

If you can build a business up big enough, it's respectable.

Will Rogers, 1879–1935, American humorist and showman

More worship the rising than the setting sun.

Plutarch, d. A.D. 431 or 432, Greek philosopher

One may return to the place of his birth; he cannot go back to his youth.

John Burroughs, 1837–1921, American political leader

Polish doesn't change quartz into a diamond.

Wilma Askinas, b. ~1924, writer

The method of the enterprising is to plan with audacity and execute with vigor.

Christian Bovee, 1820–1904, American author, lawyer

The success of most things depends upon knowing how long it will take to succeed.

Charles de Montesquieu, 1689–1755, French philosopher

All passions exaggerate: it is because they do that they are passions.

Nicholas Chamfort, 1741–1794, French writer and wit

As natural selection works solely by and for the good of each being, all corporeal and mental endowments will tend to progress toward perfection.

Charles Darwin, 1809–1882, naturalist

I am a great believer in luck. The harder I work, the more of it I seem to have.

Coleman Cox

We are all hoping and praying, and all well-intentioned people are working, for a new earth. I point out, however, that in St. John's teaching the new heaven came before the new earth. This is the law of life. Idealism precedes realism.

Milo Hudson Gates, D.D.

It has been my experience that folks who have no vices have very few virtues.

Abraham Lincoln, 1809–1865, 16th U.S. president

Beware of little expenses; a small leak will sink a great ship.

Benjamin Franklin, 1706–1790, statesman, scientist, public leader

Speculation is an effort, probably unsuccessful, to turn a little money into a lot. Investment is an effort, which should be successful, to prevent a lot of money from becoming a little.

Fred Schwed, Jr., author and investor

It is not men that interest or disturb me primarily; it is ideas. Ideas live; men die.

Woodrow Wilson, 1856–1924, 28th U.S. president

May I be wrong, for whenever men are right they are not young.

e e cummings, 1894–1962, American poet

The more original a discovery, the more obvious it seems afterward.

Arthur Koestler, 1905–1983, novelist and essayist

A simple trading rule is that if IPOs start selling below the offer price on the first day of settlement, you should stop buying them. And if you are unable to acquire them at the offer price, the deck is stacked against you.

Dean LeBaron, b. 1933, investment manager and contrarian thinker

In politics forget the truth . . . The focus is to win . . . It's not what's needed to be done . . . It's how it's made to spin.

Art Buck

A lawyer is a person who writes a 10,000-word document and calls it a "brief."

Unknown

The statement has truth but not quite enough to be true.

Francis M. Cornford, 1874–1943, British author and poet

The test of an enjoyment is the remembrance which it leaves behind.

Logan Pearsall Smith, 1865–1946, American essayist and aphorist

Nothing can be so perfect while we possess it as it will seem when remembered.

Oliver Wendell Holmes, 1841–1935, associate justice,
U.S. Supreme Court

Self-respect: the secure feeling that no one, as yet, is suspicious.

H. L. Mencken, 1880–1956, American journalist and writer

Society can exist only on the basis that there is some amount of polished lying and that no one says exactly as he thinks.

Lin Yutang, 1895–1976, Chinese-born American philologist

No man is impatient with his creditors.

> The Talmud, *body of Jewish civil and religious law*

For purposes of action, nothing is more useful than narrowness of thought combined with energy of will.

> *Henri Frederic Amiel, 1821–1881, Swiss poet*

Illusion is the first of all pleasures.

> *Voltaire, 1694–1778, French philosopher and writer*

Originality is simply a pair of fresh eyes.

> *Thomas Wentworth Storrow Higginson, 1823–1911,*
> *American writer and soldier*

The first man gets the oyster, the second man gets the shell.

> *Andrew Carnegie, 1835–1919, steel manufacturer and philanthropist*

If we will it, it is no dream.

> *Theodore Herzl, 1860–1904, Austrian author*

We do not really feel grateful toward those who make our dreams come true; they ruin our dreams.

> *Eric Hoffer, 1902–1983, American philosopher*

To try and to fail is at least to learn; to fail to try is to suffer the inestimable loss of what might have been.

> *Chester Barnard, 1886–1961, executive and author*

Whom the gods wish to destroy they first call promising.

> *Cyril Connolly, 1903–1974, critic and novelist*

If the building of a bridge does not enrich the awareness of those who work on it, then that bridge ought not be built.

> *Frantz Fanon, 1925–1961, political theorist and author*

You will never stub your toe standing still. The faster you go, the more chance there is of stubbing your toe, but the more chance you have of getting somewhere.

Charles F. Kettering, 1876–1958, engineer and inventor

Wouldn't it be much worse if life were fair and all the terrible things that happen to us happen because we really deserve them?

J. M. Straczynski

It seems to me that the thing that makes the theater worthwhile is the fact that it attracts so many people with good ideas who are constantly trying to share them with the public. Real art is illumination. It gives a man an idea he never had before or lights up ideas that were formless or only lurking in the shadows of his mind. It adds stature to life.

Brooks Atkinson, 1894–1984, American theater critic

Our aspirations are our possibilities.

Robert Browning, 1812–1889, poet

Most people like hard work. Particularly when they are paying for it.

Franklin P. Jones

Economy is in itself a great source of revenue.

Seneca, ~4 B.C.–A.D. 65, Roman statesman and philosopher

There can be no economy where there is no efficiency.

Benjamin Disraeli, 1804–1881, British prime minister, author,
1st Earl of Beaconsfield

Retail investors without an especially close relationship with their broker are better off staying away from IPO offerings altogether—and when it comes to money, "relationship" is a rather fleeting concept.

Ivo Welch, finance professor, UCLA

If your endeavors are beset by fearful odds, and you receive no present reward, go not back to error, nor become a sluggard in the race. When the smoke of battle clears away, you will discern the good you have done and receive according to your deserving.

Mary Baker Eddy, 1821–1910, American religious leader

I early found that when I worked for myself alone, myself alone worked for me; but when I worked for others also, others worked also for me.

Benjamin Franklin, 1706–1790, statesman, scientist, public leader

Persistency is what makes the impossible possible, the possible likely, and the likely definite.

Robert Half, employment agent

Profit is the ignition system of our economic engine.

Charles Sawyer, American government official

Ultimate bravery is courage of the mind.

H. G. Wells, 1866–1946, English novelist, sociologist, and historian

Ambition, energy, industry, perseverance, are indispensable requisites for success in business.

P. T. Barnum, 1810–1891, showman and businessman

Profitability is the sovereign criterion of the enterprise.

Peter Drucker, b. 1909, author and consultant

The business of America is business.

Calvin Coolidge, 1872–1933, 30th U.S. president

The law of work does seem utterly unfair—but there it is and nothing can change it: The higher the pay in enjoyment the worker gets out of it, the higher shall be his pay in money also.

Mark Twain, 1835–1910, American author

Sign in office: No one would ever have crossed the ocean if he could have gotten off the ship in the storm.

Charles F. Kettering

Opportunity has power everywhere; always let your hook be hanging— where you least expect it, there will swim a fish.

Ovid, 43 B.C.–A.D. 17, Roman poet

Men are born to succeed—not to fail.

Henry David Thoreau, 1817–1862, American naturalist and writer

We might have been—these are but common words, and yet they make the sum of life's bewailing.

Charles Lamb, 1775–1834, essayist

International Money

99 99 99

The International Money Game

Great spenders are bad lenders.

Benjamin Franklin, 1706–1790,
statesman, scientist, public leader

It is no longer possible for governments and central banks to conduct monetary policy at the national level—policy cooperation through international bodies like the International Monetary Fund (IMF) and the G-7 has become essential. The Bretton Woods system developed at the end of World War II was "government-led"—official bodies decided on exchange rates and the provision of liquidity, and oversaw the international adjustment process. Now, the system is "market-led"—major exchange rates are floating; liquidity is determined by the market; and the adjustment mechanism operates through market forces. There is an idea on the part of developing countries that prescribed behavior—democracy, human rights, environmental concerns—will lead to cheap, long-term money. However, the IMF is no longer effective on the global scene—the central issue for the international monetary system is creating a new global lender of last resort whose role is formally recognized by national governments and financial markets.

Meetings are indispensable when you don't want to do anything.

John Kenneth Galbraith, b. 1908, economist

History teaches us that men and nations behave wisely once they have exhausted all other alternatives.

Abba Eban, b. 1915, Israeli politician

The IMF annual meeting is a hothouse of rumors. All the commercial bankers in the world as well as all the governments meet there and talk about each other, and these rumors do terrible things to economies.

Denis Healey, former British Chancellor of the Exchequer, 1987

One savvy foreign trading specialist has begun calling the IMF, the Imaginary Money Fund.

Arthur Cashin, floor broker, New York Stock Exchange

Prescription for aid: Make a lot of noise, declare war on America, and then immediately surrender.

The Mouse That Roared, *the movie*

We have a firm commitment to NATO; we are a "part" of NATO. We have a firm commitment to Europe. We are a "part" of Europe.

J. Danforth Quayle, b. 1947, vice president of the United States

We have to learn to have a debate where mathematics will not dominate humanity.

James Wolfensohn, president, World Bank, October 1997

You don't want to be in the same woods as a wounded bear.

Russian proverb

The Germans had to revalue from time to time due to the surpluses and due to speculation, which was pushing the D-mark up all the time. Every time you had to choose a new parity, you had to draw conclusions about farm prices and all that. It was the Germans who really wanted a floating system, not us.

Valéry Giscard d'Estaing, b. 1926, former French president

Dinners have become a means of government, and the fates of nations are decided at a banquet.

Anthelme Brillat-Savarin, 1755–1826, French politician and gourmet

Democracy demands that all of its citizens begin the race even. Egalitarianism insists that they *finish* the race even.

Roger Price

As an international institution you have to limit your interference as much as possible to what is essential for the purpose of the institution—balance of payments, the monetary system, credit creation and exchange rates.

Johannes Witteveen, former managing director,
International Monetary Fund, 1987

A man said to the universe: "Sir, I exist!" . . . However, replied the universe, "That fact has not created in me a sense of obligation."

Stephen Crane, 1871–1900, American author, in War Is Kind

A small debt produced a debtor; a large one, an enemy.

Publilius Syrus, 1st century B.C., Roman writer

Alliance: In international politics, the union of two thieves who have their hands so deeply into each other's pocket that they cannot separately plunder a third.

Ambrose Bierce, 1842–~1914, American writer and journalist

OPEC members are among the most professional I have ever dealt with. They made a clear policy decision in the mid-'60s and later that as their financial resources were increasing they would not take those resources and recycle them to countries in deficit. They would put them in the hands of strong intermediaries—money center banks—or lend them to very high-quality issuers, like the World Bank.

Eugene Rotberg, b. ~1929, World Bank

Another generation is rapidly growing up to whom war is becoming a romantic episode once more, and I fear that many of the amusement films are helping to create that impression. It is for those whose memories are not yet shortened to work strenuously in the few years that yet remain to us to banish the unspeakable horror of war from international possibilities. [as quoted in 1929]

Margaret Bondfield, 1873–1953, English trade unionist and politician

Dependence begets subservience and venality, suffocates the germ of virtue, and prepares fit tools for the designs of ambition.

Thomas Jefferson, 1743–1826, 3rd U.S. president

In 1971, when President Nixon first adjusted the dollar against gold and then floated it: He [Paul Volcker] explained to me the action that the United States was going to take. He was basically saying that under Bretton Woods, there was no way for the dollar to be devalued, and he wanted the other currencies to appreciate against the dollar.

Yusuke Kashiwagi, Bank of Tokyo, 1987

Economic power is headstrong and vehement, and if it is to prove beneficial to mankind it must be securely curbed and regulated with prudence.

Pope Pius XI, 1857–1939, established temporal authority of the papacy over Vatican City

For the United States to launch forth on a program of building the largest navy in the world is equivalent to firing cannon which will be heard around the world, and will start a competitive armament race. Military preparedness upon the dimensions which Mr. Coolidge asks inevitably creates the military spirit. The practical results of Coolidge's proposed naval bills will be contradictory to the spirit and purpose of the anti-war pact to which the representatives of sixty nations have signed their names.

The Rev. C. Everett Wagner

There was never really a "Nixon shock." The destabilization of the Bretton Woods agreement had been coming over a long period. There was a kind of dogma by which we lived that the dollar was as good as gold. We thought, very early, with de Gaulle around 1964, that this structure would not remain stable forever. We decided to bring back some of our gold reserves that were stored in Fort Knox, because it was perfectly normal for any central bank to have in its own vaults its own reserves.

Valéry Giscard d'Estaing, b. 1926, former French president

Great men sometimes lose the reins and lose their heads. This time, let us hope that they will retain them and that when victory is assured they will sit down and reckon what the future is going to be for their countries as well as for other lands. [as quoted in 1945]

David Lloyd George, 1863–1945, British prime minister

If a conference lasts a long time, it must end in peace; no one can keep on defying his enemies all day.

Alfred Duggan, 1903–1964, author

One frightening thing about the coming peace, unless I am wrong in my reading, is that the Moscow pact, the Teheran and Yalta communiques, and the draft of the Dumbarton Oaks plan never once mentioned the name of God, though it might have been an oversight.

John P. Delaney, D.D.

Global capital markets pose the same kinds of problems that jet planes do. They are faster, more comfortable, and they get you where you are going better. But the crashes are much more spectacular.

Lawrence Summers, former secretary, U.S. Treasury Department

One of the most certain ways of bringing about international disagreement and ultimately war is to talk constantly about war as inevitable and speculate concerning when and how war is to come. America should be very slow to give expression to that kind of thought.

Walter F. George, U.S. senator

Neither Jimmy Carter nor the British had the slightest right to ask us to play the locomotive role to the world economy [in 1978].

Helmut Schmidt, b. 1918, former chancellor of Germany

Peace is not a relationship of Nations. It is a condition of mind brought about by a serenity of soul. Lasting peace can come only to peaceful people.

Horace E. De Lisser

Self-determination is not a mere phrase. It is an imperative principle of action, which statesmen will henceforth ignore at their peril.

Woodrow Wilson, 1856–1924, 28th U.S. president

Since America possesses two-thirds of the banking capital of the world, graduates annually more trained youth than all the world together; since capital and management are the agencies of employment, individual opportunity and aggregate national profits, an inevitable conclusion is that there must center in America the major industrial organization of the world. America must become the natural headquarters for manifold activities at home and abroad.

Julius H. Barnes

Today [1987] we have become accustomed to muddling through, and we know that monetary reform is very difficult. But when I came to the IMF in 1973, the United States had only relatively recently stopped convertibility of the dollar, so that the basis of the old Bretton Woods system was taken away. And that was a shock.

Johannes Witteveen, former managing director,
International Monetary Fund, 1987

The gift derives its value from the rank of the giver.

Ovid, 43 B.C.–A.D. 17, Roman poet

The great task of the peace is to work morals into it. The only sort of peace that will be real is one in which everybody takes his share of responsibility. World organizations and conferences will be of no value unless there is improvement in the relation of men to men.

Sir Frederick Eggleston

The highest use of capital is not to make more money, but to make money do more for the betterment of life.

Henry Ford, 1863–1947, American automobile manufacturer,
founder of Ford Motor Co.

The whole world is learning that treaties, constitutions, ordinances and bonds are good only to the extent that they are made coincident with basic human relationships which have the approval of that sensitive, quick acting and dominant power, the public opinion of the world.

Owen D. Young, 1874–1962, American lawyer and financier

There is more wisdom in public opinion than is to be found in Napoleon, Voltaire, or all the ministers of State, present or to come.

Charles Talleyrand, 1754–1838, French statesman

Government intervention was popular, but we viewed government intervention as just another big player. They were entitled to their view, and they could deflect the market for a while. But we knew the [currency] market was bigger than they were.

Leo Melamed, b. ~1932, former chairman, Chicago Mercantile Exchange

There is only one class in the community that thinks more about money than the rich, and that is the poor. The poor can think of nothing else. That is the misery of being poor.

Oscar Wilde, 1854–1900, Irish-British author

We may consider each generation as a separate nation, with a right, by the will of the majority, to bind themselves, but none to bind the succeeding generation, more than the inhabitants of another country.

Thomas Jefferson, 1743–1826, 3rd U.S. president

In that period of the early 1960s, the balance-of-payments problem also started to emerge, as did the need to deal with it under the Bretton Woods agreement. And we had, therefore, Operation Nudge and Twist, with the Federal Reserve trying to hold up the short rate and hold down the long rate.

Henry Kaufman, b. 1927, chief economist, Salomon Brothers

You cannot help men permanently by doing for them what they could and should do for themselves.

Abraham Lincoln, 1809–1865, 16th U.S. president

A gift much expected is paid, not given.

George Herbert, 1593–1633, British poet

Lives of great men all remind us that we can make our lives sublime, and departing, leave behind us footprints on the sands of time.

Henry Wadsworth Longfellow, 1807–1882, American poet

At a meeting in the Azores in 1971 with President Nixon and Paul Volcker: We thought that the overvaluation of the dollar should be corrected. One was to float, the other to devalue. And President Nixon accepted the idea of devaluation. It was the first devaluation since the war.

Valéry Giscard d'Estaing, b. 1926, former French president

A well-governed appetite is a great part of liberty.

Seneca, ~4 B.C.–A.D. 65, Roman statesman and philosopher

All bad precedents begin with justifiable measures.

Julius Caesar, 100–44 B.C., Roman general and statesman

Americans are uneasy with their possessions, guilty about power, all of which is difficult for Europeans to perceive because they themselves are so truly materialistic, so versed in the uses of power.

Joan Didion, b. 1934, American author

It was not tax evasion that brought clients to Switzerland; it was fear of war, revolution and inflation. A former French minister said: "Switzerland is a reflection of our mistakes," and another added, "It has saved the fortunes of the French." We had gotten the money that sought refuge, not because we were Swiss per se, but because we had escaped many of the accidents of history.

Yves Oltramare, former general partner, Lombard, Odier & CIE, 1987

Divorce: A resumption of diplomatic relations and rectification of boundaries.

Ambrose Bierce, 1842--~1914, American writer and journalist

Education is a better safeguard of liberty than a standing army.

Edward Everett, 1794–1865, American Unitarian clergyman, orator, and statesman

Everything that poverty touches becomes frightful.

Nicolas Boileau, 1636–1711, French poet

On Bretton Woods: Committees and commissions numbering anything up to 200 people, in rooms with bad acoustics, shouting through microphones, with many of those present having an imperfect knowledge of English, each wanting to get something on the record that would look well in the press at home.

John Maynard Keynes, 1883–1946, British economist, 1st Baron Keynes of Tilton

Greater is he who acts from love than he who acts from fear.

Simeon ben Eleazar

It is better to do the wrong thing than to do nothing.

Winston Churchill, 1874–1965, British prime minister

I am getting ready to see Stalin and Churchill and it is a chore. I have to take my tuxedo, tails, high hat, low hat, and hard hat.

Harry S. Truman, 1884–1972, 33rd U.S. president

I believe that every human mind feels pleasure in doing good to another.

Thomas Jefferson, 1743–1826, 3rd U.S. president

Paul Volcker is my hero; I've known him more than twenty years, and I really like him and admire him. He understands that we live in an interdependent world. I think if we could revive this kind of close friendship among these mandarins of the financial world, then we might be able to work out a better solution to many things.

Yusuke Kashiwagi, Bank of Tokyo, 1987

I feel the responsibility of the occasion. Responsibility is proportionate to opportunity.

Woodrow Wilson, 1856–1924, 28th U.S. president

I get weary of the European habit of taking our money, resenting any slight hint as to what *they* should do, and then assuming, in addition, full right to criticize us as bitterly as they may desire.

Dwight D. Eisenhower, 1890–1969, 34th U.S. president

Because of that meeting [in January 1974, during the oil crisis] I proposed the first oil facility of the International Monetary Fund to cope with the problem of these oil deficits, to enable countries to finance these deficits short-term.

Johannes Witteveen, former managing director, International Monetary Fund, 1987

If all misfortunes were laid in one common heap whence everyone must take an equal portion, most people would be contented to take their own and depart.

Socrates, 469–399 B.C., Greek philosopher

If you study the history and records of the world, you must admit that the source of justice was the fear of injustice.

Horace, 65–8 B.C., Roman poet

In general, despite all the talk about freedom, peoples and governments demand unlimited state power internally.

Jakob Burckhardt, 1818–1897, Swiss historian of art and culture

Increased means and increased leisure are the two civilizers of man.

Benjamin Franklin, 1706–1790, statesman, scientist, public leader

What was significant was that this [1971] devaluation didn't succeed in stabilizing the situation. And there was a second round, the Smithsonian agreement, which was, in fact, the beginning of the new monetary era of flotation. It was impossible to deal with this [capital] movement with fixed parities.

Valéry Giscard d'Estaing, b. 1926, former French president

Indifference is the invincible giant of the world.

Ouida (Marie Louise de la Ramée), 1839–1908, English novelist

It is better to risk saving a guilty man than to condemn an innocent one.

Voltaire, 1694–1778, French philosopher and writer

We might have a great deal of money and a great deal of wisdom, but you can't prevent earthquakes from happening or high interest rates or a recession in the West or protectionism. Yet these are variables that will affect the way the world is held together. The better part of wisdom is to understand that while we are an ethical spokesman for what *should* happen, we really can't make major changes or prevent the untoward.

Eugene Rotberg, b. ~1929, World Bank

Liberal institutions straightaway cease from being liberal the moment they are firmly established.

Friedrich Nietzsche, 1844–1900, German philosopher

The job of central banks: To take away the punch bowl just as the party is getting going.

William McChesney, U.S. Federal Reserve chairman in the 1950s

Money is as money does. If it doesn't, it isn't.

Edward Smith

Morality is a private and costly luxury.

Henry Adams, 1838–1918, American historian

Never let your sense of morals prevent you from doing what is right.

Isaac Asimov, 1920–1992, American author

No man has come to true greatness who has not felt in some degree that his life belongs to his race, and that what God gives him he gives him for mankind.

Phillips Brooks, 1835–1893, American religious leader

The idea of having unlimited convertibility between dollar and gold for central banks could not last for long. So when we had destabilization of the international monetary situation in the 1970s, it was what we expected, due to the imbalances.

Valéry Giscard d'Estaing, b. 1926, former French president

Our most valuable possessions are those which can be shared without lessening those which, when shared, multiply.

William H. Danforth

The blunting effects of slavery upon the slaveholder's moral perceptions are known and conceded the world over; and a privileged class, an aristocracy, is but a band of slaveholders under another name.

Mark Twain, 1835–1910, American author

The only way to have a friend is to be one.

Ralph Waldo Emerson, 1803–1882, American essayist and poet

Money is a kind of poetry.

Wallace Stevens, 1879–1955, American poet

The original of all great and lasting societies consisted not in the mutual good will men had toward each other, but in the mutual fear they had of each other.

Thomas Hobbes, 1588–1679, English philosopher

It has even been very difficult to get a normal quota increase for the fund; a capital increase for the World Bank is still difficult. And central banks don't do anything. The official export credit arrangements are cutting down their credit availability; they behave just like the commercial banks.

Johannes Witteveen, former managing director,
International Monetary Fund, 1987

The salvation of mankind lies only in making everything the concern of all.

Aleksandr Solzhenitsyn, b. 1918, Russian novelist

The space of play and the space of thought are the two theaters of freedom.

Eugen Rosenstock-Huessy

There are no people in the world who are so slow to develop hostile feelings against a foreign country as the Americans, and no people who, once estranged, are more difficult to win back.

Winston Churchill, 1874–1965, British prime minister

There is no art which one government sooner learns from another than that of draining money from the pockets of the people.

Adam Smith, 1723–1790, political economist

As quoted in 1987: The international financial world is changing very fast. There may be more risks, but there are also more ways to cope with risk. The U.S. dollar cannot be the single reserve currency anymore.

Yusuke Kashiwagi, Bank of Tokyo, 1987

We have always known that heedless self-interest was bad morals; we know now that it is bad economics.

Franklin D. Roosevelt, 1882–1945, 32nd U.S. president

Why is it that right-wing bastards always stand shoulder to shoulder in solidarity, while liberals always fall out among themselves?

Yevgeny Yevtushenko, b. 1933, Russian poet

You can't achieve anything without getting in someone's way. You can't be detached and effective.

Abba Eban, b. 1915, Israeli politician

[At the first economic summits,] the press didn't have a chance to interfere, and government press spokesmen had no chance to run out every half hour to tell the press what their great chancellor or their great president had just told those other six idiots. This has deteriorated; nowadays it is a meeting of the mass media, on the fringes of which you also have seven prime ministers or presidents.

Helmut Schmidt, b. 1918, former chancellor of Germany

You may proclaim, good sirs, your fine philosophy. But till you feed us, right and wrong can wait.

Bertolt Brecht, 1898–1956, German playwright

Rich man down and poor man up—they are still not even.

Yiddish proverb

Such subtle covenants have been made, that peace itself is war in masquerade.

John Dryden, 1631–1700, English author

In the world there are a lot of nations, so everything cannot go in one way.

Rong Yiren, b. ~1916, China International Trust and Investment Corp.

The agreement to use the ECU as a central bank intervention instrument was drafted by the heads of government. I had a meeting in Bremen with Schmidt and Callaghan and [others]. And it became a formal agreement in 1979. We must act on the institutional side by creating what I call a central bank of the central banks for the administration of the ECU system.

Valéry Giscard d'Estaing, b. 1926, former French president

The worst sin towards our fellow creatures is not to hate them, but to be indifferent to them; that's the essence of inhumanity.

George Bernard Shaw, 1856–1950, playwright

The price of greatness is responsibility.

Winston Churchill, 1874–1965, British prime minister

Internet Investing

99 99 99

Winning on the Web?

Profitability is for wimps.
Mike Doonesbury, comic strip character devised by
Garry Trudeau

During the second half of the 1990s and into the early days of the new millennium, investing both in and via the Internet became the new investment frontier. The potential impact of this new communications medium on business and society was reflected in a frenzy of speculation in Internet stocks, driving prices to extraordinary levels. By early 1999, investors seemed willing to pay virtually any price for Internet stocks, causing Federal Reserve chairman Alan Greenspan to warn of a "lottery mentality." A year later, such warnings finally became reality as the market for Internet stocks crashed along with many other stocks in the technology, media, and telecommunications sectors. The Internet industry is reminiscent of the emerging markets in the early to mid-1990s—the same excitement of discovery, the glamour of seemingly unbridled growth, the almost infinite demand, the element of risk.

In the internet business, profitability is for wimps. It means your business plan wasn't aggressive enough.

Mike Doonesbury, comic strip character devised by Garry Trudeau

Cyberspace is where your money is.

John Perry Barlow, cofounder of the Electronic Frontier Foundation

Hysterical "bulls" care nothing whatever about the earnings or dividend returns on a stock. The only note to which they attune their actions is the optimistic slogan, "It's going up!" and the higher it goes, the more they buy, and the more their ranks are swelled by new recruits.

Henry Howard Harper in The Psychology of Speculation, *1926*

Cyberspace: A consensual hallucination experienced daily by billions . . . unthinkable complexity . . . lines of light ranged . . . in the nonspace of the mind, clusters and constellations of data. Like city lights . . . receding . . .

William Gibson, 1850–1896, science fiction writer

The electric light is very probably a great invention and let us take it for granted that its future development will be vast. But this, unhappily, cannot be urged as a reason why the pioneer companies should be prosperous.

The Economist, *1882*

Bankers are the gatekeepers of modern capitalist development.

Joseph Alois Schumpeter, 1883–1950, Austrian-American economist

During a gold rush, the people that make the money are those selling picks and shovels.

Unknown

My grandfather told me you make more money selling information than you do following it. So let that be a warning.

Malcolm ("Steve") Forbes, Jr., b. 1947, publisher and presidential candidate

Observing that there is probably some bubble quality to the internet stock craze: I have a general rule: Whenever something becomes worth more than the whole state of California, sell it.

Alan Blinder, economics professor and former Federal Reserve governor

You can dream, create, design and build the most wonderful place in the world, but it requires people to make the dream a reality.

Walt Disney, 1901–1966, animator, film producer

A new scientific truth does not triumph by convincing its opponents, but rather because its opponents die, and a new generation grows up that is familiar with it.

Max Planck, 1858–1947, German physicist

Instead of demanding bread, as did the people of France during the French revolution, the people of the United States, in our first real economic revolution, are demanding information. [as quoted in 1933]

Carl W. Ackerman, School of Journalism, Columbia University

Anyone who is not intimately involved with the Internet and the web does so at extreme peril.

Bill Gates, b. 1955, Microsoft founder

The great accomplishments of man have resulted from the transmission of ideas and enthusiasm.

Thomas J. Watson, 1874–1956, American businessman, IBM chairman

The problem that worries you today may have been solved by a fellow craftsman yesterday. The pooling of knowledge is the surest step forward to progress.

Exchange, *publication*

What is conservatism? Is it not adherence to the old and tried, against the new and untried?

Abraham Lincoln, 1809–1865, 16th U.S. president

Graham's observations that investors pay too much for trendy, fashionable stocks and too little for companies that are out-of-favor, was on the money . . . why does this profitability discrepancy persist? Because emotion favors the premium-priced stocks. They are fashionable. They are hot. They make great cocktail party chatter. There is an impressive and growing body of evidence demonstrating that investors and speculators don't necessarily learn from experience. Emotion overrides logic time after time.

David Dreman, contrarian investor and author

Almost everything that is great has been done by youth.

Benjamin Disraeli, 1804–1881, British prime minister, author,
1st Earl of Beaconsfield

While that was true of his business and of every other business in the new Internet industry and while everybody knew it was true—that is, that cash was just being consumed at a rate and with an illogic that no one could explain much less justify—you must never, never admit it.

Michael Wolff in Burn Rate, *1998*

Hitch your wagon to a star. Let us not fag in paltry works which serve our pot and bag alone.

Ralph Waldo Emerson, 1803–1882, American essayist and poet

Nothing is more wearisome or more futile than the most antiquated of all manias: the rage to be modern.

Paul Hindemith, 1895–1963, German composer

You've become a computer freak when you spend half your plane trip with your laptop on your lap and your child in the overhead baggage compartment.

Unknown

The New York Stock Exchange has more people smoking outside at any point in the day than it takes to run our system.

Mark Yegge, chairman and CEO of NexTrade, one of the new electronic trading networks that has sprouted on the World Wide Web

An ideal cannot wait for its realization to prove its validity.

George Santayana, 1863–1952, Spanish-American poet and philosopher

How little do my countrymen know what precious blessings they are in possession of and which no other people on earth enjoy.

Thomas Jefferson, 1743–1826, 3rd U.S. president

Comment to AOL in 1993: I can buy 20% of you or I can buy all of you. Or I can go into this business myself and bury you.

Bill Gates, b. 1955, Microsoft founder

The greatest and noblest pleasure which men can have in this world is to discover new truths; and the next is to shake off old prejudices.

Frederick the Great, 1712–1786, third king of Prussia

The old say, "I remember when." The young say, "What's the news?"

Gelett Burgess, 1866–1951, American writer and illustrator

The spectacle has changed, but our eyes remain the same.

Joseph Joubert, 1754–1824, French moralist

Market efficiency is a description of how prices in competitive markets respond to new information. The arrival of new information to a competitive market can be likened to the arrival of a lamb chop to a school of flesh-eating piranha, where investors are—plausibly enough—the piranha. The instant the lamb chop [information] hits the water, there is turmoil as the fish devour the meat . . . as investors buy and sell securities in response to the news, causing prices to change. Once prices adjust, all that is left of the information is the worthless bone.

Robert C. Higgins in Analysis for Financial Management
(3rd edition, 1992)

The longer I've been in this business, the more I realize that investors really are lemmings.

Tom Maguire, "Life in the Fast Lane," Smart Money

Before the 2000 crash of Internet stocks: But I am still sitting on the sidelines, waiting to see if internet investors are playing a game of musical chairs, with the last investors being ruined. Even though I admit that I wish I had followed my friends who have made millions speculating on the internet, the last laugh is still the best laugh.

Ivo Welch, finance professor, UCLA

We must always think about things, and we must think about things as they are, not as they are said to be.

George Bernard Shaw, 1856–1950, playwright

We think too small. Like the frog at the bottom of the well. He thinks the sky is only as big as the top of the well. If he surfaced, he would have an entirely different view.

Mao Zedong, 1893–1976, Chinese soldier and Communist leader

The danger of the past was that men became slaves. The danger of the future is that men may become robots.

Eric Fromm, 1900–1980, German-American psychoanalyst

Response to AOL founders seeking venture capital in 1985: It's a dog. You should take it out in back and shoot it.

Unknown banker

We may be sure that any opposition to industrial advancement which is made by men who see political advantage in it will fail to recommend itself to the common sense of the American people. The record of electricity supply in the United States is one of continuously better service at continuously lower rates. I believe that that record can be maintained and that it will be maintained by the men who made it, not by political meddlers.

Henry Ford, 1863–1947, American automobile manufacturer, founder of Ford Motor Co.

The more people who believe something, the more apt it is to be wrong. The person who's right often has to stand alone.

Søren Kierkegaard, 1813–1855, Danish philosopher

It was necessary for us to discover greater powers of destruction than our enemies. We did. But after every war we have followed through with a new rise in our standard of living by the application of war-taught knowledge for the benefit of the world. It will be the same with the atomic bomb principles.

Thomas J. Watson, 1874–1956, American businessman, IBM chairman

All the old markers by which the price of a promising common stock could be measured had long since been passed; if a stock once valued at 100 went to 300, what on earth was to prevent it from sailing on to 400? And why not ride with it for fifty or a hundred points, with Easy Street at the end of the journey?

Frederick Lewis Allen, 1894–1956, American humorist,
in Only Yesterday

There is no squabbling so violent as that between people who accepted an idea yesterday and those who will accept the same idea tomorrow.

Christopher Morley, 1870–1957, American author

Fame usually comes to those who are thinking about something else.

Oliver Wendell Holmes, 1841–1935, associate justice,
U.S. Supreme Court

In my opinion, there is nothing new under the sun in the financial world—only different people doing the same things.

Ray DeVoe

It should not surprise us that the applications of today's financial engineer seem internally consistent, sound and almost unassailable. That would always be found after decades of reconfirmation of market and portfolio theory. But we should not be lulled into complacency by a catechism built on data of only a few decades. There will be new theory and new engineering to apply it.

Dean LeBaron, b. 1933, investment manager and contrarian thinker

A man's reach should exceed his grasp, or what's heaven for?

Robert Browning, 1812–1889, poet

As quoted in 1929: Airplane manufacturing will expand rapidly in the next few years, and it is even conceivable that we are beginning another industry which may parallel the making of automobiles.

Charles M. Schwab, 1862–1939, first president of U.S. Steel Corp.

Civilization advances by extending the number of important operations which we can perform without thinking.

Alfred North Whitehead, 1861–1947, English mathematician and philosopher

It is the child in the man that is the source of his uniqueness and creativeness, and the playground is the optimal milieu for the unfolding of his capacities and talents.

Eric Hoffer, 1902–1983, American philosopher

Online investors should remember that it is just as easy, if not more, to lose money through the click of a button as it is to make it.

Arthur Levitt, U.S. Securities and Exchange Commission chairman

Let the people know the truth and the country is safe.

Abraham Lincoln, 1809–1865, 16th U.S. president

Progress in industry depends very largely on the enterprise of deep thinking men, who are ahead of the times in their ideas.

Sir William Ellis

The most important problem that faces science today is to bring up to date our methods of transmitting and reviewing the mass of research which has accumulated through the years. We have so much knowledge that we are engulfed in a sea of publications in which we flounder. In the age of airplanes we must plow through this in square-rigged ships. We have not employed the inventions that we have to make this easier.

Vannevar Bush, 1890–1974, American engineer

Today's pioneers are building tomorrow's progress.

Thomas J. Watson, 1874–1956, American businessman, IBM chairman

We are just in the kindergarten of uncovering things and there is no down curve in science.

Charles F. Kettering, 1876–1958, engineer and inventor

Benjamin Franklin may have discovered electricity, but it was the man who invented the meter who made the money.

Earl Wilson

Asked how he would teach business students: For the final exam, I would take an Internet company and say, "How much is this worth?" And anybody that gave me an answer I would flunk.

Warren Buffett, b. 1930, American investor

Creativity is the act of bringing something new into the world, whether a symphony, a novel, a supermarket or a new casserole. It is based first on communication with oneself, then testing that communication with experience and reality.

S. I. Hayakawa, 1906–1992, American educator

Real generosity toward the future consists in giving all to what is present.

Albert Camus, 1913–1960, French journalist and philosopher

The most popular labor-saving device is still money.

Phyllis George, television personality

The reasonable man adapts himself to the world. The unreasonable one persists in trying to adapt the world to himself. Therefore, all progress depends on the unreasonable man.

George Bernard Shaw, 1856–1950, playwright

We are more ready to try the untried when what we do is inconsequential. Hence the remarkable fact that many inventions had their birth as toys.

Eric Hoffer, 1902–1983, American philosopher

Speaking at Davos prior to the 2000 crash of Internet stocks: Even people involved can't believe valuations.

Bill Gates, b. 1955, Microsoft founder

There is more to life than increasing its speed.

Mahatma Gandhi, 1869–1948, Indian nationalist and spiritual leader

There are no passengers on Spaceship Earth. Everybody's crew.

Marshall McLuhan, 1911–1980, Canadian sociologist and critic

Investment Consultants

99 99 99

Ask the Experts

Give me a pig.

Winston Churchill, 1874–1965,
British prime minister

The need of institutional investors, such as pension funds, for objective information about investment managers—their people, products, processes, performance, and principles—has led to the development of the institutional investment consulting industry. Consultants can provide a useful service, often if pushed to go beyond mere support for ideas already grasped. But they might just be needed to give credibility, especially to bodies like pension committees of boards of directors, where the staff people need more "cover."

Dogs look up to you, cats look down on you. Give me a pig. He just looks you in the eye and treats you as an equal.

Winston Churchill, 1874–1965, British prime minister

The one absolute requirement of a money manager is emotional maturity. If you don't know who you are, the stock market is an expensive place to find out.

Adam Smith, 1723–1790, political economist

Generally speaking, I think [money manager] size does have a negative impact, but there are firms—they're rare—where size has not had a great impact.

George Russell, Jr., Frank Russell Co., 1987

An actuary is someone who brings a fake bomb on a plane, because that decreases the chances that there will be another bomb on the plane.

Laurence J. Peter, 1919–1990, Canadian author and educator

A consultant is someone who takes the watch off your wrist and tells you the time.

Unknown

Just making money is not enough any more. Now we have to worry about our money making money.

Woody Allen, b. 1935, American film maker

First-class investment performance cannot be measured on a quarterly or annual basis. Outstanding investors don't work that way.

Charles Ellis, Greenwich Associates, 1987

I got a simple rule about everybody. If you don't treat me right, shame on you.

Louis Armstrong, 1900–1971, American jazz musician

If you can't say anything good about someone, sit right here by me.

Alice Roosevelt Longworth, 1884–1980, daughter of
President Theodore Roosevelt

- The economic chain is too complex with too many levels and has too many uncommitted agents.
- Institutional investment organization is the Achilles heel of success.

Dean LeBaron, quoted in Five Eminent Contrarians,
by Steven L. Mintz, 1994

Nobody knows anything.

William Goldman, b. 1931, U.S. screenwriter and novelist,
in Adventures in the Screen Trade, *1983*

If you're looking for the most important thing that we look for in a money manager selection process, it's continuity of good managers. It's the common denominator of success in money management—a dedicated group of professionals who have worked together for long periods of time. So that when they do fall into the tank, they work themselves out of it together. And if you have confidence in that group of people, then you don't terminate them when they go into the tank. You know that in due course they'll get out.

George Russell, Jr., Frank Russell Co., 1987

I don't know why a responsible board needs investment bankers at all, except for the decisions of the courts. I mean, everybody's in cahoots on this one. The courts say you have to have due diligence; you prove that you've done due diligence by hiring an investment banker, and so what's the function of a director? The directors should be doing that stuff.

Herbert A. Allen, Allen & Co., Inc.

Conceit causes more conversation than wit.

La Rochefoucauld, 1613–1680, French author

The fees paid now for so-called investment banking advice are obscene.

John Loeb, former senior partner, Loeb, Rhoades & Co., 1987

Every man who attacks my belief diminishes in some degree my confidence in it, and therefore makes me uneasy; and I am angry with him who makes me uneasy.

Samuel Johnson, 1709–1784, British author

Pension consultants have not made a difference in terms of adding value for clients. They are not able to prove that they choose better money managers.

Charles Ellis, Greenwich Associates, 1987

Mr. Clay, we have appointed you as our economic adviser; let me tell you that you are not here to tell us what to do, but to explain to us why we have done it.

Montagu Norman, governor of Bank of England, 1920–1944,
to Henry Clay, his eventual biographer

I live in company with a body, a silent companion, exacting and eternal. He it is who notes that individuality which is the seal of the weakness of our race. My soul has wings, but the brutal jailer is strict.

Eugene Delacroix, 1798–1863, French painter

In the old days the pension trustee was a fiduciary representing the employees, not the corporation. Now that distinction has been very badly blurred. Corporations are guaranteeing the pensions, making up the shortfall, so there has been a blurring of fiduciary responsibility.

Peter Vermilye, investment manager, Baring America
Asset Management Co., 1987

I use not only all the brains I have but all I can borrow.

Woodrow Wilson, 1856–1924, 28th U.S. president

It is the province of knowledge to speak, and it is the privilege of wisdom to listen.

> *Oliver Wendell Holmes, 1841–1935, associate justice,*
> *U.S. Supreme Court*

R&D to us is the ability to access data and to prove or disprove multiple correlations—to find out, for example, if we have an efficient market or not. Our responsibility to our clients is to help them improve returns and, at least, control or modify their risk.

> *George Russell, Jr., Frank Russell Co., 1987*

Never forget what a man has said to you when he was angry. If he has charged you with anything, you had better look it up.

> *Harriet Ward Beecher*

No man will take counsel, but every man will take money. Therefore, money is better than counsel.

> *Jonathan Swift, 1667–1745, English churchman and writer*

One of the most difficult things to contend with in a hospital is the assumption on the part of the staff that because you have lost your gall bladder you have also lost your mind.

> *Jean Kerr, b. 1923, American author*

I also got involved with a strange breed of people called actuaries. An actuary is described as an accountant without personality. I don't think that's true.

> *John English, b. ~1933, Ford Foundation*

Postponement: The sincerest form of rejection.

> *Robert Half, employment agent*

The art of selling is not to prove to Mr. Prospect that he is wrong, but to help him reach a decision which he, Mr. Prospect, knows is right.

John A. McMillan, Dayton Rubber Mfg. Co.

Investment managers are hyperkinetic; their behavior during trading hours makes whirling dervishes appear sedated by comparison. Indeed, the term "institutional investors" is becoming one of those self-contradictions called an oxymoron.

Warren Buffett, b. 1930, American investor

The regard one shows economy, is like that we show an old aunt, who is to leave us something at last.

William Shenstone, 1714–1763, British poet

What is the hardest task in the world? To think.

Ralph Waldo Emerson, 1803–1882, American essayist and poet

There are no answers in this business. There's just a hell of a lot of information.

George Russell, Jr., Frank Russell Co., 1987

A real friend is one who walks in when the rest of the world walks out.

Walter Winchell, 1897–1972, American newspaperman and commentator

Arrogance in persons of merit affronts us more than arrogance in those without merit. Merit itself is an affront.

Friedrich Nietzsche, 1844–1900, German philosopher

The evidence in the marketplace is overwhelming that if you are charging little, you should charge more because a low fee predicts low value, and in this field hope is very, very important.

Charles Ellis, Greenwich Associates, 1987

Few men can afford to be angry.

> *Edmund Burke, 1729–1797, English political leader*

I like to listen. I have learned a great deal from listening carefully. Most people never listen.

> *Ernest Hemingway, 1899–1961, American author*

If you want to discover your true opinion of anybody, observe the impression made on you by the first sight of a letter from him.

> *Arthur Schopenhauer, 1788–1860, German philosopher*

We needed ongoing relationships—we weren't in the business to provide a recommendation for the solution of a problem. We were on for life, as long as we did our work. There was always just a handshake until the federal government required contracts for soft-dollar arrangements.

> *George Russell, Jr., Frank Russell Co., 1987*

It is an old and true maxim that a drop of honey catches more flies than a gallon of gall. So with men, if you would win a man to your cause, first convince him that you are his sincere friend.

> *Abraham Lincoln, 1809–1865, 16th U.S. president*

Experts internalize decisions but beginners learn rules of procedure. Therefore an amateur can precisely explain what he's doing and why, while an expert often just knows when it's right.

> *Jeremy Grantham, investment manager, Grantham, Mayo, Van Otterloo*

Drawing on my fine command of language, I said nothing.

> *Robert Benchley, 1889–1945, humorist and script writer*

We bury the men who do the nation's creative work under layers of administrators and mountains of memoranda. We shrivel creativity by endless frustrations.

Admiral H. G. Rickover, 1900–1986, American naval officer

I'm a self-made man, but I think if I had it to do over again, I'd call in someone else.

Roland Young

I think I have been pitched by just about everybody in this business. I've seen every investment pitch known to man.

John English, b. ~1933, Ford Foundation

If a man does not make new acquaintances as he advances through life, he will soon find himself left alone. A man, sir, should keep his friendships in constant repair.

Samuel Johnson, 1709–1784, British author

The most valuable of all talents is that of never using two words when one will do.

Thomas Jefferson, 1743–1826, 3rd U.S. president

A man knows when he is justified, and not all the wits in the world can enlighten him on that point.

Henry David Thoreau, 1817–1862, American naturalist and writer

It is a wise man that does not waste time in regrets of yesterday.

Confucius, 551–479 B.C., Chinese philosopher

Manners are especially the need of the plain. The pretty can get away with anything.

Evelyn Waugh, 1903–1966, British author

We've worked up the Russell 1000, 2000 and 3000 U.S. stock indexes, because we found that our clients' small-cap bet average [was] about 18 or 19 percent of their equity portfolios, and the S&P 500 cover[ed] only about 2.5 percent.

George Russell, Jr., Frank Russell Co., 1987

We have cumbered the simple process of human affairs with a gigantic mass of silly negotiation, correspondence and accounting.

Bruce Barton, 1886–1957, American advertising executive and politician

Whenever an individual or a business decides that success has been attained, progress stops.

Thomas J. Watson, 1874–1956, American businessman, IBM chairman

You probably wouldn't worry about what people think of you if you could know how seldom they do.

Olin Miller

A student never forgets an encouraging private word, when it is given with sincere respect and admiration.

William Lyon Phelps, 1865–1943, American educator and critic

The investment management business creates no value, but it costs, in round numbers, 1% a year to play the game. In total, we are the market and, given the costs, we collectively must underperform.

Jeremy Grantham, investment manager, Grantham, Mayo, Van Otterloo

We judge ourselves by what we feel capable of doing, while others judge us by what we have already done.

Henry Wadsworth Longfellow, 1807–1882, American poet

It used to trouble me that the money that we were putting into the fund was going to be paid out in the year 2022, and yet we would meet with the money managers every 90 days to find out how we're doing. Maybe you don't need to meet with them annually; maybe it would be better to meet with them every five years.

John English, b. ~1933, Ford Foundation

Journalists: People who have nothing to say and know how to say it.

Karl Kraus, 1874–1936, Austrian satirist

I always have believed deeply in the importance of people and personal relationships. I still am as convinced as ever that successful long-term financial relationships are far more a matter of personal knowledge and interpersonal relationships than of just supposedly "objective" numbers and technology.

David Rockefeller, b. 1915, Chase Manhattan Bank, American financier, son of John D. Rockefeller, Jr.

Honest differences of views and honest debate are not disunity. They are the vital process of policy-making among free men.

Herbert Hoover, 1874–1964, 31st U.S. president

The purpose of life is to matter, to count, to stand for something, to have it make some difference that we lived at all.

Leo Rosten, b. 1908, American writer

We really introduced, I think, the concept of . . . a multimanager mix, diversified by style, which makes sense in an efficient market, where it's quite important to spread your bets.

George Russell, Jr., Frank Russell Co., 1987

Earnestness—that infallible sign of low metabolism.

Friedrich Nietzsche, 1844–1900, German philosopher

I've been married to one Marxist and one Fascist, and neither would take the garbage out.

Lee Grant, American actress

When someone says, "I intend to beat the market," the market he is talking about is not some neutered beast; it's the sum of all the smartest, toughest minds in this business. When you come to market to sell, the only buyers you'll find are the ones who are thrilled that you just came into the cross hairs on their sniper scopes.

Charles Ellis, Greenwich Associates, 1987

It isn't safe to sit in judgment upon another person's illusion when you are not on the inside. While you are thinking it is a dream, he may be knowing it is a planet.

Mark Twain, 1835–1910, American author

One cool judgment is worth a thousand hasty counsels. The thing to do is to supply light and not heat.

Woodrow Wilson, 1856–1924, 28th U.S. president

Investment Policy

Strategies and Styles

The best time to invest is when you have money.
Sir John Templeton, b. ~1913,
Tennessee-born British financier

Investment policy describes an institutional or individual investor's overall approach to management of their portfolio: goals, asset mix, stock selection, and investment strategy. But it does not deal with turbulence, outliers of statistical events, and major changes, and is sluggish by its nature. In the climate of the late 1990s, investment policy, founded as it is on a long-term commitment to equities, looked fine after a long bull market. But does investment policy take adequate account of the opportunities of the 1990s and the new millennium? Global investing, emerging markets, and Internet investing were, only a relatively short time ago, never conceived of as investment ideas.

About diversification: One buys two of everything and in the end owns a zoo.

> *Warren Buffett, b. 1930, American investor*

When you think the market's too high, don't do anything. And when you think a particular stock is a hell of a buy, don't do anything.

> *Charles Ellis, Greenwich Associates*

Be honest; toil constantly; be patient. Have courage and self-reliance. Be ambitious and industrious. Have perseverance, ability and judgment. Cultivate foresight and imagination.

> *Benjamin Franklin, 1706–1790, statesman, scientist, public leader*

It's not the bulls and bears you need to avoid—it's the bum steers.

> *Chuck Hillis*

Stocks don't really know who owns them and they don't care.

> *Alan Greenberg, b. 1928, Bear, Stearns & Co.*

If you don't know where you're going, you'll end up somewhere else.

> *Yogi Berra, b. 1925, baseball player, coach, and manager*

There is nothing so disastrous as a rational investment policy in an irrational world.

> *John Maynard Keynes, 1883–1946, British economist,*
> *1st Baron Keynes of Tilton*

My favorite poem is "If" by Rudyard Kipling. Well, in the middle of the takeover game, there's a lot of that in there. If you can risk everything you've got, and if you can keep your head when all those around you are losing theirs and blaming it on you. . . .

> *Carl Icahn, b. 1936, corporate raider*

A man who gives his children habits of industry provides for them better than by giving them a fortune.

Richard Whately, 1787–1863, English logician and theologian

A man's got to believe in something. I believe I'll have another drink.

W. C. Fields, 1879–1946, American comedian

A mistake in judgment isn't fatal, but too much anxiety about judgment is.

Pauline Kael, 1919–2001, American movie critic

A wise man should have money in his head, but not in his heart.

Jonathan Swift, 1667–1745, English churchman and writer

Adequate distribution of goods makes, unmakes—or remakes—all capital values!

Kenneth Goode

- In the last twenty years, the right course was to be disciplined and steady. In the next ten years, be firm in the conviction that you will only know a few things; they will change and be short term.
- The goal is real absolute terms, not relative performance.

Dean LeBaron, quoted in Five Eminent Contrarians, *by Steven L. Mintz, 1994*

I haven't heard of anybody who wants to stop living on account of the cost.

F. Mckinney Hubbard, 1868–1930

Eat less, wear less, scold less, worry less, talk less, preach less. Practice more, chew more, walk more, sleep more, smile more, read more, think more, and you'll live longer and be much happier while you live.

Silent Partner

Give me books, fruit, French wine and fine weather and a little music out of doors, played by someone I do not know. I admire lolling on a lawn by a water-lilied pond to eat white currants and see goldfish, and go to the fair in the evening if I'm good.

John Keats, 1795–1821, English poet

I had to pull back, which I did with alacrity because my principle is to survive first and make money afterwards.

George Soros, b. 1930, Budapest, financier, philanthropist, author

Gold is tested by fire, man by gold.

Chinese proverb

Grownups have a strange way of putting themselves in compartments and groups. They build up barriers . . . of religion, of caste, of color, of party, of nation, of province, of language, of custom and of wealth and poverty. Thus they live in prisons of their own making.

Jawaharlal Nehru, 1889–1964, prime minister of India

It is more shameful to distrust our friends than to be deceived by them.

La Rochefoucauld, 1613–1680, French author

It is not the greatness of a man's means that makes him independent, so much as the smallness of his wants.

William Cobbett, 1762–1835, British journalist and social reformer

Money and time are the heaviest burdens of life, and the unhappiest of all mortals are those who have more of either than they know how to use.

Samuel Johnson, 1709–1784, British author

We said that nobody should do anything that his mother would not be pleased to read about in *The New York Times*.

Leon Levy, Odyssey Partners, cofounder Oppenheimer Fund, 1987

No more important duty can be urged upon those who are entering the great theater of life than simple loyalty to their best convictions.

Edwin Chapin

No wise man ever wished to be younger.

Jonathan Swift, 1667–1745, English churchman and writer

Our great problem of the new post-war age will be not how to produce, but how to use; not how to create, but how to cooperate; not how to maim and to kill, but how to live.

Robert A. Millikan, 1868–1953, American physicist

Patience is the best remedy for every trouble.

Plautus, ~254–184 B.C., Roman playwright

Relaxation—or rest—is absolutely essential to the right working of this body of ours, and the mind as well. But the cry from so many is: "But I am too busy, I have no time for relaxation." But people take time out to go to bed when they are ill—and we all have to take time out to die! Why not then take time out to live?

George Matthew Adams

Rule No. 1: Never lose money.
Rule No. 2: Never forget Rule No. 1.

Warren Buffett, b. 1930, American investor

The best way to keep children at home is to make the home atmosphere pleasant, and let the air out of the tires.

Dorothy Parker, 1893–1967, American writer

The only big loss for the investment management profession over these years has been the disappearance of the balanced manager. The stylish cafeteria of specialized managers that we see today leads to a mishmash of risks and covariances that most clients fail to understand.

Peter L. Bernstein, b. ~1919, investment manager
and economic commentator

As quoted in 1945: The lives and happiness of our children, as far ahead as the mind can reach, depend on us today. If we succeed, posterity looking back will record that this was indeed man's finest hour.

Carl A. Berendsen

Tsze-King asked, "Is there one word which may serve as a rule of practice for all one's life?" The Master said, "Is not reciprocity such a word? What you do not want done to yourself, do not do to others."

Confucius, 551–479 B.C., Chinese philosopher

We are in the world to laugh. In purgatory or in hell we shall no longer be able to do so. And in heaven it would not be proper.

Jules Renard, 1864–1910, French novelist and playwright

Business and industry are subject to rigorous religious and moral obligations.

Vicar Richard May, Msgr. Edward Mitty, Rabbi Meyer Hager,
religious leaders in NY, 1987

We shall never have more time. We have, and we have always had, all the time there is. No object is served in waiting until next week or even until tomorrow. Keep going day in and out. Concentrate on something useful. Having decided to achieve a certain task, achieve it at all costs.

Arnold Bennett, 1867–1931, English novelist, playwright

Whatever you can lose, reckon of no account.

Publilius Syrus, 1st century B.C., Roman writer

Investment must be rational; if you can't understand it, don't do it.

Warren Buffett, b. 1930, American investor

When a man has not a good reason for doing a thing, he has one good reason for letting it alone.

Thomas Scott, American businessman

Whether it's marriage or business, patience is the first rule of success.

William Feather, 1889–1981, American author, publisher

One of my favorite sayings is that a sick portfolio is like a sidewalk burn: If you keep picking at it, it will never heal.

Robert Kirby, investment manager, Capital Guardian Trust Co., 1987

Investing is most intelligent when it is most businesslike.

Benjamin Graham, 1894–1976, value investor

More often than not stocks, bonds, gold, pork bellies etc. are neither wildly popular, nor wildly unpopular at any particular moment so it's hard to tell when the crowd gets crowded enough to oppose.

John Rothchild in The Bear Book

Anyone may so arrange his affairs that his taxes shall be as low as possible; he is not bound to choose that pattern which will best pay the Treasury; there is not even a patriotic duty to increase one's taxes.

Judge Learned Hand, 1872–1961, American jurist

Be civil to all; sociable to many; familiar with few.

Benjamin Franklin, 1706–1790, statesman, scientist, public leader

The philosophy which guided me both in making and spending money . . . is not about money, it is about the human condition.

George Soros, b. 1930, Budapest, financier, philanthropist, author

Character is that which reveals moral purpose, exposing the class of things a man chooses or avoids.

Aristotle, 384–322 B.C., Greek philosopher, educator, scientist

Contrary to popular belief, English women do not wear tweed nightgowns.

Hermione Gingold, 1897–1987, actress

Destiny is not a matter of chance, it is a matter of choice.

William Jennings Bryan, 1860–1925, politician and orator

Dogma does not mean the absence of thought, but the end of thought.

G. K. Chesterton, 1874–1936, English journalist and writer

My mother taught me that you should divide your life into three segments. In the first third of your life, you should learn. In the second third, you should earn. And in the third, you should serve.

John English, b. ~1933, Ford Foundation

Doubt of any kind cannot be resolved except by action.

Thomas Carlyle, 1795–1881, Scottish author

He who possesses most must be most afraid of loss.

Leonardo da Vinci, 1452–1519, Italian artist, architect, engineer, and scientist

I have knowingly defended a number of guilty men. But the guilty never escape unscathed. My fees are sufficient punishment for anyone.

F. Lee Bailey, American lawyer

I have no money, no resources, no hopes. I am the happiest man alive.

Henry Miller, 1891–1980, American writer

People needed a risk model, and the alpha and beta ideas of Bill Sharpe were very strong.

Barr Rosenberg, b. ~1942, Rosenberg Institutional Equity Management

Statistics show that investing your money in the stock market is nearly twice as secure as feeding it to otters.

Dave Barry, columnist

It is always well to moor your ship with two anchors.

Publilius Syrus, 1st century B.C., Roman writer

Let every man divide his money into three parts, and invest a third in land, a third in business, and a third let him keep by him in reserve.

Hebrew proverb

Money is not required to buy one necessity of the soul.

Henry David Thoreau, 1817–1862, American naturalist and writer

The reasons to build [a financial services company] from an insurance base are simple. Even a small insurance company controls a lot of assets that you normally wouldn't be able to control. The securities gains that you make out of the portfolio go into the book value of the company, and insurance companies are sold at two times book. So if I make a dollar buying and selling IBM, that's all it's worth. But once it's in the insurance company portfolio and you sell the company, you sell it for two bucks.

Gerald Tsai, Primerica Corp., 1987

My life has no purpose, no direction, no aim, no meaning, and yet I'm happy. I can't figure it out. What am I doing right?

Charles M. Schulz, 1922–2000, cartoonist, creator of Peanuts

Patience is the companion of wisdom.

St. Augustine, 354–430, early Christian church father and philosopher

Perhaps middle age is, or should be, a period of shedding shells; the shell of ambition, of material accumulations and possessions, the shell of ego.

Anne Morrow Lindbergh, 1906–2001, American poet and essayist

Speak not but what may benefit others of yourself; avoid trifling conversation.

Benjamin Franklin, 1706–1790, statesman, scientist, public leader

The best condition in life is not to be so rich as to be envied nor so poor as to be damned.

Josh Billings, 1818–1885, American author

The best cure for anger is delay.

Seneca, ~4 B.C.–A.D. 65, Roman statesman and philosopher

The best thing to give your enemy is forgiveness; to an opponent, tolerance; to a friend, your heart.

Arthur Balfour, 1848–1930, British prime minister

The most I can do for my friend is simply to be his friend.

Henry David Thoreau, 1817–1862, American naturalist and writer

We are not human beings having a spiritual experience. We are spiritual beings having a human experience.

Pierre Chardin, 1881–1955, French philosopher

If your investment is going well, follow your instincts and go with all you've got.

George Soros, b. 1930, Budapest, financier, philanthropist, author

We must ask where we are and whither we are tending.

Abraham Lincoln, 1809–1865, 16th U.S. president

Without a plan for completion, it just won't happen.

Robert Half, employment agent

Work is not of course, any more than play, the object of life; both are means to the same end.

Sir John Lubbock, 1834–1913, author and financier

Start off every day with a smile and get it over with.

W. C. Fields, 1879–1946, American comedian

Risk comes from not knowing what you are doing.

Warren Buffett, b. 1930, American investor

It is a funny thing about life; if you refuse to accept anything but the best you very often get it.

W. Somerset Maugham, 1874–1965, author

This is the lesson: Never give in . . . never, never, never, never . . . in nothing, great or small, large or petty—never give in except to convictions of honor or good taste.

Winston Churchill, 1874–1965, British prime minister

Investor Psychology

Think and Grow Rich

If you sit down at a poker table and can't spot
the sucker, get up . . . it's you.

Arnold S. Wood, investment manager,
Martingale Asset Management

B ehavioral finance is throwing more light on why people buy or sell
the stocks they do—and even why they don't buy stocks at all. People tend to see patterns in random sequences in financial data, for example; and people chase what they see as a trend but remain slow to change their opinions in the face of new evidence that runs counter to their current view of the world. Some believe that market anomalies—like calendar effects—and investor behavior are uniform around the world; that investors underprice out-of-favor stocks while at the same time being irrationally overconfident about exciting growth companies. Not only do they like to follow the crowd, but they also get pleasure and pride from owning growth stocks.

Many a man or woman who would not expect to be successful as a circus clown, opera singer, or grocer, without some kind of preparation or talent, nevertheless expects to be successful right off in the stock market—probably the most intricate and difficult game on earth. The reason for this faith in success without any special qualification is doubtless the most universal belief in luck.

Fred Kelley in Why You Win and Lose, *1930*

A psychologist is a man who watches everyone else when a beautiful girl enters the room.

Unknown

It isn't necessary to be rich and famous to be happy. It's only necessary to be rich.

Alan Alda, b. 1936, American actor

Money is better than poverty, if only for financial reasons.

Woody Allen, b. 1935, American film maker

There's a certain Buddhistic calm that comes from having . . . money in the bank.

Tim Robbins, b. 1958, American actor and film maker

Any fool can criticize, condemn, and complain—and most fools do.

Dale Carnegie, 1888–1955, motivational trainer and author

Baloney is flattery so thick it cannot be true, and blarney is flattery so thin we like it.

Bishop Fulton J. Sheen, 1895–1979, American religious leader

Conscience is the hag that rides my dreams.

John Dryden, 1631–1700, English author

The stock market is always going lower (when it is headed down) and always is going higher (when it is headed up). Sounds stupid, doesn't it? But that about expresses the public psychology. The crowd rides the trend and never gets off until they're bumped off.

Humphrey Neill, d. 1978, contrarian and author

Content makes poor men rich; discontent makes rich men poor.

Benjamin Franklin, 1706–1790, statesman, scientist, public leader

Behavioral finance is not a branch of standard finance: it is its replacement with a better model of humanity.

Meir Statman, investor, writer, professor, University of Santa Clara

Disturbed political conditions, both national and international, are more usually symptoms of depression rather than the cause of depression. Rightly or wrongly, it is human nature to blame the government for bad times.

The Royal Bank of Canada

Ever since Eve gave Adam the apple, there has been a misunderstanding between the sexes about gifts.

Nan Robertson, Pulitzer winner, feature writer

For an hundred that can bear adversity, there is hardly one that can bear prosperity.

Thomas Carlyle, 1795–1881, Scottish author

Human society is based on want. Life is based on want. Wild-eyed visionaries may dream of a world without need. Cloud-cuckoo-land. It can't be done.

H. G. Wells, 1866–1946, English novelist, sociologist, and historian

I found that money was like a sixth sense without which you could not make the most of the other five.

W. Somerset Maugham, 1874–1965, author

I have learned to seek my happiness by limiting my desires, rather than attempting to satisfy them.

John Stuart Mill, 1806–1873, economist and philosopher

To some people, the Rockefeller name implies an aura of mystery and almost magical powers of getting things done. In fact, this is generally nonsense.

David Rockefeller, b. 1915, formerly Chase Manhattan Bank,
American financier, son of John D. Rockefeller, Jr.

It is more necessary to study men than books.

La Rochefoucauld, 1613–1680, French author

Just as you are unconsciously influenced by outside advertisement, announcement, and appeal, so you can vitally influence your life from within by auto-suggestion. The first thing each morning, and the last thing each night, suggest to yourself specific ideas that you wish to embody in your character and personality. Address such suggestions to yourself, silently or aloud, until they are deeply impressed upon your mind.

Grenville Kleiser

Life is a long lesson in humility.

James M. Barrie, 1860–1937, dramatist and novelist

My young partners do the work and I do the laughing and I recommend to you the thought that there is little success where there is little laughing.

Andrew Carnegie, 1835–1919, steel manufacturer and philanthropist

The history of our race, and each individual's experience, are sown thick with evidence that a truth is not hard to kill and that a lie well told is immortal.

Mark Twain, 1835–1910, American author

The most unhappy of all men is he who believes himself to be so.

David Hume, 1711–1776, Scottish philosopher

The supreme happiness of life is the conviction that we are loved.

Victor Hugo, 1802–1885, French writer

Investment and speculation are said to be two different things, and the prudent man is advised to engage in one and avoid the other. This is something like explaining to the troubled adolescent that love and passion are two different things. He perceives that they are different but they don't seem quite different enough to clear up his problems.

Fred Schwed, Jr., in Where Are the Customers' Yachts? *1995*

The young fancy that their follies are mistaken by the old for happiness; and the old fancy that their gravity is mistaken by the young for wisdom.

C. C. Colton, 1780–1832, writer

There is no wealth but life.

John Ruskin, 1819–1900, writer and critic

There is one principle which a man must follow if he wishes to succeed, and that is to understand human nature.

Henry Ford, 1863–1947, American automobile manufacturer, founder of Ford Motor Co.

There never was a child so lovely but that his mother was glad to get him asleep.

Ralph Waldo Emerson, 1803–1882, American essayist and poet

We have enough religion to make us hate, but not enough to make us love one another.

Jonathan Swift, 1667–1745, English churchman and writer

What really flatters a man is that you think him worth flattering.

George Bernard Shaw, 1856–1950, playwright

When, against one's will, one is high pressured into making a hurried decision, the best answer is always "No," because "No" is more easily changed to "Yes," than "Yes" is changed to "No."

Charles E. Nielson

The market is both a game and a Game, i.e., both sport, frolic, fun and play, and a subject for continuously measurable options. If it is a game, then we can relieve ourselves of some of the heavy and possibly crippling emotions that individuals carry into investing, because in a game where the winning of the stake is so clearly defined, anything else becomes irrelevant.

George Goodman as "Adam Smith" in The Money Game

Where I hear somebody sigh that "Life is hard," I am always tempted to ask, "Compared to what?"

Sydney Harris, b. 1917, American journalist

Wise men are instructed by reason; men of less understanding, by experience; the most ignorant by necessity; and beasts by nature.

Cicero, 106–43 B.C., Roman orator, statesman

A little sincerity is a dangerous thing, and a great deal of it is absolutely fatal.

Oscar Wilde, 1854–1900, Irish-British author

After a certain point money is meaningless. It's the game that counts.

Aristotle Onassis, 1906–1975, Greek shipowner, business executive

All changes, even the most longed for, have their melancholy; for what we leave behind us is a part of ourselves; we must die to one life before we can enter into another!

Anatole France, 1844–1924, French novelist and critic

All seems infected that the infected spy, as all looks yellow to the jaundiced eye.

Alexander Pope, 1688–1744, English poet

American youth attributes much more importance to arriving at driver's license age than at voting age.

Marshall McLuhan, 1911–1980, Canadian sociologist and critic

When people are thinking about investing, they focus on losses because losses loom so large in their minds. They think more about losses than they do about potential gains.

Richard Thaler, b. ~1946, Chicago economics professor, investment manager

Anger is momentary madness.

Horace, 65–8 B.C., Roman poet

Bounty always receives part of its value from the manner in which it is bestowed.

Samuel Johnson, 1709–1784, British author

Few men have the natural strength to honor a friend's success without envy.

Aeschylus, 525–456 B.C., writer of Greek tragedy

Flattery is all right if you don't inhale.

Adlai E. Stevenson, 1900–1965, U.S. ambassador to the United Nations

Friends provoked become the bitterest of enemies.

Baltasar Gracian, 1601–1658, Spanish priest and writer

God must love the rich or he wouldn't divide so much among so few of them.

H. L. Mencken, 1880–1956, American journalist and writer

I believe that the power to make money is a gift from God.

John D. Rockefeller, 1839–1937, American industrialist and philanthropist

I do not dismiss the behavioral aspects that Joe [Lakonishok] and others have argued which is to say that there are all kinds of reasons from cognitive psychology that suggest that a real dog is likely to get underpriced, and maybe people know it's underpriced and they still don't want to hold it.

William F. Sharpe in Investment Gurus, *by Peter J. Tanous*

I don't like money actually, but it quiets my nerves.

Joe Louis, 1914–1981, American boxer

There are several good protections against temptations, but the surest is cowardice.

Mark Twain, 1835–1910, American author

I finally know what distinguishes man from the beasts: financial worries.

Jules Renard, 1864–1910, French novelist and playwright

I never dared to be radical when young for fear it would make me conservative when old.

Robert Frost, 1874–1963, American poet

It is sadder to find the past again and find it inadequate to the present than it is to have it elude you and remain forever a harmonious conception of memory.

F. Scott Fitzgerald, 1896–1940, novelist

It is sometimes necessary to play the fool to avoid being deceived by clever men.

La Rochefoucauld, 1613–1680, French author

It pays to be obvious, especially if you have a reputation for subtlety.

Isaac Asimov, 1920–1992, American author

I would come down firmly on Ernest Hemingway's side in his famous exchange with F. Scott Fitzgerald. As I recall this, Fitzgerald said, "The rich are very different from the rest of us." And Hemingway dryly replied, "Yes, they have more money."

David Rockefeller, b. 1915, formerly Chase Manhattan Bank, American financier, son of John D. Rockefeller, Jr.

Memory presents to us not what we choose but what it pleases.

Michel Montaigne, 1533–1592, French essayist

My belief is that to have no wants is divine.

Socrates, 469–399 B.C., Greek philosopher

My problem lies in reconciling my gross habits with my net income.

Errol Flynn, 1909–1959, actor

Next to being shot at and missed, nothing is quite so satisfying as an income tax refund.

F. J. Raymond

Our greatest foes, whom we must chiefly combat, are within.

Cervantes, 1547–1616, Spanish writer

People seem to me to be happiest when they are working for nothing and can afford to do so.

Robert Lynd, 1892–1970, American sociologist

Poor people know poor people and rich people know rich people. It is one of the few things La Rochefoucauld did not say, but then La Rochefoucauld never lived in the Bronx.

Moss Hart, 1904–1961, American dramatist

In my opinion, misconceptions and mistakes play the same role in human affairs as mutation does in biology.

George Soros, b. 1930, Budapest, financier, philanthropist, author

The heart has reasons of which the reason has no knowledge.

George Santayana, 1863–1952, Spanish-American poet and philosopher

The more money an American accumulates, the less interesting he becomes.

Gore Vidal, b. 1929, novelist

The most valuable of human possessions, next to a superior and disdainful air, is the reputation of being well-to-do. Nothing else so neatly eases one's way through life, especially in democratic countries.

H. L. Mencken, 1880–1956, American journalist and writer

The two things that people want more than sex or money are recognition and praise.

Mary Kay Ash, businesswoman

Thousands upon thousands are yearly brought into a state of real poverty by their great anxiety not to be thought poor.

William Cobbett, 1762–1835, British journalist and social reformer

People trade for both cognitive and emotional reasons. They trade because they think they have information when they have nothing but noise, and they trade because trading can bring the joy of pride. Trading brings pride when decisions turn out well, but it brings regret when decisions do not turn out well. Investors try to avoid the pain of regret by avoiding the realization of losses, employing investment advisors as scapegoats, and avoiding stocks of companies with low reputations.

Meir Statman, investor, writer, professor, University of Santa Clara

Virtue has never been as respectable as money.

Mark Twain, 1835–1910, American author

Every natural human impulse seems to be a foe to success in stocks. And that is why success is so difficult.

Fred Kelley, author and investor

What is moral is what you feel good after and what is immoral is what you feel bad after.

Ernest Hemingway, 1899–1961, American author

Who can refute a sneer?

William Paley, American media executive

You are financially secure when you can afford anything you want and you don't want anything.

Art Buck

Remember that as a teenager you are in the last stage of your life when you will be happy to hear the phone is for you.

Fran Lebowitz, b. 1946, American journalist

Have you ever noticed that many jewels make women either incredibly fat or incredibly thin?

James M. Barrie, 1860–1937, dramatist and novelist

Oftentimes we call a man cold, when he is only sad.

Henry Wadsworth Longfellow, 1807–1882, American poet

Only in opera do people die of love.

Freda Bright

You can understand people better if you look at them—no matter how old or impressive they may be—as if they are children. For most of us never mature: we simply grow taller.

Leo Rosten, b. 1908, American writer

Manias, Panics, and Crashes

Irrational Times

Memory is a great betrayer.

Anaïs Nin, 1903–1977, American writer

Financial markets are particularly susceptible to manias, panics, and crashes, where asset prices rise to extraordinary heights only for confidence and greed to turn to fear and despair, sending the market into freefall. Classic examples include the Mississippi Scheme that swept France in 1720; the South Sea Bubble that ruined thousands in England at the same time; and the Dutch tulipmania, when fortunes were made and lost on single tulip bulbs. In a buying frenzy, there is, through the effect of contagion, a universal urge to participate in the whirlwind of speculation. There might also be gambling on the upside, with some investors doubling their bets in a rising market, attracted by the thrill of winning and the whiff of danger. People succumb to the "fallacy of composition"—each individual decision can be rationalized but not the whole.

A crowd is at the mercy of all external exciting causes, the slave of the impulses which it receives.

> *Gustave Le Bon, 1841–1931, French sociologist, author,*
> *in* The Crowd: A Study of the Popular Mind

It is in the nature of a speculative boom that almost anything can collapse it.

> *John Kenneth Galbraith in* The Great Crash, *1997*

In 1929: An ex-actress in New York fitted up her Park Avenue apartment as an office and surrounded herself with charts, graphs, and financial reports, playing the market by telephone on an increasing scale and with increasing abandon.

> *Frederick Lewis Allen, 1894–1956, American humorist,*
> *in* Only Yesterday

In a buying frenzy, there is, through the effect of contagion, a universal urge to participate in the whirlwind of speculation.

> *Marc Faber, b. ~1945, investment manager based in Hong Kong*

The market is always making mountains out of molehills and exaggerating ordinary vicissitudes into major setbacks.

> *Benjamin Graham, 1894–1976, value investor*

About a new issue launched during the 1720 South Sea bubble: A company for carrying on an undertaking of great advantage, but nobody is to know what it is.

> *Unknown*

At first, as in all these gambling mania, confidence was at its height, and everybody gained. Many individuals grew suddenly rich. A golden bait hung temptingly out before the people, and one after the other, they rushed to the marts, like flies around a honeypot.

> *Charles Mackay describing 17th century Dutch tulipmania in*
> Extraordinary Popular Delusions and the Madness of Crowds, *2000*

There is hardly a more conventional subject in economic literature than financial crises.

> *Charles Kindleberger, first sentence of* Manias, Panics
> and Crashes, *1978*

At the time of the 1929 Great Crash, very few Americans were actively involved in the market. It was considered the sort of thing that racy, and rather corrupt, city slickers did. A lot of Americans, if they didn't actually cheer the Crash, felt a certain grim satisfaction. Only in the last generation have things changed. The market has been made legitimate, respectable, wholesome—the sort of place where, if you're a young man, your mother would look benignly on you for investing your money.

> *Ron Chernow, historian of finance*

When a man has a small trouble, he can laugh it off. But when he has a big trouble—a real trouble, he should go for a long walk. He should walk at least five miles quickly. That will send the blood bounding through his veins. It will take the blood out of his head. It will help to put him in control of himself.

> *George M. Cohan, 1878–1942, American composer*

Every great crisis reveals the excessive speculation of many houses which no one before suspected, and which commonly had not begun, or had not carried very far those speculations till they were tempted by daily rise of price and the surrounding fever.

> *Walter Bagehot, 1826–1877, writer, in* Lombard Street, *1873*

Having a quote machine on your desk is like having a slot machine there.

Ed Seykota

In early 1720, just before the South Sea Bubble: I can calculate the motions of heavenly bodies, but not the madness of people.

Isaac Newton, 1642–1727, English physicist

No matter how correct the forecast of the future may be, safety disappears in inverse ratio to the increased possibilities of abnormal returns; and with the factor of safety continually ignored, the final results are bound to be disastrous.

Thomas Gibson in The Cycles of Speculation, *1907*

When the world is mad, we must imitate them in some measure.

Unknown banker during the 1720 South Sea bubble

We were beginning to breathe again, and the '73–'74 break came, which I understand, proportionately, was more severe than '29, and I can believe it, because I had a stack of margin calls from my clients that was almost as big as the Beverly Hills telephone book. It literally wiped clients out and rubbed brokers out of the business.

Michael Starkman, Prudential-Bache Securities

I suppose that one reason why the road to ruin is broad, is to accommodate the great amount of travel in that direction.

Josh Billings, 1818–1885, American author

In the midst of great joy do not promise to give a man anything: in the midst of great anger do not answer a man's letter.

Chinese proverb

It is an intensely hot day, all things on land and sea being merely varieties and shapes of flame, wonderful to look upon but not wholly good to be amongst.

William Vaughn Moody, 1869–1910, American poet and playwright

It is hard to free fools from the chains they revere.

Voltaire, 1694–1778, French philosopher and writer

History teaches us that investors behave wisely . . . once they have exhausted all other alternatives.

Steve Leuthold, investment manager, The Leuthold Group

Neither great poverty nor great riches will hear reason.

Henry Fielding, 1707–1754, novelist

Nothing is so firmly believed as when we least know.

Michel Montaigne, 1533–1592, French essayist

At particular times a great deal of stupid people have a great deal of stupid money and there is speculation and there is panic.

Walter Bagehot, 1826–1877, writer

The ability to keep a cool head in an emergency, maintain poise in the midst of excitement, and to refuse to be stampeded are true marks of leadership.

R. Shannon

The covetous man never has money; the prodigal will have none shortly.

Ben Jonson, 1572–1637, English playwright and poet

As quoted in January 1929: When I hear, as I frequently do, of large sums being made in the stock market through the increasing values that are being established—and I realize that this is going on to a certain extent all over the country—I sometimes ask myself, if from one angle, it is not unfortunate. For there is only one fundamental way to create wealth, and that is through work.

Alfred P. Sloan, Jr., 1875–1966, chairman of
General Motors Corporation

The desire of one man to live on the fruits of another's labor is the original sin of the world.

James O'Brien, 1805–1864, Irish journalist and Chartist

The united voice of millions cannot lend the smallest foundation to falsehood.

Oliver Goldsmith, 1730–1774, British playwright and poet

The wayside of business is full of brilliant men who started out with a spurt, and lacked the stamina to finish. Their places were taken by patient and unshowy plodders who never knew when to quit.

J. R. Todd

There is a paradox in pride—it makes some men ridiculous, but prevents others from becoming so.

C. C. Colton, 1780–1832, writer

Though there is a limit to what a man can use, there is no limit to what he can waste.

Kenneth Burke, 1897–1993, American philosopher and literary critic

Characteristic of every investment mania is the formation of investment pools and a rising number of new issues flooding the market. During every manic phase, cash is always regarded as a totally unattractive investment alternative.

> *Marc Faber, b. ~1945, investment manager based in Hong Kong*

Times of general calamity and confusion have ever been productive of the greatest minds. The purest ore is produced from the hottest furnace, and the brightest thunderbolt is elicited from the darkest storm.

> *C. C. Colton, 1780–1832, writer*

As quoted on October 15, 1929: I expect to see the stock market a good deal higher than it is today within a few months.

> *Irving Fisher, 1867–1947, American economist*

When you have found out the prevailing passion of any man, remember never to trust him where that passion is concerned.

> *Lord Chesterfield, 1694–1773, British author and statesman,*
> *4th Earl of Chesterfield*

To a gathering of Wall Street executives: It has become evident time and again that when events become too complex and move too rapidly, as appears to be the case today, human beings become demonstrably less able to cope.

> *Alan Greenspan, b. 1926, chairman of the U.S. Federal Reserve*

Who does more earnestly long for a change than he who is uneasy in his present circumstances? And who run to create confusions with so desperate a boldness as those who having nothing to lose, hope to gain by them?

> *Sir Thomas More, 1478–1535, English politician and writer*

If you see a banker jump out of a window, jump after him—there's sure to be a profit in it.

Voltaire, 1694–1778, French philosopher and writer

Nothing is more dangerous than an idea when it is the only one we have.

Alain, 1868–1951, French philosopher

The best liar is he who makes the smallest amount of lying go the longest way.

Samuel Butler, 1612–1680, English author

Graham's conviction rested on certain assumptions. First, he believed that the market frequently mispriced stocks. This mispricing was most often caused by human emotions of fear and greed. At the height of optimism, greed moved stocks beyond their intrinsic value, creating an overpriced market. At other times, fear moved prices below intrinsic value, creating an undervalued market.

Robert G. Hagstrom, b. 1956, in The Warren Buffett Way, *1997*

The degree of one's emotion varies inversely with one's knowledge of the facts—the less you know the hotter you get.

Bertrand Russell, 1872–1970, British philosopher and mathematician

The things we remember best are those best forgotten.

Baltasar Gracian, 1601–1658, Spanish priest and writer

There is no passion of the human heart that promises so much and pays so little as revenge.

Henry Wheeler Shaw, 1818–1885, American author

There is nothing more irrational than a man who is rationally irrational.

Lecomte Du Nouy

Things do change. The only question is that since things are deteriorating so quickly, will society and man's habits change quickly enough?

Isaac Asimov, 1920–1992, American author

Markets invariably move to undervalued and overvalued extremes because human nature falls victim to greed and/or fear.

William Gross in Everything You've Heard About Investing Is Wrong!, 1997

When I am angry with myself, I criticize others.

E. W. Howe, 1853–1937, American writer

Our memories are independent of our wills. It is not easy to forget.

Richard B. Sheridan, 1751–1816, Irish dramatist

Crowds are somewhat like the Sphinx of ancient fable: it is necessary to arrive at a solution of the problems offered by their psychology or resign ourselves to being devoured by them.

Gustav Le Bon, 1841–1931, French sociologist, author, The Crowd: A Study of the Popular Mind

Character is not made in a crisis—it is only exhibited.

Dr. Robert Freeman

The language of excitement is at best picturesque. You must be calm before you can utter oracles.

Henry David Thoreau, 1817–1862, American naturalist and writer

Never speak to a fasting man.

> *John Clarke, 1609–1676, American clergyman and physician*

Major manias are usually once-a-generation affairs and lead to some serious economic damage once they come to an end.

> *Marc Faber, b. ~1945, investment manager based in Hong Kong*

I suppose there is not a man in the world who, when he becomes a knave for the sake of $1000, would not rather have remained an honest man for half the money.

> *Georg C. Lichtenberg, 1742–1799, German physicist and philosopher*

Most people *know* that there is no such thing as luck, but it is difficult to find anyone who does not *believe* in it.

> *Raoul de Sales*

A fool and her money are soon courted.

> *Helen Rowland, 1875–1950, American journalist*

Market Efficiency

99 99 99

Prices and Information

The time to buy is when blood is running in the streets.

Baron Nathan Rothschild, 1777–1836,
German banker

The efficient market hypothesis (EMH) says that at any given time, asset prices fully reflect all available information—that price movements do not follow any patterns or trends. This means that past price movements cannot be used to predict future price movements. Rather, prices follow what is known as a "random walk," an intrinsically unpredictable pattern. In the world of the strong form EMH, trying to beat the market becomes a game of chance not skill. A central challenge to the EMH is the existence of market anomalies: reliable, widely known, and inexplicable patterns in returns, such as the January effect. In reality, markets are neither perfectly efficient nor completely inefficient. All are efficient to a certain degree, but some more than others.

Do not argue with the market, for it is like the weather; though not always kind, it is always right.

Kenneth E. Walden

Most so-called anomalies don't seem anomalous to me at all. They seem like nuggets from a gold mine, found by one of the thousands of miners all over the world.

Fischer Black, pioneer of options pricing

The stock market is not an abstract animal. It's a lot of people out there making decisions. And whenever you make one or don't make one, you're making a bet against what all those other people are doing.

Peter L. Bernstein, b. ~1919, investment manager
and economic commentator

Adam was but human—this explains it all. He did not want the apple for the apple's sake, he wanted it only because it was forbidden. The mistake was in not forbidding the serpent; then he could have eaten the serpent.

Mark Twain, 1835–1910, American author

One dollar invested on a "Black Friday" is worth ten dollars invested on any other day.

Julius Westheimer's father

First, there are considerable questions regarding the long-run dependability of these [predictable] effects. Many could be the result of "data snooping," letting the computer search through the data sets of past securities prices in the hopes of finding some relationships . . . some statistically significant correlations . . . [and] published work is probably biased in favor of reporting anomalous results rather than boring confirmations of randomness.

Burton Malkiel in A Random Walk Down Wall Street,
7th edition, 1999

The sensibility of man to trifles, and his insensibility to great things, indicates a strange inversion.

Blaise Pascal, 1623–1662, French philosopher

However, [capital market theory] shook all of us up. We graduate students had been trained to think of only a single random variable, with its own mean and variance, but now we had to talk about covariance.

Barr Rosenberg, b. ~1942, Rosenberg Institutional Equity Management

Man is not the creature of circumstances, circumstances are the creature of man.

Benjamin Disraeli, 1804–1881, British prime minister, author,
1st Earl of Beaconsfield

An "efficient" market is defined as a market where there are large numbers of rational, profit-maximizers actively competing, with each trying to predict future market values of individual securities, and where important current information is almost freely available to all participants.

Eugene F. Fama, b. 1939, Chicago finance professor
who coined the term EMH

Nature gives to every time and season some beauties of its own; and from morning to night, as from the cradle to the grave, is but a succession of changes so gentle and easy that we can scarcely mark their progress.

Charles Dickens, 1812–1870, novelist

Nothing in this world can one imagine beforehand, not the least thing. Everything is made up of so many unique particulars that cannot be foreseen.

Rainer Maria Rilke, 1875–1926, German poet

Clearly the price considered most likely by the market is the true current price; if the market judged otherwise, it would quote not this price, but another price higher or lower.

Louis Bachelier

The irrationality of a thing is no argument against its existence, rather a condition of it.

Friedrich Nietzsche, 1844–1900, German philosopher

The efficient market hypothesis is disarmingly simple to state, has far-reaching consequences for academic pursuits and business practice and yet it is surprisingly resilient to empirical proof or refutation.

Andrew Lo, MIT finance professor

The pursuit of truth shall set you free—even if you never catch up with it.

Clarence Darrow, 1857–1938, American lawyer

Many of the predictable patterns that have been discovered may simply be the result of data mining—the result of beating the data set in every conceivable way until it finally confesses. There may be little confidence that these relationships will continue in the future.

Burton Malkiel in A Random Walk Down Wall Street,
7th edition, 1999

We know accurately only when we know little; with knowledge doubt increases.

Johann Goethe, 1749–1832, German writer

Academic research has become much more empirical now. It's not terribly surprising that in these last ten years academics are discovering anomalies. [In the late 1970s], they were discovering efficiencies. And they haven't started explaining the anomalies yet; they are just saying they are there, so let's design a strategy to exploit them. The academics have gone to the brokerage houses.

Dean LeBaron, b. 1933, investment manager and contrarian thinker

All genuine progress results from finding new facts.

Wheeler McMillen

It is not easy to transform the resulting opportunities to trade profitably against the market consensus into superior portfolio performance. Unless the active investor understands what really goes on in the trading game, he can easily convert even superior research information into the kind of performance that will drive his clients to the poorhouse . . . why aren't more active investors consistently successful? The answer lies in the cost of trading.

Jack Treynor, "What Does It Take to Win the Trading Game?"
Financial Analysts Journal

Only two things are infinite, the universe and human stupidity, and I'm not sure about the former.

Albert Einstein, 1879–1955, German-American scientist

As for the floor [NYSE] members, my impression was they were very isolated. I mean, they're down there in a community within a community.

James Needham, b. ~1932, former chairman, New York Stock Exchange

Start keeping a diary. Write down every time you are convinced that the market is going up or down. After a few years, you will realize that your insights are worth nothing. Once you realize that, it becomes much easier to float on that ocean we call the market.

Meir Statman, "To Sell or Not?" The Wall Street Journal

The efficient market is a state of nature dreamed up by theoreticians. Neat, elegant, even majestic, it has nothing to do with the real world of uncertainty in which you and I must make decisions every day we are alive.

Peter L. Bernstein, b. ~1919, investment manager and economic commentator

A half truth is a whole lie.

Yiddish proverb

A man is judged by his friends, for the wise and the foolish have never agreed.

Baltasar Gracian, 1601–1658, Spanish priest and writer

An age cannot be completely understood if all the others are not also. The song of history can only be sung as a whole.

Ortega y Gasset, 1883–1955, Spanish philosopher

The results of studying 66,100 consensus estimates of Wall Street analysts from 1974 to 1991:
- Consensus forecasts, revised as recently as two weeks prior to the end of the [subject] quarter . . . deviate significantly and consistently from actual earnings.
- Even on a volatility-adjusted basis, analysts err indiscriminately across industries.
- On average, large earnings surprises are the rule rather than the exception.

- Analysts, money managers, and investors appear to ignore the industry's poor forecasting record, although it questions the viability of many important stock valuation methods.

  David Dreman and Michael A. Berry, "Analyst Forecasting Errors and Their Implications for Security Analysis," Financial Analysts Journal

Don't lay any certain plans for the future; it is like planting toads and expecting to raise toadstools.

Josh Billings, 1818–1885, American author

Economic theory needs to be fundamentally reconsidered. There is an element of uncertainty in economic processes that has been largely unaccounted for.

George Soros, b. 1930, Budapest, financier, philanthropist, author

Experience has shown, and the true philosophy will always show, that a vast, perhaps the largest portion of the truth arises from the seemingly irrelevant.

Edgar Allan Poe, 1809–1849, writer

Stocks are usually more than just the abstract "bundles of returns" of our economic models. Behind each holding may be a story of family business, family quarrels, legacies received, divorce settlements, and a host of other considerations almost totally irrelevant to our theories of portfolio selection. That we abstract from all these stories in building our models is not because the stories are uninteresting but because they may be too interesting and thereby distract us from the pervasive market forces that should be our principal concern.

Merton Miller, b. 1923, Chicago finance professor and Nobel laureate

Growing old is no more than a bad habit which a busy man has no time to form.

André Maurois, 1885–1967, French novelist and biographer

The capital market theory argued that a portfolio that reflected the whole market would be efficient for someone who held consensus beliefs. Furthermore, it also meant that the market portfolio had minimum risk, in the sense that it got rid of all the diversifiable risk. It was obvious that this was a simplistic thing, but people took it as a beautiful and elegant description of what it was about risk that really mattered.

Barr Rosenberg, b. ~1942, Rosenberg Institutional Equity Management

Rule of life: Vital papers will demonstrate their vitality by moving from where you left them to where you can't find them.

Unknown

I'm a passive investor. All stocks. I believe in efficient markets. I know nothing about stock picking. I don't trust anyone else to interpret the data better than myself so I don't believe the opportunities are there to beat the market.

Eugene F. Fama, b. 1939, Chicago finance professor who coined the term EMH

Honesty is often in the wrong.

Lucan, A.D. 39–65, Roman poet

Elaborate tests of the correlation of successive prices, runs, and filter rules find some weak relationships, but they are not sufficient to generate trading profits after taking account of transactions costs.

Sidney Cottle, Roger F. Murray, and Frank E. Block in Graham and Dodd's Security Analysis, *5th edition*

The course of every intellectual, if he pursues his journey long and unflinchingly enough, ends in the obvious, from which the nonintellectuals have never stirred.

Aldous Huxley, 1894–1963, British writer

Human society is ordered, productive and in accord with human dignity only if it is based on truth.

Pope John XXIII, 1881–1963, convenor of the Second Vatican Council

The central proposition of charting is absolutely false, and investors who follow its precepts will accomplish nothing but increasing substantially the brokerage charges they pay. There has been a remarkable uniformity in the conclusions of studies done on all forms of technical analysis. Not one has consistently outperformed the placebo of a buy-and-hold strategy.

Burton Malkiel in A Random Walk Down Wall Street, *7th edition, 1999*

I care about truth not for truth's sake, but for my own.

Samuel Butler, 1612–1680, English author

I suppose you could never prove to the mind of the most ingenious mollusk, that such a creature as a whale could exist.

Ralph Waldo Emerson, 1803–1882, American essayist and poet

In formal logic, a contradiction is the signal of a defeat. But in the evolution of real knowledge it marks the first step in progress towards a victory. This is one great reason for the utmost toleration of variety of opinion.

Alfred North Whitehead, 1861–1947, English mathematician and philosopher

Fact is that most seasonal tendencies are only "statistically significant"—meaning you can write a dissertation on the subject, but don't try to make money on it . . . Institutions, unlike most of you, close their books at the end of the year and tally up their gains and losses so they can prepare their report cards. If a stock has been the subject of bad news and has done poorly, they may throw it out, even if it is now a cheap stock; they don't want prospective investors to think they pick losers.

Laszlo Birinyi, Jr., "The Window Dressing Anomaly," Forbes

Life is full of infinite absurdities, which, strangely enough, do not even need to appear plausible, because they are true.

Pirandello, 1867–1936, Italian author

Nature never quite goes along with us. She is somber at weddings, sunny at funerals, and she frowns on ninety-nine out of a hundred picnics.

Alexander Smith, 1830–1867, Scottish poet and writer

Nine-tenths of the serious controversies which arise in life result from misunderstandings; result from one man not knowing the facts which to the other man seem important, or otherwise failing to appreciate his point of view.

Justice Louis D. Brandeis, 1856–1941, associate justice,
U.S. Supreme Court

In each action we must look beyond the action at our past, present and future state, and at others whom it affects, and see the relations of all those things. And then we shall be very cautious.

Blaise Pascal, 1623–1662, French philosopher

Outside of a dog a book is a man's best friend. Inside a dog it is too dark to read.

Groucho Marx, 1890–1977, comedian

Many [market anomalies] can be explained away. When transactions costs are taken into account, the fact that stock prices tend to over-react to news, falling back the day after good news and bouncing up the day after bad news, proves unexploitable: price reversals are always well within the bid-ask spread. Others, such as the small-firm effect, work for a few years and then fail for a few years. Others prove to be merely proxies for the reward for risk taking.

Frontiers of Finance survey, The Economist

The one who thinks over his experiences most, and weaves them into systematic relations with each other, will be the one with the best memory.

William James, 1842–1910, American philosopher and psychologist

The rain falls upon the just and the unjust alike; a thing which would not happen if I were superintending the rain's affairs. No, I would rain softly and sweetly on the just, but if I caught a sample of the un-just outdoors I would drown him.

Mark Twain, 1835–1910, American author

To know that we know what we know, and that we do not know what we do not know, that is true knowledge.

Confucius, 551–479 B.C., Chinese philosopher

In an efficient market, competition among the many intelligent par-ticipants leads to a situation where, at any point in time, actual prices of individual securities already reflect the effects of information based both on events that have already occurred and on events which, as of now, the market expects to take place in the future. In other words, in an efficient market at any point in time the actual price of a security will be a good estimate of its intrinsic value.

Eugene F. Fama, b. 1939, Chicago finance professor
who coined the term EMH

Wall Street: A thoroughfare that begins in a graveyard and ends in a river.

Unknown

I have reviewed all the recent research proclaiming the demise of the efficient-market theory and purporting to show that market prices are, in fact, predictable. My conclusion is that such obituaries are greatly exaggerated and the extent to which the stock market is usefully predictable has been vastly overstated.

Burton Malkiel, Princeton finance professor

What are we without the help of that which does not exist?

Georg Hegel, 1770–1831, German philosopher

The evidence reveals repeated patterns of irrationality, inconsistency, and incompetence in the ways human beings arrive at decisions and choices when faced with uncertainty.

Peter L. Bernstein in Against the Gods, *1996*

As quoted on October 27, 1997; the Dow was down 550 points: It was very orderly. It was a systematic meltdown of testing new bottoms.

Arthur Hogan, equity trader, Morgan Stanley

You don't get anything clean without getting something else dirty.

Cecil Baxter

You never need think you can turn over any falsehood without a terrible squirming and scattering of the horrid little population that dwells under it.

Oliver Wendell Holmes, Sr., 1809–1894, American author
and medical doctor

The first thing to realize is that modern portfolio theory says nothing about which stocks you should buy. It talks about how you should build a portfolio based upon your expectations. Portfolio theory doesn't take a position on market efficiency.

Barr Rosenberg, b. ~1942, Rosenberg Institutional Equity Management

We are all prisoners of cell biology.

H. B. Peari

Peter Principle #9: When even the analysts are bored, it's time to start buying.

Peter Lynch, investment manager, in Beating the Street, *1994*

Do what we can, summer will have its flies.

Ralph Waldo Emerson, 1803–1882, American essayist and poet

To every thing there is a season, and a time to every purpose under heaven: A time to be born, and a time to die; a time to plant, and a time to pluck up that which is planted; a time to kill, and a time to heal; a time to break down, and a time to build up; a time to weep, and a time to laugh; a time to mourn, and a time to dance.

Ecclesiastes 3:1–4, The Bible

The truth is out there.

The X Files, *1990s television series*

Mutual Funds

99 99 99

Mutual Benefits

Mutual funds, one of the great success stories of the bull market that started in the early 1980s, allow individual investors to get exposure to many asset classes, geographical markets, and investment styles. Nevertheless, some experts believe that most investors would be considerably better off purchasing a low expense index fund than trying to select an active fund manager who appears to have a "hot hand." They recommend an index fund that invests in the entire stock market, which is "diversified across almost every publicly held corporation in America; essentially untouched by human hands; nearly bereft of costly portfolio turnover; remarkably cost-efficient; and extraordinarily tax-effective."

The most fundamental decision of investing is the allocation of your assets. How much should you own in stocks? How much should you own in bonds? How much should you own in cash reserves? According to a recent study, that decision has accounted for an astonishing 94 percent of the differences in total returns achieved by institutionally managed pension funds.

John C. Bogle, b. 1929, founder of the Vanguard Funds

What we take for virtue is often nothing but an assemblage of different actions, and of different interests, that fortune or our industry knows how to arrange.

La Rochefoucauld, 1613–1680, French author

In literature as in love, we are astonished at what is chosen by others.

André Maurois, 1885–1967, French novelist and biographer

Ninety percent of what passes for brilliance or incompetence in investing is the ebb and flow of investment style—growth, value, small, foreign.

Jeremy Grantham, investment manager, Grantham, Mayo, Van Otterloo

Past performance is no indicator of future results. Fund historical performance does not promise the same results in the future.

SchwabNOW disclaimer

My role at the firm was to be the "partner in charge of outer space." I was thinking about what would happen several years hence.

Leon Levy, Odyssey Partners, cofounder Oppenheimer Fund, 1987

We need education in the obvious more than investigation in the obscure.

Oliver Wendell Holmes, 1841–1935, associate justice,
U.S. Supreme Court

Just before the 1973 collapse of IOS: "Bernie," Robert Vesco said, "They're not going to blow my brains out. They're going to blow your brains out. You're the one who sold them the funds."

Bernard Cornfeld, Investors Overseas Services, 1987

They [Investors Overseas Services, IOS, Bernard Cornfeld's trusts] held a conference, *Pacem in Terris*, which was a mixture of religion, finance and moralizing. It was really strange. I must say they were fabulous at publicity.

Yves Oltramare, former general partner, Lombard, Odier & CIE, 1987

Don't be disquieted in time of adversity. Be firm with dignity and self-reliant with vigor.

Chiang Kai-shek, 1887–1975, Chinese political leader

An investor cannot earn superior profits from stocks simply by committing to a specific category or style. He can earn them only by carefully evaluating facts and continuously exercising discipline.

Warren Buffett, b. 1930, American investor

Change is the investor's only certainty.

T. Rowe Price, growth investor

There are only two or three human stories, and they go on repeating themselves as fiercely as if they had never happened before.

Willa Cather, 1873–1947, American novelist

We became quite bearish at the firm in the late '60s, early '70s. The trouble was, we got sucked back in the '72–'73 advance. The Nifty Fifty just tore everybody's guts out, but it was a performance game, and if you didn't own the Nifty Fifty, you were behind.

Edward (Ned) Johnson III, b. 1930, chairman, Fidelity Investments

If you aspire to the highest place it is no disgrace to stop at the second, or even the third.

Cicero, 106–43 B.C., Roman orator, statesman

Few things are impracticable in themselves, and it is for want of application rather than of means than men fail of success.

La Rochefoucauld, 1613–1680, French author

Obsession with broad diversification is the sure road to mediocrity. Most people who own more than two mutual funds are over-diversified.

John Neff, investment manager, Wellington Management

Variety is the very spice of life, that gives it all its flavour.

William Cowper, 1731–1800, British poet

It has amazed me that the most incongruous traits should exist in the same person and, for all that, yield a plausible harmony.

Somerset Maugham, 1874–1965, author

Commenting on whether paying higher fees for mutual funds results in higher returns: If you pay the executives at Sara Lee more, it doesn't make the cheesecake less good. But with mutual funds, it comes directly out of the batter.

Don Phillips (Morningstar president) in U.S. News & World Report, *July 8, 1996*

Democracy is the most difficult form of government, because it is the form under which you have to persuade the largest number of persons to do anything in particular.

Woodrow Wilson, 1856–1924, 28th U.S. president

Genuine morality is preserved only in the school of adversity; a state of continuous prosperity may easily prove a quicksand to virtue.

Friedrich von Schiller, 1759–1805, German poet, playwright, and critic

It's pretty hard to find what does bring happiness. Poverty and wealth have both failed.

Kin Hubbard, 1868–1930, American humorist and journalist

How quickly investors flock to better-performing mutual funds, even though financial researchers have shown that the "hot" funds in one time period very often turn out to be the poorest performers in another.

David Dreman in The New Contrarian Investment Strategy, *1998*

Today's hero is often tomorrow's blockhead.

Peter L. Bernstein, b. ~1919, investment manager and economic commentator

I was a technician at Putnam, and the fund managers were giving me an unusually hard time one day. I told them "Yes; the boss just called me into his office, and said I had been making a lot of mistakes recently. He added that if I kept it up they'd have to give me a fund to run."

Walter Deemer, market strategist

The abolition of fixed commissions on Mayday meant there was no more free lunch—you had to be out scratching for a living. There was an apocryphal story in those days that the president of the Pru was at a cocktail party and met an institutional salesman who made more money than he did, and he thought that if that was so, there must be something really rotten with the system.

Leon Levy, Odyssey Partners, cofounder Oppenheimer Fund, 1987

A salesman who stands still runs no danger of making a false step. But he will have to watch out that he doesn't get stepped on by the hustlers who are out after business.

New England Pilot

He who, by an exertion of mind or body, adds to the aggregate of enjoyable wealth, increases the sum of human knowledge, or gives to human life higher elevation or greater fullness—he is, in the larger meaning of the words, a "producer," a "working man," a "laborer," and is honestly earning honest wages.

Henry George, 1839–1897, American social reformer

If you aren't fired with enthusiasm, you will be fired with enthusiasm.

Vince Lombardi, 1913–1970, American football coach,
Green Bay Packers

When a man has put a limit on what he will do, he has put a limit on what he can do.

Charles M. Schwab, 1862–1939, first president of U.S. Steel Corp.

Whatever method you use to pick stocks of stock mutual funds, your ultimate success or failure will depend on your ability to ignore the worries of the world long enough to allow your investments to succeed. It isn't the head but the stomach that determines the fate of the stock-picker.

Peter Lynch, investment manager, in Beating the Street, *1994*

That the love of money is the root of all evil can, conceivably, be disputed. What is not in doubt is that the pursuit of money, or an enduring association with it, is capable of inducing not only bizarre but ripely perverse behavior.

John Kenneth Galbraith, b. 1908, economist

We had our first international investment trust in 1950; we were among the first to launch an international investment service in English and to develop institutional expertise; and we were the first foreign firm to join the New York Stock Exchange.

Yves Oltramare, former general partner, Lombard, Odier & CIE, 1987

Of all the countries in the world, America is that in which the spread of ideas and of human industry is the most continual and most rapid.

Alexis de Tocqueville, 1805–1859, French historian and political philosopher

What really matters is what you do with what you have.

Shirley Lord

The ultimate goal of the educational system is to shift to the individual the burden of pursuing his own education.

John Gardner, b. 1912, American government official

The most important message of this book is to stay invested in stocks. This is extremely difficult for many investors, especially during bear markets. As a result, they jump into and out of even the best funds as market conditions change, dramatically lowering their returns. It does little good to purchase the right stocks or funds if the next time the market trembles you find yourself scurrying to the safety of money market assets.

Jeremy J. Siegel in Stocks for the Long Run, *1994*

Passions are less mischievous than boredom, for passions tend to diminish, boredom to increase.

Jules Barbey d'Aurevilly, 1808–1889, French writer

It is with rivers as it is with people: the greatest are not always the most agreeable nor the best to live with.

Henry Van Dyke, 1852–1933, American clergyman and writer

It never occurs to fools that merit and good fortune are closely united.

Johann Goethe, 1749–1832, German writer

The important thing is to know how to take all things quietly.

Michael Faraday, 1791–1867, British physicist

In 30 years in this business, I do not know anybody who has done it successfully and consistently, nor anybody who knows anybody who has done it successfully and consistently. Indeed, my impression is that trying to do market timing is likely, not only not to add value to your investment program, but to be counterproductive.

John C. Bogle, b. 1929, as quoted in A Random Walk Down Wall Street *by Burton Malkiel*

Knowledge may give weight, but accomplishments give lustre, and many more people see than weigh.

Lord Chesterfield, 1694–1773, British author and statesman, 4th Earl of Chesterfield

How many people live on the reputation of the reputation they might have made!

Oliver Wendell Holmes, 1841–1935, associate justice, U.S. Supreme Court

There is no strong performance without a little fanaticism in the performer.

Ralph Waldo Emerson, 1803–1882, American essayist and poet

Many [market anomalies] have disappeared [because] attention has been drawn to them. One example is the partial disappearance of the illogical discount on closed-end funds in America (known in Britain as investment trusts), since Princeton University's Burton Malkiel drew attention to it in his book *A Random Walk Down Wall Street*. The activities of traders exploiting an inefficiency cause it to disappear.

Frontiers of Finance survey, The Economist

What signifies the ladder, provided one rise and attain the end?

Charles Sainte-Beuve, 1804–1869, French critic

If money is your only hope for independence, you will never have it. The only real security that a man can have in this world is a reserve of knowledge, experience and ability.

Henry Ford, 1863–1947, American automobile manufacturer, founder of Ford Motor Co.

Social progress makes the wellbeing of all more and more the business of each.

Henry George, 1839–1897, American social reformer

I created the institutional trading committee because it was important that the Fidelitys and Dreyfuses of our industry that supported the exchange be represented. Still, the members were angry about that. They said: "You're letting our competitors into the building [NYSE]. That guy Needham is a Trojan horse."

James Needham, b. ~1932, former chairman, New York Stock Exchange

Money is a terrible master but an excellent servant.

P. T. Barnum, 1810–1891, showman and businessman

We were a company without distribution. If we let that go on, there would be no company left.

Edward (Ned) Johnson III, b. 1930, chairman, Fidelity Investments

A person under the firm persuasion that he can command resources virtually has them.

Livy, 59 B.C.–A.D. 17, Roman historian

Among the portfolio managers of giant insurance companies, bank trust departments and mutual funds, I have sometimes found that market know-how decreases as the surroundings become more plush.

William A. Kent

I saw that the institutions were beginning to call the shots and that even in the '60s you could project what would happen on Mayday. The institutions became larger and stronger than the brokerage firms and were eventually able to force discounts.

Leon Levy, Odyssey Partners, cofounder Oppenheimer Fund, 1987

Many people take no care of their money till they come nearly to the end of it, and others do just the same with their time.

Johann Goethe, 1749–1832, German writer

The secret of success is constancy of purpose.

Benjamin Disraeli, 1804–1881, British prime minister, author,
1st Earl of Beaconsfield

No liberal man would impute a charge of unsteadiness to another for having changed his opinion.

Cicero, 106–143 B.C., Roman orator, statesman

A principle of policy once established, be it sound or unsound, is almost sure, through evolution, to exert an influence far beyond that created at the time of its original inception.

Alfred P. Sloan, Jr., 1875–1966, chairman of
General Motors Corporation

The United States is the only country where it takes more brains to figure your tax than to earn the money to pay it.

Edward J. Gurney

If you look at a fifteen-year time frame, using mutual fund data, mutual funds basically outperform the S&P. We are of the opinion, as are most sponsors, that over a long period of time, active managers can add value.

George Russell, Jr., Frank Russell Co., 1987

From a tax point of view you're better off raising horses or cattle than children.

Patricia Schroeder, b. 1940, American congresswoman

Ideas are best sold one at a time. People seem to resist them in batches. They get mental indigestion. One idea at a time, properly "packaged," is understandable, commands action, and oftener than not gets itself enthusiastically adopted.

The Brake Shoe Party Line

You can't advertise today and quit tomorrow. You're not talking to a mass meeting. You're talking to a parade.

Bruce Barton, 1886–1957, American advertising executive
and politician

Even the best investment managers do not always have great results. There is no man for all seasons in this business.

John English, b. ~1933, Ford Foundation

The trouble with the rat race is that even if you win, you're still a rat.

Lily Tomlin, b. 1939, actress

If you cannot win, make the one ahead break the record.

Keene Thrusts

Inflation is not all bad. After all, it has allowed every American to live in a more expensive neighborhood without moving.

Alan Cranston, b. 1914, U.S. senator

He who governed the world before I was born shall take care of it likewise when I am dead. My part is to improve the present moment.

John Wesley, 1703–1791, English religious leader

The methods and approaches in capitalist management, if they can survive for so long, must have their merits.

Rong Yiren, b. ~1916, China International Trust and Investment Corp.

There was a great inflation in the 1970s; an asset boom in the 1980s; a more widely shared prosperity in the 1990s. More people tended their portfolios. Fewer voted.

David Warsh, Boston Globe *columnist*

Performance Measurement

❞ ❞ ❞

Measure Up!

You can't manage what you can't measure.

William Hewlett, National Inventors
Hall of Fame, 1992

We live in an age of measurement—how high, how heavy, how much, how many? Academic studies suggest great caution with the predictability of investment returns: The results of one period cannot be predicted by another. Teachers of science typically urge students not to record measurements to a greater degree of precision than their crude instruments allow, because error rather than precision results. Performance measurement almost always fails standard statistical tests of significance and can hardly ever be projected forward. In terms of selecting investment managers on the basis of short-term performance indicators, it may be better to pick a solid long-term performer that has underperformed in the last couple of years.

Money managers have created their own nightmare by saying, "Boy, look at the February we had." They call about March 3.

Robert Kirby, investment manager, Capital Guardian Trust Co., 1987

Money is a stupid measure of achievement but unfortunately it is the only universal measure we have.

Charles P. Steinmetz, 1865–1923, mathematician and engineer

The years teach much which days never know.

Ralph Waldo Emerson, 1803–1882, American essayist and poet

If at first you do succeed—try to hide your astonishment.

Harry F. Banks

I shall tell you a great secret, my friend. Do not wait for the last judgment, it takes place every day.

Albert Camus, 1913–1960, French journalist and philosopher

Destiny: A tyrant's authority for crime and a fool's excuse for failure.

Ambrose Bierce, 1842–~1914, American writer and journalist

A man is not finished when he is defeated. He is finished when he quits.

Richard Nixon, 1913–1994, 37th U.S. president

We made too many wrong mistakes.

Yogi Berra, b. 1925, baseball player, coach, and manager

If you have no confidence in self you are twice defeated in the race of life.

Marcus Garvey, 1887–1940, American social reformer

If you look at people who've been ahead of the market for five years, their chances of being ahead for the next five years are not very good— only a little better than random.

Barr Rosenberg, b. ~1942, Rosenberg Institutional Equity Management

Fame is a vapor, popularity an accident, riches take wings. Only one thing endures, and that is character.

Horace Greeley, 1811–1872, American politician and writer

Success is full of promise till men get it and then it is last year's nest from which the bird has flown.

Henry Ward Beecher, 1813–1887, American religious leader and reformer

There is no young man or grown man living who cannot do more than he thinks he can.

Henry Ford, 1863–1947, American automobile manufacturer, founder of Ford Motor Co.

It is a mistake to fancy ourselves greater than we are, and to value ourselves at less than we are worth.

Johann Goethe, 1749–1832, German writer

Malice is a greater magnifying glass than kindness.

Lord Halifax, 1661–1715, English wit and politician

The best is good enough.

German proverb

The jests of the rich are ever successful.

Oliver Goldsmith, 1730–1774, British playwright and poet

Laughter is not a bad beginning for a friendship, and it is the best ending for one.

Oscar Wilde, 1854–1900, author

The thing that is most interesting to me is that every one of the managers is able to give me a chart that shows me that he was in the first quartile or the first decile. I have never had a prospective manager come in and say, "We're in the fourth quartile or bottom decile."

John English, b. ~1933, Ford Foundation

The superior man is distressed by the limitations of his ability; he is not distressed by the fact that men do not recognize the ability that he has.

Confucius, 551–479 B.C., Chinese philosopher

To be unduly elated if you win, or unduly depressed when you lose, is a sign that you are carrying too much sail and not enough ballast.

Kodak *magazine*

It is not goodness to be better than the worst.

Seneca, ~4 B.C.–A.D. 65, Roman statesman and philosopher

What others think of us would be of little moment did it not, when known, so deeply tinge what we think of ourselves.

Paul Valéry, 1871–1945, French writer

Whoever serves his country well has no need of ancestors.

Voltaire, 1694–1778, French philosopher and writer

I have found that it is much easier to make a success in life than to make a success of one's life.

G. W. Follin

You will become as small as your controlling desire; as great as your dominant aspiration.

James Allen, 1849–1925, American novelist

A man's life is interesting primarily when he has failed—I well know. For it's a sign that he tried to surpass himself.

Georges Clemenceau, 1841–1929, French statesman

An ounce of performance is worth more than a pound of preachment.

Elbert G. Hubbard, 1856–1915, American writer and businessman

Every man has a right to be conceited until he is successful.

Benjamin Franklin, 1706–1790, statesman, scientist, public leader

We live in a spelling bee culture where the demand is for factual accuracy and everybody overlooks the absence of art or meaning in what's said . . . too many people send letters to Nero telling he was fingering his fiddle wrong. This passion for data is a way of avoiding coming to terms with things.

Mark Harris

We live in deeds, not years; in thoughts, not figures on a dial. We should count time by heart throbs. He most lives who thinks most, acts the best.

Philip James Bailey, 1816–1902, English poet

Glory is fleeting, but obscurity is forever.

Napoleon Bonaparte, 1769–1821, French general

I care not what others think of what I do, but I care very much about what I think of what I do: That is character!

Theodore Roosevelt, 1858–1919, 26th U.S. president

Whosoever does not know how to recognize the faults of great men is incapable of estimating their perfections.

Voltaire, 1694–1778, French philosopher and writer

I was sorry to hear my name mentioned as one of the great authors, because they have a sad habit of dying off. Chaucer is dead, so is Milton, so is Shakespeare, and I am not feeling very well myself.

Mark Twain, 1835–1910, American author

If I could drop dead right now, I'd be the happiest man alive.

Samuel Goldwyn, 1882–1974, American movie producer

If misery loves company, then triumph demands an audience.

Brian Moore, b. 1921, Irish novelist

It's great to be great, but it's greater to be human.

Will Rogers, 1879–1935, American humorist and showman

In the school of stock market experience, vacation time never counts.

James L. Fraser, author, publisher, and contrarian thinker

One who is contented with what he has done will never become famous for what he will do.

Christian Bovee, 1820–1904, American author, lawyer

A man is in general better pleased when he has a good dinner upon his table, than when his wife talks Greek.

Samuel Johnson, 1709–1784, British author

Our greatest glory consists not in never failing, but in rising every time we fall.

Oliver Goldsmith, 1730–1774, British playwright and poet

Success is never final and failure never fatal. It's courage that counts.

George F. Tilton

The longer we dwell on our misfortunes, the greater is their power to harm us.

Voltaire, 1694–1778, French philosopher and writer

The only conquests which are permanent and leave no regrets are our conquests over ourselves.

Napoleon Bonaparte, 1769–1821, French general

Vanity plays lurid tricks with our memory.

Joseph Conrad, 1857–1924, Polish-British author

You can't expect to win unless you know why you lose.

Benjamin Lipson

If you mean to keep as well as possible, the less you think about your health the better.

Oliver Wendell Holmes, Sr., 1809–1894, American author
and medical doctor

Never have so many [money managers] made so much money by achieving so little. We've contributed a negative result in the aggregate, and we've been paid like Croesus for it. You'd think, in due course, retribution or regression to the mean would reel us all in.

Robert Kirby, investment manager, Capital Guardian Trust Co., 1987

Winning isn't the most important thing; it's everything.

Vince Lombardi, 1913–1970, American football coach,
Green Bay Packers

Success is when you get what you want. Happiness is when you want what you get.

Unknown

You can develop in yourself the manners, tastes and habits which you most admire in others. The man you most like to meet is the type of man you ought to be.

Grenville Kleiser

The autumn of the beautiful is beautiful.

Latin proverb

Success is the ability to go from failure to failure with no loss of enthusiasm.

Winston Churchill, 1874–1965, British prime minister

Too much of a good thing can be wonderful.

Mae West, 1892–1980, actress

If you get simple beauty and naught else, you get about the best thing God invents.

Robert Browning, 1812–1889, poet

Politics and Investing

꠹ ꠹ ꠹

Governments and Markets

There can be no legislation against stupidity.
Fred Schwed, Jr., author and investor

What effects do politics have on economics? How can investors analyze political risks and assess their likely effects on equity returns? Stock markets are influenced by major financial events (for example, interest rates), by major fiscal events (for example, government budgets), and by major political events (for example, a "presidential cycle" in U.S. equity markets). Politics is usually thought to influence economic outcomes. But is it more often the other way around, with markets leading politics?

It is difficult to make our material condition better by the best laws, but it is easy enough to ruin it by bad laws.

Theodore Roosevelt, 1858–1919, 26th U.S. president

Good markets make for lackluster politics—and vice versa.

David Warsh, Boston Globe *columnist*

Politicians don't move the economy, the economy moves the politicians.

Richard Russell, author of Dow Theory Letters, *newsletter*

The world doesn't stop functioning because of changes in government.

Eugene Rotberg, b. ~1929, World Bank

Among politicians the esteem of religion is profitable; the principles of it are troublesome.

Benjamin Whitecote

A liberal is a person whose interests aren't at stake at the moment.

Willis Player

I can remember way back when a liberal was one who was generous with his own money.

Will Rogers, 1879–1935, American humorist and showman

I'm in favor of letting the status quo stay as it is.

Wisconsin legislator

The problem came when negotiated rates came along in 1975 [Mayday], and people who continued to try to do block trading found out that the percentages were now against them. It was just a losing, losing proposition, because the commissions were sliced so much that the vigorish was gone. Anybody who says they make money in block trading is, in my opinion, either joking or not telling the truth.

Alan Greenberg, b. 1928, Bear, Stearns & Co.

A public right cannot be changed by private agreement.

Maxim of Law

All progress and growth is a matter of change, but change must be growth within our social and government concepts if it should not destroy them.

Herbert Hoover, 1874–1964, 31st U.S. president

Taxes are not levied for the benefit of the taxed.

Robert Heinlein, 1907–1988, American author

Ancient laws remain in force long after the people have the power to change them.

Aristotle, 384–322 B.C., Greek philosopher, educator, scientist

The oil countries used to have a lot of liquidity; now they have less. So Arab banks will not be able to grow, even if their capital base is good enough. You have to have permanent deposits, not deposits subject to the war in Iran and Iraq or to a private sector which isn't meeting its commitments.

Abdulla Saudi, founder, Arab Banking Corp. (ABC), 1987

Communism always victimizes the strong. Property victimizes the weak.

Henry Adams, 1838–1918, American historian

Every advance in social organization requires some surrender of individual freedom by the majority and the ultimate coercion of a destructive minority.

Owen D. Young, 1874–1962, American lawyer and financier

Freedom without obligation is anarchy; freedom with obligation is democracy.

Earl Riney

Great evils befall the world when the powerful begin to copy the weak. The desperate devices which enable the weak to survive are unequaled instruments of oppression and extermination in the hands of the strong.

Eric Hoffer, 1902–1983, American philosopher

As for the exchange's [NYSE] floor committee, by the time I left the exchange [1976] I put a complete end to it. It was one of my "hidden agenda items." It was to eliminate the way that stocks were allocated to specialists. They had real power. I wanted to put an end to the stock allocation system, and I did that.

James Needham, b. ~1932, former chairman, New York Stock Exchange

Justice consists in doing no injury to men; decency in giving them no offence.

Cicero, 106–43 B.C., Roman orator and statesman

John Adams and Thomas Jefferson were political enemies, but they became fast friends. And when they passed away on the same day, the last words of one of them was, "The country is safe. Jefferson still lives." And the last words of the other was, "John Adams will see that things go forward."

Harry S. Truman, 1884–1972, 33rd U.S. president

I think we have more machinery of government than is necessary, too many parasites living on the labor of the industrious.

Thomas Jefferson, 1743–1826, 3rd U.S. president

I've never taken the view that the world of poetry and the world of politics are so far apart. I think politicians and poets share at least one thing, and that is that their greatness depends upon the courage with which they face the challenges of life.

John F. Kennedy, 1917–1963, 35th U.S. president

The whole conglomerate movement happened in the '60s. In those days everybody was concerned about antitrust. No one was concerned with the United States' competitive position in the world. There were people in this country, including professors at the Wharton School, who wanted to see IBM broken up—because it was too competitive. It didn't do anything illegal. It just tried harder. Maybe the greatest company that has ever been built—and people in this country wanted to tear it apart.

Saul Steinberg, founder, Reliance Group Holdings, 1987

As soon as government management begins, it upsets the natural equilibrium of industrial relations, and each interference only requires further bureaucratic control until the end is the tyranny of the totalitarian state.

Adam Smith, 1723–1790, political economist

What has always made the state a hell on earth has been precisely that man has tried to make it his heaven.

Friedrich Hölderlin, 1770–1843, German poet

When the state is most corrupt, then laws are most multiplied.

Tacitus, ~A.D. 56–120, Roman orator, politician, and historian

As quoted in 1945: We have forgotten in America that a democracy is the most difficult kind of government to maintain. It is the hardest kind of government under which to live. It is hardest to maintain because of the widespread political corruption to which it so easily lends itself. Our drift today toward complete totalitarian bureaucracy is one that threatens immediately the very freedoms for which our own boys are dying.

Ernest R. Palen, D.D.

About raising interest rates in 1981: There was a conflict between the Bundesbank and the government, and it was a conflict Schmidt could only lose. The government had, at that time, a very low reputation and a high budget deficit.

Karl Otto Pöhl, president, Deutsche Bundesbank

The worst country to be poor in is America.

Arnold Toynbee, 1889–1975, British historian

It's a great country, but you can't live in it for nothing.

Will Rogers, 1879–1935, American humorist and showman

There are plenty of good five-cent cigars in the country. The trouble is they cost a quarter. What the country really needs is a good five-cent nickel.

Franklin Pierce Adams, 1881–1960, American journalist and humorist

As quoted in January 1933: If you will make me the unemployment Mussolini of this country, I agree to organize and train an army of men and women now unemployed to present a nation-wide educational campaign to create a legitimate demand for goods.

Roger W. Babson, 1875–1967, American financial statistician

Each scandal brings additional regulations and laws. And the more laws you have, the more people believe that what is *not* prohibited is legal, so the more loopholes people find.

Yves Oltramare, former general partner, Lombard, Odier & CIE, 1987

Tact consists in knowing how far to go in going too far.

Jean Cocteau, 1889–1963, French author

Tax reform is when you take the taxes off things that have been taxed in the past and put taxes on things that haven't been taxed before.

Art Buchwald, b. 1925, American newspaper columnist

Tact is the ability to tell someone to go to hell in such a way that they look forward to the trip.

Unknown

The art of taxation consists in so plucking the goose as to obtain the largest amount of feathers with the least possible amount of hissing.

J. B. Colbert, 1619–1683, French government official

I know you believe you understand what you think I said, but I am not sure you realize that what you heard is not what I meant.

Alan Greenspan, b. 1926, chairman of the U.S. Federal Reserve

It was very clear to me in the early '70s that Mayday was coming. That was in the days of give-ups. You made so much money that you could afford to take part of your income and just send a check to somebody else. One thing you can be sure about in terms of excesses is that someone has to come along and correct them. At one point I was advocating that we ease into negotiated rates with a system tied to volume. The options were us managing the change or Washington managing the change.

Donald Marron, b. ~1934, Paine Webber

Let Wall Street get a nightmare, and the whole country has to help get them in bed again.

Will Rogers, 1879–1935, American humorist and showman

In a land which is distinguished for freedom of speech, freedom of religion, freedom from want and freedom from fear, any lack of a freedom of job opportunity isn't going to set well with the men who have fought to save us on the battlefields of the world.

Henry Ford, 1863–1947, American automobile manufacturer,
founder of Ford Motor Co.

It is a general error to suppose the loudest complainers for the public to be the most anxious for the welfare.

Edmund Burke, 1729–1797, English political leader

The way to crush the bourgeoisie is to grind them between the millstones of taxation and inflation.

Vladimir I. Lenin, 1870–1924, Russian revolutionary

In some ways, the whole decade from the late '60s into the '70s can be seen as a breaking down of various "clubs" on Wall Street. There were "Catholic" firms and "Jewish" firms and "WASP" firms. There was a sort of gentleman's agreement: You'd not have Catholics working for a WASP firm and certainly not Jews.

Leon Levy, Odyssey Partners, cofounder Oppenheimer Fund, 1987

As quoted in 1929: It is America, not Moscow, that has shown the worker how he can get what he most desires—a steadily rising standard of living.

Philip Kerr, English socialist and author

Judging from the main portions of the history of the world, so far, justice is always in jeopardy.

> *Walt Whitman, 1819–1892, American poet*

Laws should be like clothes. They should be made to fit the people they are meant to serve.

> *Clarence Darrow, 1857–1938, American lawyer*

Necessity is the plea for every infringement of human freedom. It is the argument of tyrants; it is the creed of slaves.

> *William Pitt, 1708–1778, British prime minister*

The Hongkong Bank was viewed as anticompetitive. But that was because we just happened to be damned successful.

> *Michael Sandberg, former chairman, Hongkong and Shanghai Banking Corp., 1987*

No political leader operates without courtiers who mould him— deciding what and whom he sees, providing him with the thoughts he thinks. I find the greatest use of all in talking to the courtiers of the candidate. You get a vision of America as it comes to him.

> *Theodore H. White, 1915–1986, American political journalist*

Politics has got so expensive that it takes lots of money to even get beat with.

> *Will Rogers, 1879–1935, American humorist and showman*

Rich bachelors should be heavily taxed. It is not fair that some men should be happier than others.

> *Oscar Wilde, 1854–1900, Irish-British author*

A government which robs Peter to pay Paul can always count on
Paul's support.

George Bernard Shaw, 1856–1950, playwright

We were like pathologists with respect to American business.

Stanley Sporkin, U.S. Securities and Exchange Commission, 1987

Since a politician never believes what he says, he is surprised when
others believe him.

Charles de Gaulle, 1890–1970, French president

The future of nations cannot be frozen. The forces which will arise out
of this war cannot be foreseen. If we are going to accomplish anything
in our time we must approach our problem in the knowledge that
there is nothing rigid or immutable in human affairs. History is a
story of growth, decay and change. If no provision, no allowance is
made for change by peaceful means, it will come anyway—and with
violence.

Herbert Hoover, 1874–1964, 31st U.S. president

In our complex world, there cannot be fruitful initiative without government, but unfortunately, there can be government without initiative.

Bertrand Russell, 1872–1970, British philosopher and mathematician

The secret point of money and power in America is neither the things
that money can buy nor power for power's sake but absolute personal
freedom, mobility, privacy.

Joan Didion, b. 1934, American author

Response to a question about whether the Democrats will retake either house of Congress anytime soon: Actually, the interesting question for '98 is, if we have a balanced budget agreement and we achieve various other bipartisan objectives, it's far from clear to me what the Democrats who are running for Congress will be arguing for or against.

Robert Reich, b. 1946, American economist and former secretary of labor

Wipe out college—the Electoral College, that is. From all I've read, studied and thought about the matter, I can't find one good reason why the President and Vice President shouldn't be elected by popular vote.

Malcolm Forbes, 1919–1990, publisher and author

Politics is the art of looking for trouble, finding it everywhere, diagnosing it incorrectly, and applying the wrong remedies.

Groucho Marx, 1890–1977, comedian

There are no warlike peoples—just warlike leaders.

Ralph J. Bunche, 1904–1971, American statesman

Trade and commerce, if they were not made of india-rubber, would never manage to bounce over the obstacles which legislators are continually putting in their way; and, if one were to judge these men wholly by the effects of their actions and not partly by their intentions, they would deserve to be classed and punished with those mischievous persons who put obstructions on the railroads.

Henry David Thoreau, 1817–1862, American naturalist and writer

There is a well-documented "presidential cycle" in U.S. equity markets, which highlights favorable market forces in the fourth year of a presidential term. The suggestion is that political powers favor expansionary policies to attract voters. And then, after the election, regardless of the outcome, markets tend to retrench to compensate for the politically induced pre-election policy.

Dean LeBaron, b. 1933, investment manager and contrarian thinker

The hardest thing in the world to understand is the income tax.

Albert Einstein, 1879–1955, German–American scientist

English inventor Michael Faraday conceived and built the first electric motor, then tried to get the backing of Prime Minister Gladstone. "What possible good is it?" asked Gladstone. Faraday's reply changed Gladstone's attitude: "Some day you'll be able to tax it."

Unknown

Our lack of concern for our nation on election day becomes official the day after.

Cullen Hightower

I'm proud to be paying taxes in the United States. The only thing is, I could be just as proud for half the money.

Arthur Godfrey, 1903–1983, entertainer

Even today [1987], Germany is way behind France and England in privatization and opening markets to the public.

Yves Oltramare, former general partner, Lombard, Odier & CIE, 1987

We expected substantive provisions in this tax bill—what we have, instead, is a herd of mice.

Barber Conable, U.S. representative, 1965–1985

In constitutional states liberty is compensation for heavy taxation; in despotic states the equivalent of liberty is light taxes.

Charles de Montesquieu, 1689–1755, French philosopher and author

He was the consummate politician; he didn't lie, neither did he tell the truth.

John Lundberg

How can you trust people who are poor and own no property? . . . Inequality of property will exist as long as liberty exists.

Alexander Hamilton, 1755–1804, American statesman

All of these developments give me at least as much pause in looking ahead as in looking backward. Nevertheless, I am heartened by some signs that the current mortgaging of the future for the present may be causing a period of serious and constructive national and international reflection.

David Rockefeller, b. 1915, formerly Chase Manhattan Bank,
American financier, son of John D. Rockefeller, Jr.

I personally have lived through ten presidential campaigns, but I must say the eleventh makes me feel like I lived through twenty-five.

John F. Kennedy, 1917–1963, 35th U.S. president

I wonder what our world would be like if men always had sacrificed as freely to prevent wars as to win them.

Frank A. Clark

The people never give up their liberties but under some delusion.

Edmund Burke, 1729–1797, English political leader

In politics there is a cultivated distinction between lies and deceit.

Art Buck

To me, one of the most significant things about ERISA is that it made corporate America aware of how important the pension fund really was. In the years before ERISA, the pension fund was really thought of as a sideline.

John English, b. ~1933, Ford Foundation

It's discouraging how hard it is for a President to slice away large chunks of a $305 billion budget.

Gerald Ford, b. 1913, 38th U.S. president

No man is good enough to govern another man, without that other's consent.

Abraham Lincoln, 1809–1865, 16th U.S. president

Of all debts, men are least willing to pay taxes. What a satire is this on government!

Ralph Waldo Emerson, 1803–1882, American essayist and poet

Radicalism itself ceases to be radical when absorbed mainly in preserving its control over a society or an economy.

Eric Hoffer, 1902–1983, American philosopher

The making of profits is only the ways and means for the extension of economic development through which people's living standards can be lifted, not our ultimate goal.

Rong Yiren, b. ~1916, China International Trust and Investment Corp.

Some degree of abuse is inseparable from the proper use of everything.

James Madison, 1751–1836, 4th U.S. president

The man for whom law exists—the man of forms, the conservative—is a tame man.

Henry David Thoreau, 1817–1862, American naturalist and writer

The only thing worse than taking from the poor is persuading them to give beyond their means.

Benjamin Lichtenberg

The only way to solve the traffic problems of the country is to pass a law that only paid-for cars are allowed to use the highways.

Will Rogers, 1879–1935, American humorist and showman

Nixon was resigning. It was August of '74. He was resigning every day, and every day he didn't resign, the stock market hit new lows. Interest rates were only 12 percent, but there was no money, because the Fed put such limits on the growth of money that you couldn't borrow money in the United States. So you had to borrow money in Europe, and the Eurodollar rate was 21 percent. That was the real cost of money.

Saul Steinberg, founder, Reliance Group Holdings, 1987

The victim of too severe a law is considered a martyr, rather than a criminal.

Charles Caleb Colton, 1780–1832, writer

There is nothing so bad but it can masquerade as moral.

Walter Lippmann, 1889–1974, American journalist

To whom nothing is given, of him nothing can be required.

Henry Fielding, 1707–1754, novelist

Economic stimulation that encourages the increased expenditures of the rich has an aspect of soundness that is lacking in expenditures on behalf of the undeserving poor.

John Kenneth Galbraith, b. 1908, economist

When we had to make the decision about the exchange's position to accept the commission's [SEC] edict that on May 1, 1975, there would be competitive rates, the board came back [ultimately], and they all voted to accept the SEC's decision.

James Needham, b. ~1932, former chairman, New York Stock Exchange

Without government a nation would instantly collapse. With too much government it takes considerably longer.

Cullen Hightower

Liberty has never come from Government. Liberty has always come from the subjects of it. The history of liberty is a history of resistance. The history of liberty is a history of limitations of governmental power, not the increase of it.

Woodrow Wilson, 1856–1924, 28th U.S. president

Law is born from despair of human nature.

Ortega y Gasset, 1883–1955, Spanish philosopher

Hell hath no fury like a vested interest masquerading as a moral principle.

Barber Conable, U.S. representative, 1965–1985

It's like 1938. Everybody said there would be a war, but nobody knew what exactly would start it. The problems will create not only financial but psychological difficulties. The masses are not going to adjust psychologically; the political system will modify itself and become more of a dictatorship. It's very dangerous.

Yves Oltramare, former general partner, Lombard, Odier & CIE, 1987

In necessary things, unity; in doubtful things, liberty; in all things, charity.

Richard Baxter, 1615–1691, English clergyman and writer

American history is longer, larger, more various, more beautiful, and more terrible than anything anyone has ever said about it.

James Baldwin, 1924–1987, novelist

Every man is a reformer until reform tramps on his toes.

Edgar Watson (Ed) Howe, 1853–1937, American journalist and author

In a war of ideas it is people who get killed.

Stanislaus J. Lec, 1909–1966

The theory we all held at the time was very straightforward: The only way to regulate an industry as strong and effective and with so many bright people as the securities industry was to let competition work as distinguished from regulation. We basically were not comfortable with regulation; we didn't trust how it could be turned or corrupted.

Eugene Rotberg, b. ~1929, World Bank

Law can never make us as secure as we are when we do not need it.

Alexander M. Bickel

My reading of history convinces me that most bad government results from too much government.

Thomas Jefferson, 1743–1826, 3rd U.S. president

Who ever hears of fat men heading a riot?

Washington Irving, 1783–1859, American author

Political institutions are a superstructure resting on an economic foundation.

Vladimir I. Lenin, 1870–1924, Russian revolutionary

If politicians and scientists were lazier, how much happier we should all be.

Evelyn Waugh, 1903–1966, British author

Who controls the past controls the future; who controls the present controls the past.

George Orwell, 1903–1950, novelist

A balanced budget cannot be,
Amend the process as you will
The dripping snouts within the trough
Will not forgo the tasty swill.

Art Buck

It has been said that to one who is good, the whole world becomes good. This is true so far as the individual is concerned. But goodness becomes dynamic only when it is practiced in the face of evil. If you return good for good only, it is a bargain and carries no merit, but if you return good for evil, it becomes a redeeming force. The evil ceases before it and it goes on gathering volume and momentum like a snowball till it becomes irresistible.

Mahatma Gandhi, 1869–1948, Indian nationalist and spiritual leader

Quantitative Investing

99 **99** **99**

Damned Lies and Statistics

Don't do equations with Greek letters in them.
Warren Buffett, b. 1930, American investor

The essence of quantitative investing is crunching numbers. Anything that can go into a digital computer is fair input. And since computers are mostly digital and linear programs are rigid, "quant" analysis tends to be repetitively structured and rich in reliance on back testing. The central themes of quant investing are that history reveals enduring patterns of price behavior, which can be unlocked by statistical techniques; that risk of loss is closely related to volatility, which is related to return; and that management of risk, return, covariance, and time frames can be usefully predictable. Even quantitative back testing is intuitive data mining—determining what patterns exist in a finite sample of numbers. Investment strategies based on hindsight often fail.

Read Ben Graham and Phil Fisher, read annual reports, but don't do equations with Greek letters in them.

Warren Buffett, b. 1930, American investor

Everything should be made as simple as possible, but not simpler.

Albert Einstein, 1879–1955, German-American scientist

It does not do to leave a live dragon out of your calculations, if you live near him.

J. R. R. Tolkien, 1892–1973, British author

The life or death of the ship and all her precious human freight may hang on the delinquency of one man at some moment years before.

B. C. Forbes, 1880–1954, editor and publisher

Once you have missed the first buttonhole you'll never manage to button up.

Johann Goethe, 1749–1832, German writer

In the kingdom of the blind, the one-eyed king can still goof up.

Laurence J. Peter, 1919–1990, Canadian author and educator

A poet can survive everything but a misprint.

Oscar Wilde, 1854–1900, Irish-British author

And though it is obviously more difficult to get superior *information* on a company, the crux of the matter is superior *judgment*, to know what to look for, recognize it when you see it and know how to weigh it.

Peter Vermilye, investment manager, Baring America Asset Management Co., 1987

The worth and value of knowledge is in proportion to the worth and value of its object.

Samuel Taylor Coleridge, 1772–1834, British poet

Emphatic and reiterated assertion, especially during childhood, produces in most people a belief so firm as to have a hold even over the unconscious.

Bertrand Russell, 1872–1970, British philosopher and mathematician

Because quants can handle more variables they can't resist using them. They can easily end by throwing in the kitchen sink and drowning in detail and data mining.

Jeremy Grantham, investment manager, Grantham, Mayo, Van Otterloo

A programmer is someone who solves a problem you didn't know you had in a way you don't understand.

Unknown

Language—a form of organized stutter.

Marshall McLuhan, 1911–1980, Canadian sociologist and critic

A mathematician is a blind man in a dark room looking for a black cat, which isn't there.

Charles Darwin, 1809–1882, naturalist

It is the mark of a truly intelligent person to be moved by statistics.

George Bernard Shaw, 1856–1950, playwright

Results? Why, man, I have gotten a lot of results. I know several thousand things that won't work.

Thomas A. Edison, 1847–1931, inventor and industrialist

The errors of a wise man make your rule,
Rather than the perfections of a fool.

William Blake, 1757–1827, British poet and artist

Always acknowledge a fault frankly. This will throw those in authority off their guard and give you an opportunity to commit more.

Mark Twain, 1835–1910, American author

Nothing is really work unless you would rather be doing something else.

James M. Barrie, 1860–1937, dramatist and novelist

Ever since our love for machines replaced the love we used to have for our fellow man, catastrophes proceed to increase.

Man Ray, 1890–1976, American artist

History is not a Xerox machine.

Steve Leuthold, investment manager, The Leuthold Group

We have to do with the past only as we can make it useful to the present and the future.

Frederick Douglass, 1817–1895, American social reformer

Security analysts have enormous difficulty in performing their basic function of forecasting earnings prospects for the companies they follow. Bluntly stated, the careful estimates of security analysts (based on industry studies, plant visits, etc.) do very little better than those that would be obtained by simple extrapolation of past trends.

Burton Malkiel in A Random Walk Down Wall Street,
5th edition, 1990

You can never plan the future by the past.

Edmund Burke, 1729–1797, English political leader

No truth so sublime but it may be seen to be trivial tomorrow in the light of new thoughts.

Ralph Waldo Emerson, 1803–1882, American essayist and poet

When the interval between the intellectual classes and the practical classes is too great, the former will possess no influence, the latter will reap no benefit.

Thomas Buckle, 1821–1862, English historian

Pension fund managers continue to make decisions with their eyes firmly fixed in the rear-view mirror.

Warren Buffett, b. 1930, American investor

Do not look back. It will neither give you back the past nor satisfy your daydreams. Your duty, your reward, your destiny are here and now.

Dag Hammarskjöld, 1905–1961, secretary-general of the United Nations

I know of no way of judging of the future but by the past.

Patrick Henry, 1736–1799, American political leader

The past which is so presumptuously brought forward as a precedent for the present, was itself founded on some past that went before it.

Madame de Staël, 1766–1817, French writer, literary patron, and critic

Success isn't found by sifting the ashes of the past, but by being among the first to explore and cultivate the fertile fields of the future.

Arnold Glasow, American humorist

Sometimes I feel that there is so much emphasis today put on massaging the infinite amount of data available that people get distracted from identifying the critical variables. The qualitative distinctions get lost in the computer evaluations. I think it's important to superimpose fundamental research on top of what comes up on the screen.

Peter Vermilye, investment manager, Baring America
Asset Management Co., 1987

A topologist is a man who doesn't know the difference between a coffee cup and a doughnut.

Unknown

One word sums up probably the responsibility of any vice president, and that one word is "to be prepared."

J. Danforth Quayle, b. 1947, vice president of the United States

I know this world is ruled by Infinite Intelligence. It required Infinite Intelligence to create it and it requires Infinite Intelligence to keep it on its course. Everything that surrounds us—everything that exists— proves that there are Infinite Laws behind it. There can be no denying this fact. It is mathematical in its precision.

Thomas A. Edison, 1847–1931, inventor and industrialist

The strange beating together of hands has no meaning. To me it is very disturbing. We try to make sounds like music, and then in between comes this strange sound.

Leopold Stokowski, 1882–1977, American conductor

Knowledge without wisdom is a load of books on the back of an ass.

Japanese proverb

Thousands of quant man-hours are sucked into solving intricate math problems, rather than cruder but still effective techniques. On every discussion room wall should hang the motto: "There are no points for elegance."

Jeremy Grantham, investment manager, Grantham, Mayo, Van Otterloo

Man must be disciplined, for he is by nature raw and wild.

Immanuel Kant, 1724–1804, philosopher

One has to dismount from an idea and get into the saddle again at every parenthesis.

Oliver Wendell Holmes, 1841–1935, associate justice,
U.S. Supreme Court

In public we say the race is to the strongest; in private we know that a lopsided man runs the fastest along the little side-hills of success.

Frank Moore Colby, 1865–1925, American writer and humorist

When she was good, she was very, very good; and when she was bad, she was better.

Mae West, 1892–1980, actress

Frank and explicit—that is the right line to take when you wish to conceal your own mind and confuse the minds of others.

Benjamin Disraeli, 1804–1881, British prime minister, author,
1st Earl of Beaconsfield

The way Bernard Shaw believes in himself is very refreshing in these atheistic days when so many believe in no God at all.

Israel Zangwill, 1864–1926, British author

By concentrating on precision one arrives at technique; but by concentrating on technique one does not arrive at precision.

Bruno Walter, 1876–1962, German-American conductor

Perfection of means and confusion of goals seem, in my opinion, to characterize our age.

Albert Einstein, 1879–1955, German-American scientist

A statistician is someone who is good with numbers but lacks the personality to be an accountant.

Unknown

All knowledge resolves itself into probability.

David Hume, 1711–1776, Scottish philosopher

The world is not interested in the storms you encountered, but did you bring in the ship?

William McFee

Hard work is damn near as overrated as monogamy.

Huey P. Long, 1893–1935, American political leader

Work is hard if you're paid to do it, and it's pleasure if you pay to be allowed to do it.

Finley Peter Dunne, 1867–1936, American humorist and journalist

Joy in one's work is the consummate tool.

Phillips Brooks, 1835–1893, American religious leader

The question "Who ought to be boss?" is like asking "Who ought to be the tenor in the quartet?" Obviously, the man who can sing tenor.

Henry Ford, 1863–1947, American automobile manufacturer, founder of Ford Motor Co.

If you torture the data long enough, it will confess to anything.

Darrell Huff in How to Lie with Statistics, *1954*

Risk Management

" " "

Risky Business

A nickel ain't worth a dime anymore.
Yogi Berra, b. 1925, baseball player, coach,
and manager

The role of derivatives for managing risk through the financial markets is frequently misunderstood. Yet these instruments—futures, options, and a multitude of variations—are packages of the basic components of risk: they more than anything else traded come close to the theoretically ideal instruments for the trading of risk. Derivatives can turn stocks into bonds and vice versa, and can pinpoint, very precisely, specific risks and returns that are packaged within a complex structure. Risk management is essential in a modern market economy.

I don't know where speculation got a bad name, since I know of no forward leap which was not fathered by speculation.

John Steinbeck, 1902–1968, novelist

All speculations, and even the most conservative investments, have some slight element of risk. All lines of business are more or less a gamble; marriage is a gamble; political preferment is a gamble; in fact nearly everything in life, including our very existence, is an uncertainty; yet people are not thereby discouraged from entering into any and all of these ventures. Those who look only for certainties have far to search and little to find in this world.

Henry Howard Harper in The Psychology of Speculation, *1926*

Let us watch well our beginnings, and results will manage themselves.

Alexander Clark

This old world we're livin' in
Is mighty hard to beat.
You get a thorn with every rose,
But aren't the roses sweet!

Frank L. Stanton, 1857–1927, American journalist and poet

The membership of the Merc felt [certain things hurt their future] such as the onion debacle of [the 1950s], when corners and squeezes [manipulation] allowed that market to go down the tubes.

Leo Melamed, b. ~1932, former chairman, Chicago Mercantile Exchange

If a pig could pray, it would pray for swill. What do you pray for?

B. C. Forbes, 1880–1954, editor and publisher

Assumptions keep us awake nights.

Earl Shorris

Defeat ceases when the ghost stops dancing.

Deena Metzger

Life is a school of probability.

Walter Bagehot, 1826–1877, writer

Get the things you like, lest you be compelled to like the things you get.

George Bernard Shaw, 1856–1950, playwright

We really thought it [options] added value. It created a new way of dealing with risks and rewards and a new and much more flexible way of adjusting the risk-reward parameters in your portfolio. It became central to managing risk on Wall Street. There had been options before [1973], but no liquidity.

Robert Rubin, b. ~1940, Goldman, Sachs, former U.S. Treasury secretary

A wise old trainer, asked for some advice on winning races, said, "Well, sir, the thing to do is get out in front at the start and improve your position from there on."

Exchange, publication

A burden in the bush is worth two in your hands.

James Thurber, 1894–1961, American humorist

So with slight efforts, how should one obtain great results? It is foolish even to desire it.

Euripides, ~484–406 B.C., Greek dramatist, tragic poet

No man is quite sane. Each has a vein of folly in his composition—a slight determination of blood to the head, to make sure of holding him hard to some one point which he has taken to heart.

Ralph Waldo Emerson, 1803–1882, American essayist and poet

Nobody's problem is ideal. Nobody has things just as he would like them. The thing to do is to make a success with what material I have. It is sheer waste of time and soul-power to imagine what I would do if things were different. They are not different.

Dr. Frank Crane

There is no way any professor of economics or minister of the church can tell you what your risk tolerance should be.

Paul Samuelson, b. 1915, American Nobel laureate for economics

There's nothing so comfortable as a small bankroll. A big one is always in danger.

Wilson Mizner, 1876–1933, researcher

Security is mostly a superstition. It does not exist in nature, nor do the children of men as a whole experience it. Avoiding danger is no safer in the long run than outright exposure. The fearful are caught as often as the bold. Faith, alone defends.

Helen Keller, 1880–1968, American writer

A person who doubts himself is like a man who would enlist in the ranks of his enemies and bear arms against himself. He makes his failure certain by himself being the first person to be convinced of it.

Alexander Dumas, 1802–1870, French novelist and playwright

It's the old Catch-22. In this business it's like running an opera house. You've got to have the best prima donnas in it, and if you have them, they are temperamental, they don't like to be managed, and yet if you want the business to succeed, you have to manage them. You have to have a creative tension.

Robert Genillard, former chairman, Credit Suisse White Weld, 1987

There is an audience for every play; it's just that sometimes it can't wait long enough to find it.

Shirley Booth, 1898–1992, American actress

To speculate in Wall Street when you are not an insider is like buying cows by candlelight.

Daniel Drew, 1797–1879, American businessman

Work and play are words used to describe the same thing under differing conditions.

Mark Twain, 1835–1910, American author

Every great mistake has a halfway moment, a split second when it can be recalled and perhaps remedied.

Pearl Buck, 1892–1973, American writer

Deliberate with caution, but act with decision; and yield with graciousness, or oppose with firmness.

Charles Hole

Unless you're on the inside [1967], you don't know what is going to happen tomorrow, because the market seems to go contrary to the dictates of supply and demand. It's hard enough to be right just on the basis of supply and demand in futures. And if you add to that the element of corners and squeezes, the public wouldn't have a chance.

Leo Melamed, b. ~1932, former chairman,
Chicago Mercantile Exchange

When I was 40, my doctor advised me that a man in his forties shouldn't play tennis. I heeded his advice carefully and could hardly wait until I reached 50 to start again.

Hugo L. Black, 1886–1971, associate justice, U.S. Supreme Court

Error of opinion may be tolerated where reason is left free to combat it.

Thomas Jefferson, 1743–1826, 3rd U.S. president

Don't be afraid to take a big step if one is indicated. You can't cross a chasm in two small jumps.

David Lloyd George, 1863–1945, British prime minister

The greatest mistake you can make in life is to be continually fearing you will make one.

Elbert G. Hubbard, 1856–1915, American writer and businessman

Risk could be canned and sold like tomatoes. Different investors place different prices on risk. If you are able, as it were, to buy risk from one investor cheaply and sell it to another investor dearly, you can make money without taking any risk yourself.

Michael Lewis, investor, author, in Liar's Poker, *1989*

My idea of risk taking is frying bacon while I am naked.

Ross Levin

No horse can go as fast as the money you put on it.

Earl Wilson

If you are patient in one moment of anger, you will escape 100 days of sorrow.

Chinese proverb

About common stocks: It is often easier to tell what will happen to the price of a stock than how much time will elapse before it happens.

Philip Fisher in Common Stocks and Uncommon Profits and Other Writings, *1957*

Time's fun when you're having flies.

> *Kermit the Frog, muppet created by Jim Henson*

Little drops of water wear down big stones.

> *Russian proverb*

Anything will give up its secrets if you love it enough.

> *George Washington Carver, 1864–1943, American scientist*

To be alive at all involves some risk.

> *Harold MacMillan, 1894–1986, British prime minister*

Risk is the chance of loss, and for most of history it was viewed as that. There is a chance I'm going to lose. But in the capitalist system, risk is also an opportunity. Nothing ventured, nothing gained is as important to keep in mind as the fear that if I don't manage my affairs, I can get wiped out.

> *Peter L. Bernstein, b. ~1919, investment manager*
> *and economic commentator*

As I grow to understand life less and less, I learn to love it more and more.

> *Jules Renard, 1864–1910, French novelist and playwright*

Visits always give pleasure—if not the arrival, the departure.

> *Portuguese proverb*

A bank is a place where they lend you an umbrella in fair weather and ask for it back again when it begins to rain.

> *Robert Frost, 1874–1963, American poet*

I think as long as there are risks, there will be losses. If the day ever comes when there are no risks, there will also be no profits.

Robert Rubin, b. ~1940, Goldman, Sachs, former
U.S. Treasury secretary

The sure way to miss success is to miss the opportunity.

Victor Chasles

We relaunched [1982] the S&P 500 with a pretty famous marketing plan called 15 Minutes, Please. We urged every member of the exchange to stay 15 Minutes, Please, in the S&P [futures] pit.

Leo Melamed, b. ~1932, former chairman, Chicago Mercantile Exchange

Each crop is totally destroyed three times in the pits at the Chicago Board of Trade before it is harvested.

Unknown

The Business Roundtable . . . were lobbying on Capitol Hill in the '70s and the early '80s and saying, "Leave us alone—acquisitions are just the free-enterprise system working at its best." Then along came [Drexel junk bond king Mike] Milken, and that's when you found out that the little company could get the big company. And that's when those guys went back up on the Hill and said, "The big one getting the little one is free enterprise; the little one getting the big one is un-American."

T. Boone Pickens, Jr., Mesa (Petroleum) LP, 1987

The intellectual function of trouble is to lead men to think. The depression is a small price to pay if it induces us to think about the cause of the disorder, confusion and insecurity which are the outstanding traits of our social life.

John Dewey, 1859–1952, American philosopher

When foreign brokers brought derivatives to Japanese financial institutions, it was like the white man bringing firewater to the Indians.

George Soros, b. 1930, Budapest, financier, philanthropist, author

Modern man must descend the spiral of his own absurdity to the lowest point; only then can he look beyond it. It is obviously impossible to get around it, jump over it, or simply avoid it.

Vaclav Havel, b. 1936, Czech president

Big leverage supports the investor as big rope supports a hanged man.

Steve Leuthold, investment manager, The Leuthold Group

Who drinks on credit gets twice as drunk.

Turkish proverb

Weakness cannot co-operate with anything.

Dwight D. Eisenhower, 1890–1969, 34th U.S. president

Polonius in *Hamlet*:
Neither a borrower nor a lender be;
For loan oft loses both itself and friend,
And borrowing dulls the edge of husbandry.

William Shakespeare, 1564–1616, English poet, playwright

Futures has always had a sordid history, at all the exchanges. It looks like a gambling casino, and therefore it is used as a scapegoat. When anything goes wrong in the world, it is easy to pick on futures and say it is their fault. We have proved time and time again that it isn't our fault. They have had soybean examinations.

Leo Melamed, b. ~1932, former chairman, Chicago Mercantile Exchange

When Dr. Johnson defined patriotism as the last refuge of a scoundrel, he ignored the enormous possibilities of the word reform.

Roscoe Conkling, 1829–1888, American political leader

It's a funny thing, this human nature! It clings to a man with such persistence.

Henrik Ibsen, 1828–1906, Norwegian playwright

The wise man will make more opportunities than he finds.

Roger Bacon, ~1220–1292, English philosopher and scientist

We are ready for any unforeseen event that may or may not occur.

J. Danforth Quayle, b. 1947, vice president of the United States

Gus [Levy, Goldman senior partner] told me, "All you've done is develop a new way to lose money."

Robert Rubin, b. ~1940, Goldman, Sachs, former U.S. Treasury secretary

The man does better who runs from disaster than he who is caught by it.

Homer, ~9th–8th century B.C., Greek poet

Men of mettle turn disappointments into helps, as the oyster turns into pearls the sand which annoys it.

Orison Swett Marden

It is a curious fact about British Islanders, who hate drill and have not been invaded for nearly a thousand years, that as danger comes nearer and grows they become progressively less nervous; when it is imminent they are fierce, when it is mortal they are fearless.

Winston Churchill, 1874–1965, British prime minister

Faced with crisis, the man of character falls back on himself.

Charles de Gaulle, 1890–1970, French president

The hurricane is not more or less likely to hit because more hurricane insurance has been written. In the financial markets this is not true. The more people write financial insurance, the more likely it is that a disaster will happen, because the people who know you have sold the insurance can make it happen. So you have to monitor what other people are doing.

Victor Haghani, professor

The academics who lent luster to the LTCM board were merely a modern incarnation of the aristocrats who until recently lent a veneer of respectability to shaky British boards. Brilliance in mathematical modeling is no better qualification for the board, it seems, than brain-dead lineage.

John Plender, Financial Times *columnist*

An unprejudiced mind is probably the rarest thing in the world; to nonprejudice I attach the greatest value.

Andre Gide, 1869–1951, French author

Absence makes the heart grow fonder . . . of someone else!

John McGinley

People have tried to mimic what we have here, and sure, there is a little bit of Chicago in Singapore, a little bit of Chicago in London. But in Chicago, you've got the real thing [the Mercantile Exchange].

Leo Melamed, b. ~1932, former chairman, Chicago Mercantile Exchange

The academic world [was] once a comforting source of Keynesian dogma and confirming memories of the automatic relationship between risk and loss. [Now] the youngsters had taken over the academic world, too.

Peter L. Bernstein, b. ~1919, investment manager and economic commentator

We cannot overstate our debt to the past, but the moment has the supreme claim.

Ralph Waldo Emerson, 1803–1882, American essayist

Only a fool tests the depth of the water with both feet.

African proverb

Half the failures in life arise from pulling in one's horse as he is leaping.

A. W. Hare, 1792–1834, clergyman and author

Everyone can recognize history when it happens. Everyone can recognize history after it has happened; but only the wise man knows at the moment what is vital and permanent, what is lasting and memorable.

Winston Churchill, 1874–1965, British prime minister

Short Selling

Selling Short

In fair weather prepare for foul.
Thomas Fuller, 1654–1734, doctor and writer

"Going long" in investment means buying it in the expectation of a future price rise. "Going short" is the opposite: selling something you do not own in the hope of buying it back more cheaply in the future. When you go long, your loss is limited to what you paid for the stock. But when you go short, your losses are potentially without limit as the buyback price may rise ever higher above the price at which you sold. Why sell short? The obvious answer is to profit from the impending decline of an overpriced stock. But shorting requires a tough-minded pessimism, a contrarian turn of mind, or a "gloom and doom" view of the world.

Procrastination is opportunity's natural assassin.

Victor Kiam, 1926–2001, entrepreneur

Ultimately, all of us (portfolio managers) will experience a debilitating, confidence-destroying bear market where everything hits the fan at once, where essentially everyone is a loser—except for a few of those obnoxious short sellers.

Steve Leuthold, investment manager, The Leuthold Group

We ought not to look back unless it is to derive useful lessons from past errors, and for the purpose of profiting by dearly bought experience.

George Washington, 1732–1799, 1st U.S. president

Wall Street's graveyards are filled with men who were right too soon.

William Hamilton

Success makes a fool seem wise.

H. G. Bohn, 1796–1884, English publisher

It's an impossible situation, but it has possibilities.

Samuel Goldwyn, 1882–1974, American movie producer

It is just as hard to do your duty when men are sneering at you as when they are shooting at you.

Woodrow Wilson, 1856–1924, 28th U.S. president

A lot of people have asked me how short I am. Since my last divorce, I think I'm about $100,000 short.

Mickey Rooney, b. 1920, actor

I've probably shorted more stock than anybody alive in these last twenty years. I should readily add that it's a dubious distinction. I mean, I [haven't] gotten rich necessarily in shorting stocks.

Michael Steinhardt, investment manager, Steinhardt Partners, 1987

I made my money by selling too soon.

Bernard Baruch, 1870–1965, American financier and statesman, adviser to presidents, and popular sage

The only thing that hurts more than paying an income tax is not having to pay an income tax.

Lord Dewar, 1864–1930, British distiller and author

Everyone complains of his memory, no one of his judgment.

La Rochefoucauld, 1613–1680, French author

A single idea, if it is right, saves us an infinity of experiences.

Jacques Maritain, 1882–1973, philosopher and author

The sower may mistake and sow his peas crookedly; the peas make no mistake but come up and show his line.

Ralph Waldo Emerson, 1803–1882, American essayist and poet

When anyone gets something for nothing, someone else gets nothing for something.

Unknown

Anger is never without a reason, but seldom with a good one.

Benjamin Franklin, 1706–1790, statesman, scientist, public leader

I must decline your invitation owing to a subsequent engagement.

Oscar Wilde, 1854–1900, Irish-British author

Time drinketh up the essence of every great and noble action which ought to be performed but is delayed in the execution.

Veeshnoo Sarma

Nothing hurts more than the friendly letter that one never got around to writing.

Brendan Francis Behan, 1923–1964, Irish author and playwright

It's odd to think we might have been
Sun, moon and stars unto each other;
Only I turned down one little street
As you went up another.

Fanny Heaslip Lea

No one on Wall Street has ever figured out how to time stocks' swings perfectly. Most people, in fact, fail miserably at timing.

Tom Petruno, LA Times

The public man needs but one patron, namely, the lucky moment.

Edward Bulwer-Lytton, 1803–1873, British author

We will sell no wine before its time.

Orson Welles for Ernest and Julio Gallo Wines

Opportunity has power over all things.

Sophocles, 496–406 B.C., Athenian tragedian

Wild oats will get sown some time, and one of the arts of life is to sow them at the right time.

Richard Le Gallienne, 1866–1947, British writer

Time flies like an arrow; fruit flies like a banana.

Groucho Marx, 1890–1977, comedian

Kindness is in our power, but fondness is not.

Samuel Johnson, 1709–1784, British author

Few rich men own their own property. The property owns them.

Robert Ingersoll, 1833–1899, American lawyer

If thou art rich, thou art poor for, like an ass, whose back with ingots bows, thou bearest thy heavy riches but a journey and death unloads thee.

William Shakespeare, 1564–1616, English poet, playwright

He who foresees calamities, suffers them twice over.

Portius

To survive in the financial markets sometimes means beating a hasty retreat.

George Soros, b. 1930, Budapest, financier, philanthropist, author

When you come to a fork in the road, take it.

Yogi Berra, b. 1925, baseball player, coach, and manager

There are two ways of meeting difficulties: you alter the difficulties, or you alter yourself to meet them.

Phyllis Bottome, 1884–1963, Anglo-American novelist

Men, whose trade is rat-catching, love to catch rats; the bug destroyer seizes on his bug with delight; and the suppressor is gratified by finding his vice.

Sydney Smith, 1771–1845, British religious leader and writer

In a philosophical dispute, he gains most who is defeated, since he learns most.

Epicurus, 341–270 B.C., Greek philosopher

Sound opinions are valueless. What matters is who holds them.

Karl Kraus, 1874–1936, Austrian satirist

No evil is without its compensation. The less money, the less trouble; the less favor, the less envy. Even in those cases which put us out of wits, it is not the loss itself, but the estimate of the loss that troubles us.

Seneca, ~4 B.C.–A.D. 65, Roman statesman and philosopher

Except a person be part coward, it is not a compliment to say he is brave.

Mark Twain, 1835–1910, American author

He makes no friend who never made a foe.

Alfred, Lord Tennyson, 1809–1892, English poet

Let us not be needlessly bitter: certain failures are sometimes fruitful.

E. M. Cioran, b. 1911, French philosopher

Gnawing on bones of contention provides little nourishment.

Arnold Glasow, American humorist

Very specific and personal misfortune awaits those who presume to believe that the future is revealed to them.

John Kenneth Galbraith, b. 1908, economist

When we are tired, we are attacked by ideas we conquered long ago.

Friedrich Nietzsche, 1844–1900, German philosopher

Sure the stock market is a good indicator of the business cycle. It forecast six of the last four recessions.

Paul Samuelson, b. 1915, American Nobel laureate for economics

February, the shortest month in the year, is also the worst.

Italian proverb

Do not let yourself be tainted with a barren skepticism.

Louis Pasteur, 1822–1895, French biochemist

Never buy at the bottom, and always sell too soon.

Jesse L. Livermore

Any man who is a bear on the future of this country will go broke.

J. P. Morgan, 1837–1913, American businessman

He who sells what isn't his'n,
Buys it back or goes to prison.

Fred Schwed, Jr., author and investor

She always believed in the old adage—leave them while you're looking good.

Anita Loos, 1893–1981, American writer

Technical Analysis

99 99 99

Charts, Graphs, and Random Walks

Chance favors the prepared mind.
Louis Pasteur, 1822–1895, French biochemist

There are essentially two ways of analyzing investments: fundamental analysis and technical analysis. With the former, investors try to calculate the value of an asset, comparing the present value of the likely future cash flows with its current price. With the latter, they focus exclusively on the asset's price data, asking what its past price behavior indicates about its likely future price behavior. Market strategists believe that history tends to repeat itself. They make price predictions on the basis of published data, looking for patterns and correlations, assessing trends, support, and resistance levels. The true objective of technical analysis is to determine whether the ingredients of a healthy bull market are present—and to watch out for possible warning flags before a major decline or bear strikes.

A fact is a fact and is always the same. An opinion may vary with what you had for dinner.

Charles F. Kettering, 1876–1958, engineer and inventor

There is no room both for field and matter, because field is the only reality.

Albert Einstein, 1879–1955, German-American scientist

Get your facts first, and then you can distort them as much as you please.

Mark Twain, 1835–1910, American author

Otto Eckstein and I started Data Resources [in the late '60s], based on the same idea: that all these people with these growing amounts of money were very interested in other ways of looking at the environment in which they were managing it.

Donald Marron, b. ~1934, Paine Webber

You don't want analysts in a bear market and you don't need them in a bull market.

Gerald M. Loeb

No picture of life can have any veracity that does not admit the odious facts.

Ralph Waldo Emerson, 1803–1882, American essayist and poet

Not believing in force is the same as not believing in gravity.

Leon Trotsky, 1879–1940, Russian revolutionary

When it's time to buy, you won't want to.

Walter Deemer, market strategist

In matters of conscience, first thoughts are best; in matters of prudence, last thoughts are best.

Robert Hall, 1764–1831, English clergyman

We had some unique criteria for picking research analysts. First of all, I thought that only young fellows would be good analysts, because anybody who was still an analyst and had lived through the 1930s would have a distorted and unduly pessimistic view of the world.

Leon Levy, Odyssey Partners, cofounder Oppenheimer Fund, 1987

In a 1921 decision: A page of history is worth a volume of logic.

Oliver Wendell Holmes, 1841–1935, associate justice,
U.S. Supreme Court

A great memory does not make a mind, any more than a dictionary is a piece of literature.

John Henry Cardinal Newman, 1801–1890, English theologian

He who has not a good memory should never take upon himself the trade of lying.

Michel Montaigne, 1533–1592, French essayist

Some people do not become thinkers simply because their memories are too good.

Friedrich Nietzsche, 1844–1900, German philosopher

The secret of a good memory is attention, and attention to a subject depends upon our interest in it. We rarely forget that which has made a deep impression on our minds.

Tryon Edwards, 1809–1894

Memory is the mother of all wisdom.

Aeschylus, 525–456 B.C., writer of Greek tragedy

Happiness is not something you experience, it's something you remember.

> *Oscar Levant, 1906–1972, U.S. pianist and composer*

There's hope a great man's memory may outlive his life half a year.

> *William Shakespeare, 1564–1616, English poet, playwright*

Analysts were way undercompensated relative to salesmen—or you could say the marketing guys were way overcompensated.

> *Barry Good, oil analyst, Morgan Stanley & Co.*

Knowledge comes by taking things apart: analysis. But wisdom comes by putting things together.

> *John A. Morrison*

More erroneous conclusions are due to lack of information than to errors of judgment.

> *Justice Louis D. Brandeis, 1856–1941, associate justice,*
> *U.S. Supreme Court*

Stocks are bought on expectations, not facts.

> *Gerald M. Loeb*

Those who do not study history are doomed to repeat it.

> *George Santayana, 1863–1952, Spanish-American poet and philosopher*

The Holocaust was an obscene period in our nation's history. I mean in this century's history. But we all lived in this century. I didn't live in this century.

> *J. Danforth Quayle, b. 1947, vice president of the United States*

Most ignorance is vincible ignorance. We don't know because we don't want to know.

Aldous Huxley, 1894–1963, English writer

To study history means submitting to chaos and nevertheless retaining faith in order and meaning. It is a very serious task, possibly a tragic one.

Hermann Hesse, 1877–1962, German novelist and poet

A moment's insight is sometimes worth a life's experience.

Oliver Wendell Holmes, 1841–1935, associate justice, U.S. Supreme Court

The simplest schoolboy is now familiar with truths for which Archimedes would have sacrificed his life.

Ernest Renan, 1823–1892, French philosopher and historian

To be angry is to revenge the faults of others on ourselves.

Alexander Pope, 1688–1744, English poet

A prince who will not undergo the difficulty of understanding must undergo the danger of trusting.

Lord Halifax, 1661–1715, English wit and politician

One realizes the full importance of time only when there is little of it left. Every man's greatest capital asset is his unexpired years of productive life.

P. W. Litchfield

Men are not flattered by being shown that there has been a difference of purpose between the Almighty and them.

Abraham Lincoln, 1809–1865, 16th U.S. president

What has not been examined impartially has not been well examined. Skepticism is therefore the first step toward truth.

Denis Diderot, 1713–1784, French thinker and writer

The more we study, the more we discover our ignorance.

Percy Bysshe Shelley, 1792–1822, British poet

A man must have a certain amount of intelligent ignorance to get anywhere.

Charles F. Kettering, 1876–1958, engineer and inventor

About technical analysts of the 1960s: Mostly, they were introverts dealing in the hen scratching and wiggles of lines on semi-log charts posted on sliding wallboards in their offices. Managers and analysts would walk into their environments the way one would approach a reader of tea leaves—apprehensive but hopeful.

Dean LeBaron, b. 1933, investment manager and contrarian thinker

The trouble with plays these days is that they're too easy to understand.

Robert Allen Arthur

My definition of a guru is someone who is lucky enough to be quoted in the right publication at the right time saying the right thing.

Herb Greenberg, The Street

How many young geniuses we have known, and none but ourselves will ever hear of them for the want in them of a little talent!

Ralph Waldo Emerson, 1803–1882, American essayist and poet

At a dinner honoring Nobel Prize winners: I think this is the most extraordinary collection of talent, of human knowledge, that has ever been gathered together at the White House—with the possible exception of when Thomas Jefferson dined alone.

John F. Kennedy, 1917–1963, 35th U.S. president

A war of ideas can no more be won without books than a naval war can be won without ships. Books, like ships, have the toughest armor, the longest cruising range, and mount the most powerful guns.

Franklin D. Roosevelt, 1882–1945, 32nd U.S. president

Education is a weapon, whose effect depends on who holds it in his hands and at whom it is aimed.

Joseph Stalin, 1879–1953, Soviet leader

If a little knowledge is dangerous, where is the man who has so much as to be out of danger?

Thomas H. Huxley, 1825–1895, British zoologist

One of the most striking differences between a cat and a lie is that a cat has only nine lives.

Mark Twain, 1835–1910, American author

Life is what happens to us while we are making other plans.

Thomas La Mance

Never let the future disturb you. You will meet it if you have to, with the same weapons of reason which today arm you against the present.

Marcus Aurelius, A.D. 121–180, Roman emperor

Nothing is done. Everything in the world remains to be done or done over.

Lincoln Steffens, 1866–1936, American author

A great many people have asked how I manage to get so much work done and still keep looking so dissipated.

> *Robert Benchley, 1889–1945, humorist and script writer*

If a man is worth knowing at all, he is worth knowing well.

> *Alexander Smith, 1830–1867, Scottish poet and writer*

My own business always bores me to death. I prefer other people's.

> *Oscar Wilde, 1854–1900, Irish-British author*

We seldom saw any Wall Street research and laughed at most of what we did see.

> *Peter L. Bernstein, b. ~1919, investment manager*
> *and economic commentator*

Thinking is the hardest work there is, which is the probable reason why so few engage in it.

> *Henry Ford, 1863–1947, American automobile manufacturer,*
> *founder of Ford Motor Co.*

Through zeal, knowledge is gotten, through lack of zeal, knowledge is lost.

> *Buddha, ~563–483 B.C., founder of Buddhism*

Details often kill initiative, but there have been few successful men who weren't good at details. Don't ignore details. Lick them.

> *William B. Given, Jr.*

ingle ells, ingle ells . . . Something is missing.

> *Advertisement for J&B Scotch Whiskey*

I remember being very skeptical about the start of the bull market in 1982, asking the technical department, "Has any bull market ever started in this way?" I don't think I got an answer back from the technical department for about four months, when it was obvious what the answer was.

Edward (Ned) Johnson III, b. 1930, chairman, Fidelity Investments

I am a great friend of analysis. "Why" and "How" are such useful questions that they cannot be uttered too often.

Napoleon Bonaparte, 1769–1821, French general

We should not only master questions, but also act upon them, and act definitely.

Woodrow Wilson, 1856–1924, 28th U.S. president

Life is not a problem to be solved, but a reality to be experienced.

Søren Kierkegaard, 1813–1855, Danish philosopher

A chain of logical argument is totally incomprehensible to crowds, and for this reason it is permissible to say that they do not reason or that they reason falsely and are not influenced by reasoning.

Gustave Le Bon, 1841–1931, French sociologist and author of
The Crowd: A Study of the Popular Mind

If you can think of something which is connected with something without thinking of the something it is connected to, then you have a legal mind.

Thomas Reed Powell

No one really understands the grief or joy of another. We always imagine that we are approaching some other, but our lines of travel are actually parallel.

Franz Schubert, 1797–1828, Austrian composer

I don't think anyone should write his autobiography until after he's dead.

> *Samuel Goldwyn, 1882–1974, American movie producer*

Trust, when not sought after, rarely comes to light.

> *Oliver Wendell Holmes, 1841–1935, associate justice,*
> *U.S. Supreme Court*

Only the shallow know themselves.

> *Oscar Wilde, 1854–1900, Irish-British author*

The mind is its own place, and in itself can make a heaven of Hell, a hell of Heaven.

> *John Milton, 1608–1674, English poet*

When a man's knowledge is not in order, the more of it he has the greater will be his confusion.

> *Herbert Spencer, 1820–1903, British philosopher*

Nothing is particularly hard if you divide it into small jobs.

> *Henry Ford, 1863–1947, American automobile manufacturer,*
> *founder of Ford Motor Co.*

To those who are alive, I suggest that every opportunity be taken to find out what is going on around you. Do not be satisfied to know merely the details of your little job. If you are addressing envelopes, take an interest in the names you write, their source, their accuracy and the results obtained from the mailings. An inquiring mind soon becomes an outstanding mind.

> *Santa Fe* magazine

A disciplined conscience is a man's best friend. It may not be his most amiable, but it is his most faithful monitor.

Henry Ward Beecher, 1813–1887, American religious leader, reformer

Virtue is its own punishment.

Aneurin Bevan, 1897–1960, British politician

I think my analytical abilities are rather deficient, but I do have a very strong critical faculty. I am not a professional security analyst. I would rather call myself an insecurity analyst.

George Soros, b. 1930, Budapest, financier, philanthropist, author

It is not of so much consequence what you say, as how you say it.

Alexander Smith, 1830–1867, Scottish poet and writer

These numbers are not my own. They are from someone who knows what he is talking about.

Wisconsin legislator

Statistics are no substitute for judgment.

Henry Clay, 1777–1852, American statesman

There are lies, damned lies and statistics.

Mark Twain, 1835–1910, American author

If you have anything of importance to tell me, for God's sake begin at the end.

Sara J. Duncan, Canadian author

To wisdom belongs the intellectual apprehension of eternal things; to knowledge, the rational knowledge of temporal things.

St. Augustine, 354–430, early Christian church father and philosopher

The credibility, or the certain truth of a matter of fact, does not immediately prove anything concerning the wisdom or goodness of it.

Joseph Butler, 1692–1752, English theologian

One of the virtues of being very young is that you don't let the facts get in the way of your imagination.

Sam Levinson

The great tragedy of science—the slaying of a beautiful hypothesis by an ugly fact.

Thomas H. Huxley, 1825–1895, British zoologist

Value Investing

99 99 99

Value, Value, Value

Value (like beauty) is in the eye of the beholder.
Dean LeBaron, b. 1933, investment manager
and contrarian thinker

A caricature of the investment world divides it into two camps: value investors, who buy stocks that have fallen in price in the belief that the rest of the market has missed a bargain; and growth or momentum investors, who buy stocks that have gone up in the hope that they turn out to have been "cheap at any price." Value investors dispute the efficient market hypothesis, which suggests that prices reflect all available information, and see investment opportunities created by discrepancies between stock price and the underlying value of company assets.

Lord Henry Wooton in The Picture of Dorian Gray, *1891:* Nowadays, people know the price of everything and the value of nothing.

Oscar Wilde, 1854–1900, Irish-British author

Lethargy bordering on sloth remains the cornerstone of our investment style.

Warren Buffett, b. 1930, American investor

Value investors: People who place a very high value on having the last laugh. In exchange for the privilege, they have missed out on a lot of laughs in between.

Michael Lewis, investor, author, in The New New Thing, *1999*

If we assume that it is the habit of the market to overvalue common stocks which have been showing excellent growth or are glamorous for some other reason, it is logical to expect that it will undervalue— relatively, at least—companies that are out of favor because of unsatisfactory developments of a temporary nature. This may be set down as a fundamental law of the stock market, and it suggests an investment approach that should be both conservative and promising.

Benjamin Graham, 1894–1976, value investor

What has been the fashion once, will come into fashion again.

Japanese proverb

I have seen no trend towards value investing in the 35 years I've practiced it. There seems to be some perverse human characteristic that likes to make easy things difficult.

Warren Buffett, b. 1930, American investor

In the midst of winter, I finally learned that there was in me an invincible summer.

Albert Camus, 1913–1960, French journalist and philosopher

Style is always in fashion.

Wilma Askinas, b. ~1924, writer

Enthusiasm is a virtue rarely to be met with in seasons of calm and unruffled prosperity.

Thomas Chalmers, 1780–1847, Scottish theologian and preacher

Because people are simple-minded in how they try to understand what goes on in the market, they like to own what is comfortable instead of what's uncomfortable. They make big errors in valuation. Therefore, if you really understand this, you can make money as a value investor.

Peter L. Bernstein, b. ~1919, investment manager
and economic commentator

I hate admitting that my enemies have a point.

Salman Rushdie, b. 1947, British novelist of Indian descent

If history books were the key to riches, the Forbes 400 would consist of librarians.

Warren Buffett, b. 1930, American investor

A classic is something that everybody wants to have read and nobody wants to read.

Mark Twain, 1835–1910, American author

About things on which the public thinks long it commonly attains to think right.

Samuel Johnson, 1709–1784, British author

Good nature is often a mere matter of health.

Henry Ward Beecher, 1813–1887, American religious leader, reformer

If the business does well, the stock eventually follows.

Warren Buffett, b. 1930, American investor

Dividend yield: Outdated concept once used in valuing stocks.

Steve Leuthold, investment manager, The Leuthold Group

Confronted with the challenge to distil the secret of sound investment into three words, we venture the motto, MARGIN OF SAFETY.

Benjamin Graham, 1894–1976, value investor

Because one mistake breeds another, he who buys too high will sell too low.

Leo Dworsky

Don't try to buy at the bottom and sell at the top. This can't be done—except by liars.

Bernard Baruch, 1870–1965, American financier and statesman, adviser to presidents, and popular sage

Value investing: A search for discrepancies between the *value* of a business and the *price* of small pieces of that business in the market.

Warren Buffett, b. 1930, American investor

Cheat me in the price, but not in the goods.

Thomas Fuller, 1654–1734, doctor and writer

A thing of beauty is a joy forever;
Its loveliness increases; it will never
Pass into nothingness.

John Keats, 1795–1821, English poet

Ask thy purse what thou shouldst spend.

Scottish proverb

Luxury must be comfortable, otherwise it is not luxury.

Gabrielle Chanel, 1883–1971, French fashion designer

Far away in the sunshine are my highest inspirations. I may not reach them, but I can look up and see the beauty, believe in them and try to follow where they lead.

Louisa May Alcott, 1832–1888, author

It is not given to human beings to have such talent that they can just know everything about everything all the time. But it is given to human beings who work hard at it—who look and sift the world for a mispriced bet—that they can *occasionally* find one. And the wise ones bet heavily when the world offers them that opportunity. They bet big when they have odds. And the rest of the time, they don't. It's just that simple.

Charles Munger, b. ~1925, long-time friend and partner of Warren Buffett

You pay a very high price in the stock market for a cheery consensus. Uncertainty actually is the friend of the buyer of long-term values.

Warren Buffett, b. 1930, American investor

It is difficult to set bounds to the price unless you first set bounds to the wish.

Cicero, 106–43 B.C., Roman orator, statesman

Why are divorces so expensive? Because they're worth it.

Kurt Leuthold

Frugality is founded on the principle that all riches have limits.

Edmund Burke, 1729–1797, English political leader

Happiness is a dividend on a well-invested life.

Duncan Stuart

The man who tips a shilling every time he stops for petrol is giving away annually the cost of lubricating his car.

J. Paul Getty, 1892–1976, oil tycoon

Everything concerning markets and economies—and everything else for that matter—regresses from extremes towards normal faster than people think (e.g., sales growth, profitability, management skill, investment styles, and good fortune).

Jeremy Grantham, investment manager, Grantham, Mayo, Van Otterloo

If a man has any brains at all, let him hold on to his calling, and, in the grand sweep of things, his turn will come at last.

William McCune

Time has no divisions to mark its passage. There is never a thunderstorm or blare of trumpets to announce the beginning of a new month or year. Even when a new century begins it is only we mortals who ring bells . . .

Thomas Mann, 1875–1955, German author

Experience is a dead loss if you cannot sell it for more than it cost you.

Northwestern National News

The object of work is living, experience, happiness. All that money can do is buy us some one else's work in exchange for our own.

Henry Ford, 1863–1947, American automobile manufacturer, founder of Ford Motor Co.

I am a marvelous housekeeper. Every time I leave a man I keep his house.

Zsa Zsa Gabor, b. 1919, American actress

Looking at bargains with a pure commercial view, someone is always cheated; but seen with a simple eye both seller and buyer always win.

Ray Stannard Baker, pseudonym David Grayson, 1870–1946, American journalist and author

I am a better investor because I am a businessman, and a better businessman because I am an investor.

Warren Buffett, b. 1930, American investor

Savings represent much more than mere money value. They are the proof that the saver is worth something in himself. Any fool can waste; any fool can meddle; but it takes something more of a man to save and the more he saves the more of a man he makes of himself. Waste and extravagance unsettle a man's mind for every crisis; thrift, which means some form of self restraint, steadies it.

Rudyard Kipling, 1865–1936, British author

An investment operation is one which upon thorough analysis promises safety of principal and an adequate return. Operations not meeting these requirements are speculative.

Benjamin Graham, 1894–1976, value investor

After several failures, I finally remembered some advice I once got from a golf pro: "Practice doesn't make perfect; practice makes permanent." Therefore I revised my strategy and tried to buy good businesses at fair prices rather than fair businesses at good prices.

Warren Buffett, b. 1930, American investor

In the long run, most people will find themselves better fixed if they will invest not on the basis of large returns and high interest rates, but on the soundness of the company, its prospects for the future, and hold what they buy for permanent investment. Trying to "beat the market" is a losing game for the vast majority.

A. P. Giannini, 1870–1949, American banker,
established Bank of America

Failures either do not know what they want, or jib at the price.

W. H. Auden, 1907–1973, British poet

The longer I live the more beautiful life becomes. The earth's beauty grows on men. If you foolishly ignore beauty, you'll soon find yourself without it. Your life will be impoverished. But if you wisely invest in beauty, it will remain with you all the days of your life.

Frank Lloyd Wright, 1869–1959, architect

There is no finer investment than putting milk into babies.

Winston Churchill, 1874–1965, British prime minister

Why, money isn't everything to an Englishman. There are other considerations when he marries, for instance, fondness for the girl.

Dowager Duchess of Roxburghe

We have found that there is a force at work in our common stockholdings which tends ever toward increasing their princip[al] value.

Edgar Lawrence Smith in Common Stocks as Long Term Investments, *1925*

Berkshire buys when the lemmings are heading the other way.

Warren Buffett, b. 1930, American investor

On a cold day it is very easy to borrow a fan.

Chinese proverb

It is not size that counts in business. Some companies with $500,000 capital are making more profits than other companies with $5,000,000. Size is a handicap unless efficiency goes with it.

Herbert N. Casson

The secret of all victory lies in the organization of the nonobvious.

Oswald Spengler, 1880–1936, German philosopher

My father asserted that there was no better place to bring up a family than in a rural environment. There's something about getting up at 5 am, feeding the stock and chickens, and milking a couple of cows before breakfast that gives you a life-long respect for the price of butter and eggs.

William Vaughn Moody, 1869–1910, American poet and playwright

Value investing has always had a hidden but serious risk—the 60-year flood. The so-called price/book effect (and the small stock effect) sound like a free lunch, but, in 1929–33, 20% of all companies went bankrupt. They were not the large high quality blue chips but small "cheap stocks" with low price/book ratios.

Jeremy Grantham, investment manager, Grantham, Mayo, Van Otterloo

I want to be able to understand my mistakes. This means I only do things I completely understand.

Warren Buffett, b. 1930, American investor

Too caustic? To hell with the cost. If it's a good picture, we'll make it anyway.

Samuel Goldwyn, 1882–1974, American movie producer

If you have a harem of forty women, you never get to know any of them very well.

Warren Buffett, b. 1930, American investor

Venture Capital

99 99 99

Nothing Ventured

Diamonds are only lumps of coal that stuck to
their jobs.

B. C. Forbes, 1880–1954, editor and publisher

Venture capital is essentially the institutionalization of private investment. Wealthy private investors, sometimes called *business angels*, and venture capital companies and funds typically put money into
startups in their early stages of development. A general rule for returns
from venture capital investments is that 40% will be complete losses;
30% will be "living dead;" while the remaining 30% may generate sub-
stantial returns on the original investment. While the winners might win
big, they often take much longer to emerge than the losers. The challenge
can be even greater at the height of a bull market with too much money
chasing too few great ideas.

Success or failure in business is caused more by mental attitude than by mental capacities.

Walter D. Scott

Real difficulties can be overcome; it is only the imaginary ones that are unconquerable.

Theodore N. Vail, 1845–1920, AT&T president

If you cannot make money on one dollar—if you do not coax one dollar to work hard to you, you won't know how to make money out of one hundred thousand dollars.

E. S. Kinnear

Failure is, in a sense, the highway to success, inasmuch as every discovery of what is false leads us to seek earnestly after what is true, and every fresh experience points out some form of error which we shall afterward carefully avoid.

John Keats, 1795–1821, English poet

In business and politics, indifference is fatal.

William Feather, 1889–1981, American author, publisher

In truth, people can generally make time for what they choose to do: it is not really the time but the will that is lacking.

Sir John Lubbock, 1834–1913, author and financier

Touch a thistle timidly, and it pricks you; grasp it boldly, and its spines crumble.

William S. Halsey

Aggressive fighting for the right is the greatest sport in the world.

Theodore Roosevelt, 1858–1919, 26th U.S. president

Know what thou canst work at, and work at it like a Hercules.

Thomas Carlyle, 1795–1881, Scottish author

It is always the adventurers who accomplish great things.

Charles de Montesquieu, 1689–1755, French philosopher and author

To be a great autocrat you must be a great barbarian.

Joseph Conrad, 1857–1924, Polish-British author

Men will let you abuse them if only you will make them laugh.

Henry Ward Beecher, 1813–1887, American religious leader and reformer

Absolute faith corrupts as absolutely as absolute power.

Eric Hoffer, 1902–1983, American philosopher

Don't condescend to unskilled labor. Try it for half a day first.

Brooks Atkinson, 1894–1984, American theater critic

A good horse should be seldom spurred.

Thomas Fuller, 1654–1734, doctor and writer

Some see private enterprise as a predatory target to be shot, others as a cow to be milked, but few are those who see it as a sturdy horse pulling the wagon.

Winston Churchill, 1874–1965, British prime minister

Venture capital investments are like inefficiently priced stocks, with two differences. First because there are no short-selling mechanisms, a venture capitalist, like a commodity investor, faces potential overpricing. Second, unlike stocks, which represent existing assets, an early-stage venture capital project may be an idea.

James H. Scott, Jr., "Managing Asset Classes," Financial Analysts Journal, January-February 1994

You see things; and you say "Why?" But I dream things that never were; and I say "Why not?"

George Bernard Shaw, 1856–1950, playwright

A new idea is delicate. It can be killed by a sneer or a yawn; it can be stabbed to death by a quip and worried to death by a frown on the right man's brow.

Charles Brower

Of all the icy blasts that blow on love, a request for money is the most chilling and havoc-wreaking.

Gustave Flaubert, 1821–1880, French author

Nothing in fine print is ever good news.

Unknown

What the large print giveth, the small print taketh away.

Unknown

The belief in the existence of opportunities to achieve economic equality has had a longer and more vital tradition in American history than has been the case anywhere else.

Louis Hacker

There is no solution for any of our problems except in men. If you want to plan for a year, plant grain. If you want to plan for a decade, plant trees. If you want to plan for a century, plant men.

Chinese proverb

In venture capital, the lemons ripen before the plums.

William Hambrecht, investment banker, cofounder, Hambrecht & Quist

We are not permitted to choose the frame of our destiny. But what we put into it is ours.

Dag Hammarskjöld, 1905–1961, secretary-general of the United Nations

Business progressiveness is dependent on competition. New methods and new ideas are the outgrowth of the spirit of adventure, of individual initiative, and of individual enterprise. Without adventure there is no progress.

Herbert Hoover, 1874–1964, 31st U.S. president

Man never rises to great truths without enthusiasm.

Marquis de Vauvenargues, 1715–1747, French moralist

Everyone has talent at twenty-five. The difficulty is to have it at fifty.

Edgar Degas, 1834–1917, French impressionist painter

Action does not always bring happiness, but there is no happiness without it.

Benjamin Disraeli, 1804–1881, British prime minister, author,
1st Earl of Beaconsfield

Trying is the touchstone to accomplishment.

Paul von Ringelheim

Regret for the things we did can be tempered by time; it is regret for the things we did not do that is inconsolable.

Sidney J. Harris

Fear not that thy life shall come to an end, but rather fear that it shall never have a beginning.

John Henry Cardinal Newman, 1801–1890, English theologian

Activity makes more men's fortunes than cautiousness.

Marquis de Vauvenargues, 1715–1747, French moralist

Injustice is relatively easy to bear; what stings is justice.

H. L. Mencken, 1880–1956, American journalist and writer

This business must be learned from the bottom up. Anyone who has not lost a company and not fired friends is not a venture capitalist.

Stanley Pratt, "Current Opportunities and Future Prospects-Part 1," Investing in Venture Capital, The Institute of Chartered Financial Analysts, 1989.

I've been surprised at the support we got from the Street when we reestablished Weeden & Co. Wall Street is a forgiving place.

Donald Weeden, president and CEO, Weeden & Co., 1987

I could not point to any need in childhood as strong as that for a father's protection.

Sigmund Freud, 1856–1939, psychoanalyst

Hope is the only good thing that disillusion respects.

Marquis de Vauvenargues, 1715–1747, French moralist

Money is of no value; it cannot spend itself. All depends on the skill of the spender.

Ralph Waldo Emerson, 1803–1882, American essayist and poet

The use of money is all the advantage there is in having money.

Benjamin Franklin, 1706–1790, statesman, scientist, public leader

Be not penny-wise: riches have wings; sometimes they fly away of themselves, and sometimes they must be set flying to bring in more.

Sir Francis Bacon, 1561–1626, poet, dramatist, thinker

Never invest your money in anything that eats or needs repainting.

Billy Rose, 1899–1966, American impresario and songwriter

All work and the enjoyment of its fruits must be in common.

Francois-Noël Babeuf, 1760–1797, French revolutionary

Let the man who has to make his fortune in life remember this maxim: Attacking is the only secret. Dare and the world always yields; or if it beats you sometimes, dare it again and it will succumb.

William Makepeace Thackeray, 1811–1866, British author

The sage does not care to hoard. The more he uses for the benefit of others, the more he possesses himself. The more he gives to his fellow-men, the more he has of his own.

Chinese proverb

Talk not of wasted affection; affection never was wasted.

Henry Wadsworth Longfellow, 1807–1882, American poet

The person who minds nobody's business but his own is probably a millionaire.

Unknown

The much-maligned idle rich have received a bad rap: They have maintained their wealth while many of the energetic rich—aggressive real estate operators, corporate acquirers, oil drillers, etc.—have seen their fortunes disappear.

Warren Buffett, b. 1930, American investor

All men's gains are the fruit of venturing.

Herodotus, ~484–425 B.C., Greek historian

Some of us look to the Prophet Gabriel to redeem our future life, but it is Prophet Profit that will redeem this life. This might explain to some the basic reason for American prosperity under private owner-ship as compared to the failures of government operation and manage-ment of industry.

B. A. Javits

In business the earning of profit is something more than an incident of success. It is an essential condition of success; because the continued absence of profit itself spells failure.

Justice Louis D. Brandeis, 1856–1941, associate justice,
U.S. Supreme Court

We must remember that only through business activity can the gov-ernment receipts be increased, and it is time to begin to encourage capital to come out of hiding to seek profitable investment and em-ployment. This encouragement can only be accomplished by ceasing through legislative means a policy to soak the rich, for in such encour-agement we are enabled not only to be generous to the poor, but to be of genuine help to them.

William Guggenheim

If you do things by the job, you are perpetually driven: the hours are scourges. If you work by the hour, you gently sail on the stream of time, which is always bearing you on to the haven of pay, whether you make any effort, or not.

Charles Dudley Warner, 1829–1900, American author

Profit is a byproduct of work; happiness is its chief product.

Henry Ford, 1863–1947, American automobile manufacturer, founder of Ford Motor Co.

When money is primary, life is a blank book.

Robert Half, employment agent

Conditions never get so bad in this country but that a man who works can get business.

Laurence J. Peter, 1919–1990, Canadian author and educator

Every customer was once a prospect, every prospect once a stranger. Moral: Get acquainted.

Unknown

Believe that life is worth living and your belief will help create the fact.

William James, 1842–1910, American philosopher and psychologist

Blessed is he who has found his work; let him ask no other blessedness.

Thomas Carlyle, 1795–1881, Scottish author

He can inspire a group only if he himself is filled with confidence and hope of success.

Floyd V. Filson

The important thing is this: To be able at any moment to sacrifice what we are for what we could become.

Charles Du Bos, 1882–1939, French critic

Life begets life. Energy creates energy. It is only by spending oneself that one becomes rich.

Sarah Bernhardt, 1844–1923, French actress

What great thing would you attempt if you knew you could not fail?

Robert Schuller

The creative person, in all realms of life, is like a child who dares to inquire beyond the limits of conventional answers.

Paul Tillich, 1886–1965, German theologian

I wish you all the joy that you can wish.

William Shakespeare, 1564–1616, English poet, playwright

Name Index

Keyword Index